Christianity

Christianity

5000 Years of History and Development

Gary A. Stilwell, Ph.D.

To Herb

iUniverse, Inc.
New York Lincoln Shanghai

Christianity
5000 Years of History and Development

iUniverse, Inc.

For information address:
iUniverse, Inc.
2021 Pine Lake Road, Suite 100
Lincoln, NE 68512
www.iuniverse.com

ISBN: 0-595-33376-1 (Pbk)
ISBN: 0-595-66878-X (Cloth)

Printed in the United States of America

For my Mother, Virginia Pauline Stilwell

My own St. Monica

Acknowledgments

Christianity: 5000 Years of History and Development, and the course of lectures that preceded it, is partially an attempt, among other reasons, to resolve some of the historical ambiguities of the development of Christianity to my own satisfaction.

Another purpose for its production was to condense an entire 5000-year history into a concise and comprehensible snapshot. The interested non-specialist may see the task of researching such a vast amount of information as too daunting to initiate. Hopefully, this relatively slim volume will ease that task and encourage the reader to pursue more in-depth studies among the dozens of available sources recommended in the footnotes and bibliography.

There were many friends, colleagues and family members whose help in creating this work was tremendous. I wish to thank David Worley, Judy Roberts, Carla Cramer, Dr. Dennis Duke, Dr. Maudine Blair, and my son, Keith Stilwell, for their diligent reading, proofing and suggestions for improvement to the text. My most ardent supporter and confidant is my wife, Barbara Ann Stilwell, for whose help I am most grateful.

This work is a further development of a class I taught at the Florida State University Academy. Therefore, I must also offer much gratitude to my students who endured as the first test subjects.

As much as I would like to blame the good people noted above for all remaining errors and problems in the book, I, alas, must retain responsibility for the lot.

Contents

Table of Figures

PREFACE

In the Gospel according to Mark, we have Jesus saying:

> The time is fulfilled, and the Kingdom of God has come near; repent, and believe in the gospel (1:14–15).
>
> To you has been given the secret of the kingdom of God, but for those outside, everything comes in parables; in order that they may indeed look but not perceive, and may indeed listen but not understand; so that they may not turn again, and be forgiven (4:11–12).

These passages beg to be interpreted. In them are the core teachings of the early Christian community. What does it mean that "the time is fulfilled?" What exactly is "the Kingdom of God?" How is it "come near?" And, what exactly is the "gospel?"

In the second verse, how are we to understand the "secret?" Why are there insiders and outsiders? Who are those the speaker desires that they not understand and, therefore, not be forgiven?

In the History part (Part II) of this book, we will see the events that lead up to the questions raised by the first verse. In the Development part (Part III), we will see the early development that leads to the second verses.

Here, we can address the meaning of the term "gospel." It means good news. In the Bible, it was the Greek word εὐαγγέλιον and translated into Latin as *evangelium* (which meant good telling). When the Bible was translated centuries later into an archaic form of English, it was godspell (good story). It finally came to later English as gospel. Now, do we know what it is? No, all we can say is that we know some technical etymology of the term. We cannot say what the good news was, and this has been debated by scholars of all stripes as to its exact meaning.

Unfortunately, it depends on which part of the Bible you read that determines what you believe concerning the good news. This is a simple example of what I mean when I make the claim that the Bible is ambiguous. Very early, this ambiguity led to factions within the Jesus movement and has since produced over 3000 distinct Christian factions throughout the world today.

PART I

Orientation and Introductory Information

The Academic Study of Religion

Why Study Religion?

One might fairly ask, "Why study religion at all?"

One appropriate answer could be that it is simply a fascinating subject like any other area of interest a person might have. However, more importantly, it has attributes that go beyond most other subjects, some of which are:

> Religion deals with ultimate questions. Just as science attempts to discover the ultimate reality of the universe, so does religion in its own way. The way of science appeals to validation of its tenets through the material and physical senses whereas, the way of religion appeals to non-material, non-sensual, and intuitive validation. If one holds only to the empirical physical evidence of the senses then the faith-based study of religion would literally make no sense. Even so, there are still ample reasons for the academic study of religion as a sociological phenomenon. Nevertheless, science's forte and its limitation is addressing the how and what of things; whereas, the various religions attempt to address the why of things.
>
> Most of the world's population is involved in some kind of religious of activity, and anything that important to billions of our fellow citizens is well worthy of examination. See **Fig. 1** below for the top six religious identifications.
>
> We cannot really understand a society without understanding the nature of its religion. European society of the Middle Ages is incomprehensible without knowing the religion of the Roman Catholic Church. More current and pressing is the world-wide threat of terrorism caused by Islamic fundamentalism. Although the religion of Islam itself is not responsible for the current horrors, understanding the terrorists requires that we understand the potential for fanactical adherence to any fundamentalist religion.

We cannot understand much of the arts without knowing the religious foundation upon which they are built. How can we appreciate a Bach Mass if we know nothing of the religious rite it celebrates? Michelangelo's David and the Sistine chapel murals would be meaningless without knowing the Bible stories that provided his themes.

Religious Identification	Approximate Population
Christianity	2,070,000,000
Islam	1,250,000,000
Hinduism	840,000,000
No Religion	780,000,000
Buddhism	370,000,000
Atheists	150,000,000

Fig. 1 Top six religious groups of the world (a composite of sources)

Religion as an Object of Critical Analysis

The academic study of religion differs greatly from a faith-based study. Terms like "critical" and "analysis" are used to describe the method of study. Scholars have devised specific criteria (hence, critical) for judging the factual historicity of religious data. Just as in the physical sciences, data are analyzed (i.e., broken down into component parts) in order to better understand them. This type of study introduces notions that may run counter to many cherished beliefs that we have acquired by attending church, synagogue, mosque or temple.

There are few ways to soften the blow you might feel from inquiring into an objective examination of any religion's history and developments except to, perhaps, disconnect your faith from its objective history. For the religious skeptic, this is easily done, not so for the believer. Many academic historians are themselves members of a particular faith and they employ many schemes to accomplish this disconnect. The most readily available and simplest one is to accept the facts of critical analysis as presented; yet, remain conscious of the possibility that the course of history and the hand of man may indeed be guided by divine inspiration.

Through history many great religious figures have taken this approach to explain the apparent contradictions between their faith and empirical facts. The great Church Father, St. Augustine, is an excellent example of one who did so. When faced with the anthropomorphisms and other crudities of the Bible, he refused to accept Christianity until he was led to believe that the Bible must be taken symbolically and that much in it is in the form of allegory. The modern person would do well to emulate him.

All religions have a myth of their origin. The term "myth" is used in religious studies as meaning a story that contains significant truths that cannot be explained in ordinary factual statements. Origin myths and other myths of any religion while casting some light on the religion's history are inappropriate for the historian's use at face value.

Based on strictly historical evidence, the historian's task is to trace how religions started and how they developed. Our task, in this work, will be to trace the 5000-year history and development of Christianity.

Some Important Definitions

Most terms and phrases will be defined as needed in context. However, throughout this book, there will be *three running themes* that are defined here as follows:

Theodicy—From the Greek *Theos Dike* (Θεός δίκη) meaning the Justice of God. It may be summed up with the phrase: "Why do bad things happen to good people?"

Eschatology—The study of the Last Things, *Ta Eschaton* (τα̉έσχατον). This encompasses religious ideas concerning the end of the world, the end of time, and the death of the individual.

Cosmology—The study of the universe (cosmos), from the Greek *Kosmos Logos* (κόσμος λόγος). In religion, this involves a study of creation and ties closely to the other two concepts above.

Because of their ubiquitous use and possible misunderstanding, two additional terms are explained here:

Myth—A religious model, from the Greek *muthos* (μύθος) meaning a story, which in religion has come to mean a story that teaches a spiritual truth and is believed to be a real representation of encounters with ultimate and/or sacred reality. It almost always describes an ancient time and place where Superhuman Beings are the main characters of the story.

Apocalypticism—These are eschatological beliefs concerning revelations about the Deity breaking into history. It usually signifies the abrupt end of time (as we know it) followed by the intervention of God in world affairs, a final judgment on human beings, and the salvation of the faithful. The end of this age brings on the age to come in which those elected to be saved will rule with God in a renewed heaven and earth.

The religion under study here, Christianity, falls into the category of monotheism, as do the other great religions of the West—Judaism, and Islam. There are many other categories of religion, some of which will be mentioned as we examine the history of Christianity. For that reason, the major ones are defined in the table **Fig. 2** below:

Category	Cryptic Definition	Example
Dynamism	A few natural objects are seen as having power	Primitive*
Animism	Most or all natural objects are inhabited by spirits	primitive
Polytheism	The many gods are considered to be in charge of natural objects	Greeks
Pantheism	God is in and equated with all natural things	Hinduism**
Dualism	There are two equal or nearly equal gods	Zoroastrianism
Henotheism	Other gods are recognized but only "our" god is supreme	Israelites
Deism	A supreme being is responsible for initiating everything	Enlightenment
Monotheism	A supreme being has a personal interest in his creation	Judaism

* Primitive is not meant to be derogatory, and would include many ancient and modern tribal societies on every continent. ** Hinduism runs the gamut of religious types depending on the sect, so only some Hindus are pantheists.

Fig. 2 Categories of religion

Most of the above categories are examples of theisms: The belief in personalized gods or spirits that are considered worthy of worship. These gods are thought to have human-like emotions and an interest in interaction with human beings. The non-theistic religious types (Dynamism, Animism, and Deism) reject these anthropomorphic characteristics.

For the final definition, I will graphically, in **Fig. 3**, illustrate the key terms in the title of this book—History and Development:

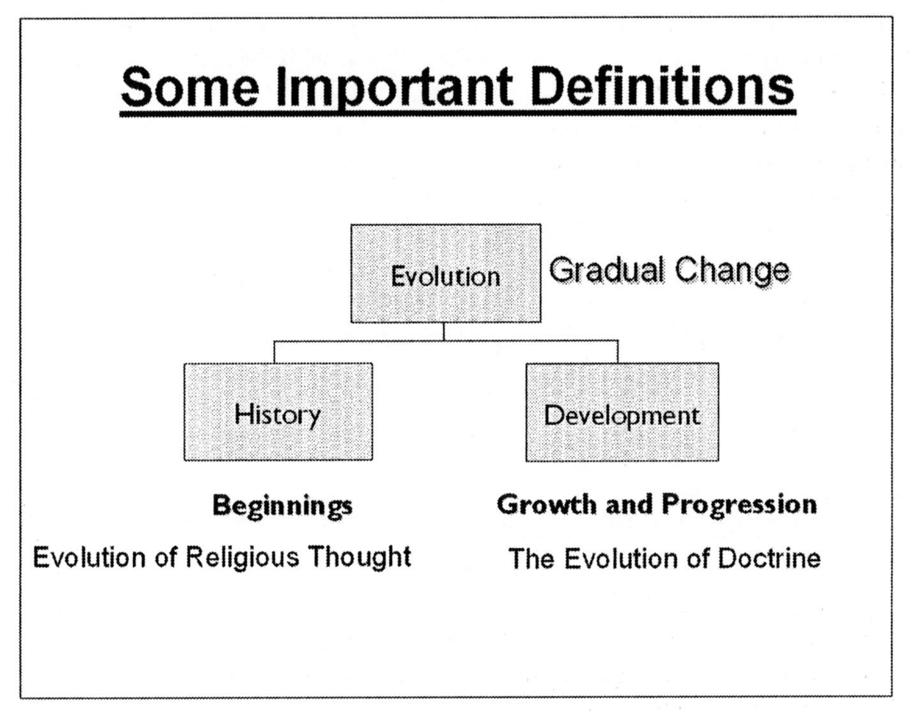

Fig. 3 Definitions of Evolution

From the above definitions, we see that the title of this book could have more simply been given as *Christianity: 5000 Years of Evolution*. Although completely accurate, that title would obfuscate my intent, which is to describe the 3000 years of <u>history</u> leading up to the time of Jesus of Nazareth and the 2000 years of subsequent <u>development</u>.

Orientation in Ancient Places and Times

Ancient Places

All of the history and early development activity discussed in this book takes place around the Mediterranean basin. We will start with the ancient civilizations of Mesopotamia (the land between the rivers) and Egypt. Then, we will look at the religion of the Persians and the reforms of Persia's greatest religious figure, Zarathustra (Zoroaster to the Greeks). Next we will examine the civilizations that have been described as the two parents that gave birth to Christianity: ancient Israel and ancient Greece. Finally, we will see the conduit through which Christianity flowed—that of the Greco-Roman empire.

Two maps below (**Fig. 4** and **Fig. 5**) graphically orient us to the places of interest to the history of Christianity, in the world, and in the Middle East

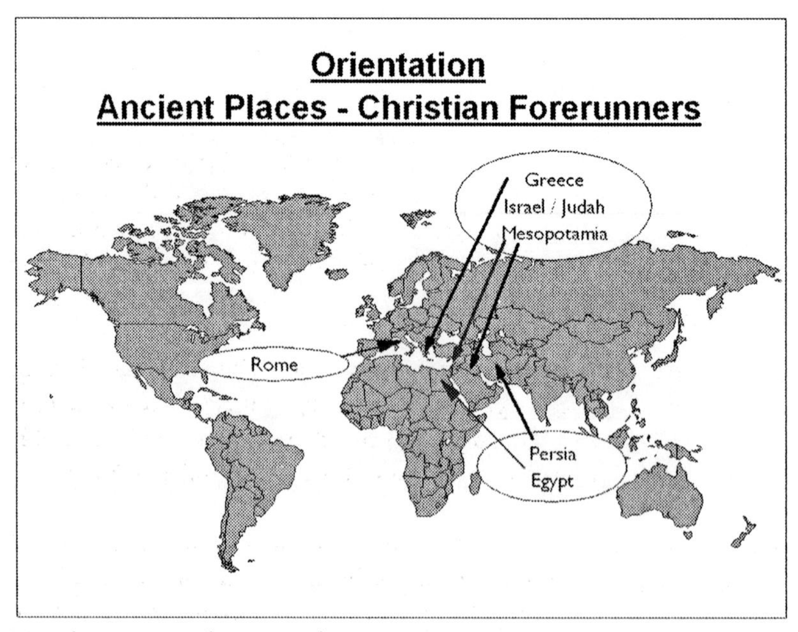

Fig. 4 Ancient Places—Christian Forerunners

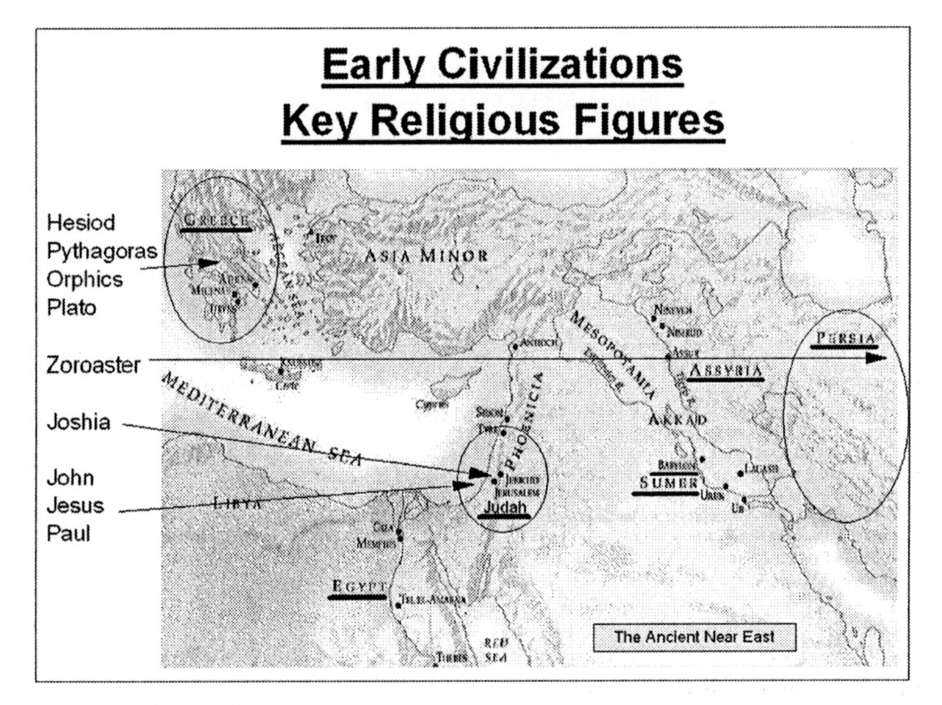

Fig. 5 Early Civilizations—Religious Figures

Ancient Times

It might prove instructional to place our inquiry in its larger setting, since we are going to explore just the first 5000 years of Christian history and development. How does that amount of time compare with the total history of civilization? How does it compare to the amount of the time since the advent of the first humans to the present day?

Compare the age of the earth and the solar system to our 5000-year time sliver of interest. Go all the way and set it against the entire known existence of the universe itself. Need it stop there? Probably not, since there is no scientific prohibition against postulating an eternal substrate out of which our universe arose.

Now, add location to that vista. Out of a potential eternity of time and infinity of space, we are narrowing to an infinitesimal dot in the scheme of things. We are only seeing a minute 5000-year span of time in a littoral geography around the Mediterranean Sea.

Infinitesimal though it may be, it is nevertheless of the vastest importance. For it is in this time and place that human beings looked out into their world and asked questions that, heretofore, had not been asked. They wanted to understand who they were, where they came from, why they were here, and where they might be going. These are the ultimate questions and in this work we will look at their answers.

So, our time frame of interest in this book will be but a tiny fragment of universal history. Our study is concerned with the past 5000 years out of some 12,000 years of human civilization. Human beings have been around for at least 4,000,000 years out of the 4,500,000,000 years of the earth's existence (and three times that for the existence of our observable universe).

Why, then, are we so interested in such a small slice of time? We are anthropocentric! Our concern is for mankind and only mankind with our unique mental and emotion capabilities; we are the center of the universe. However, it is only recently that we have been able to look into the heavens and into ourselves and ask: "What else is there in time and place? Are we all there is and is this all we get?" Not to overly belabor the issue, however, the chart and graphic (**Fig. 6** and **Fig.** 7) below suggest just how small our area of interest is.

Era	Origin
The Known Universe	15 Billion Years Ago
Our Solar System	4.5 Billion Years Ago
Human Prehistory	>4 Million Years Ago
Early Human Civilizations	12 Thousand Years Ago
Events Under Study Here	3000 BCE to Present Day

Fig. 6 Time Frame

The figure, Fig. 7, below shows three different time scales:

- the bottom scale shows the time from 5 Billion years before the present (BP) to the present;
- the middle scale shows 1/10th of that time, from 500 Million BP to the present;
- the top scale shows 1/500th of the middle scale (1/5000th of the bottom scale), from 1 million BP to the present.

If we compared the age of the earth to a 24-hour clock, our time under study in this book would have started at 1/10th of a second till Midnight.

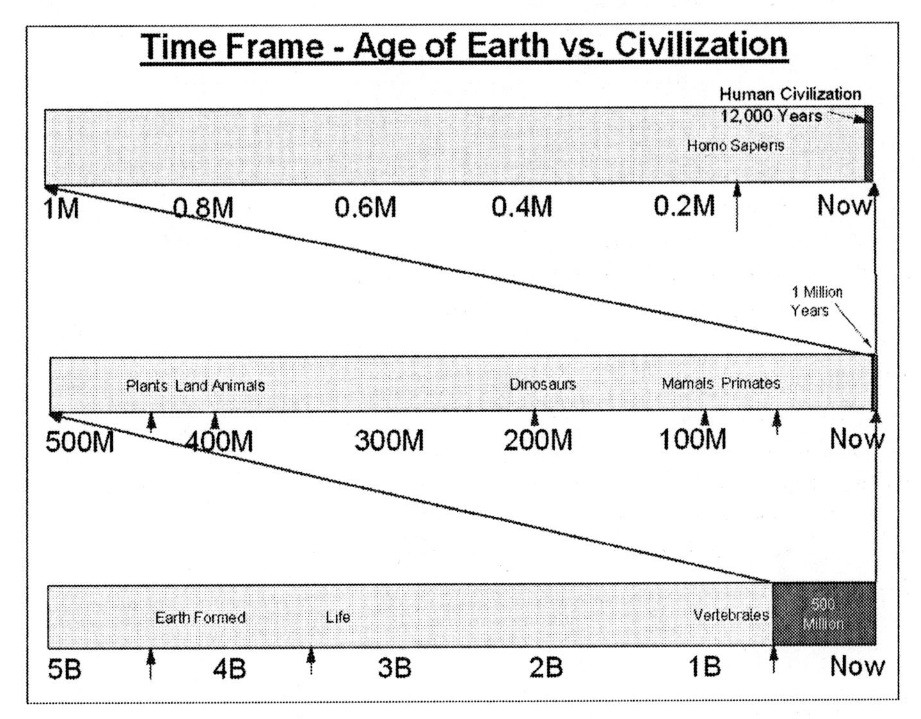

Fig. 7 Time Frame—Age of the Earth vs. Civilization

As a quick overview, some places/entities/persons and times BCE (Before the Common Era) are given in **Fig. 8** below:

Place/Entity/Person	**Date BCE**
Vertebrates	500,000,000
Primates	50,000,000
Hominids	4,000,000
Homo Sapiens	250,000
Neanderthal	120,000
Modern Humans	100,000
Human Agriculture	12,000

Place/Entity/Person	Date BCE
Mesopotamia	3000
Egypt—Old Kingdom	2500
Akhenaten	1500
Moses	1300
Zoroaster	1200
David	1000
Josiah	600
Exile	587
Orphics	500
Plato	385
Alexander	323
Daniel	165
Essenes	100
John the Baptist	10
Jesus	4

Fig. 8 Key Places/Entities/Persons and Dates

In order to illustrate the expanse of time involved (even in our small reference frame), see the Timeline chart **Fig. 16**—at the beginning of Part II—for a linear scale containing places and persons of interest to this inquiry.

Religions Before Christianity

We can go far back in time and find evidence of religious activity. Archeological burial sites from over 50,000 years ago show that people were burying their dead with some sort of rite. Everyday items of importance to the dead person were buried with him, and in all likelihood, these items were meant to be used by the dead person in some sort of an afterlife.

It would seem that from very early in our humanity there were intimations of immortality. A person cannot readily be conscious of his or her existence and envision a time when he or she does not exist. Over the millennia, these concepts waxed and waned with the prevailing disposition of any given society. We'll see that even our recent religions under consideration have gone through a series of visions of the afterlife—from none at all or as only a shadowy ghost, to that of a spiritual existence, to that of walking the earth once again.

Our search for the foundations of Christianity will reach back only to about 5000 years ago when the earliest civilization (in the land between the rivers Tigris and Euphrates) was entering the pages of history.

Figure, **Fig. 9**, below shows the very approximate time of origin and subsequent development of our subjects:

Religion	**Origin—Development**
Mesopotamian	3200 BCE
Sumerian, Old Babylonian	
Egyptian	2900 BCE
Persian/Zoroastrianism	1200 BCE
Israelite	1800–600 BCE
Greek	700–300 BCE
Early Judaism	600 BCE–70 CE

Religion	Origin—Development
Rabbinical Judaism	70 CE–present
Early Christianity	30–500 CE
Medieval Christianity	500–1500 CE
Islam	600–present
Modern Christianity	1500–present

Fig. 9 Major Religions and Approximate Time frame of Origins

World Religions Today

There are approximately six billion people in the world today and most of them claim to believe in some religion.

Fig. 10 below graphically illustrates the breakdown of religious claimants. **Fig. 11** shows the distributions of the four largest religions on a world map.

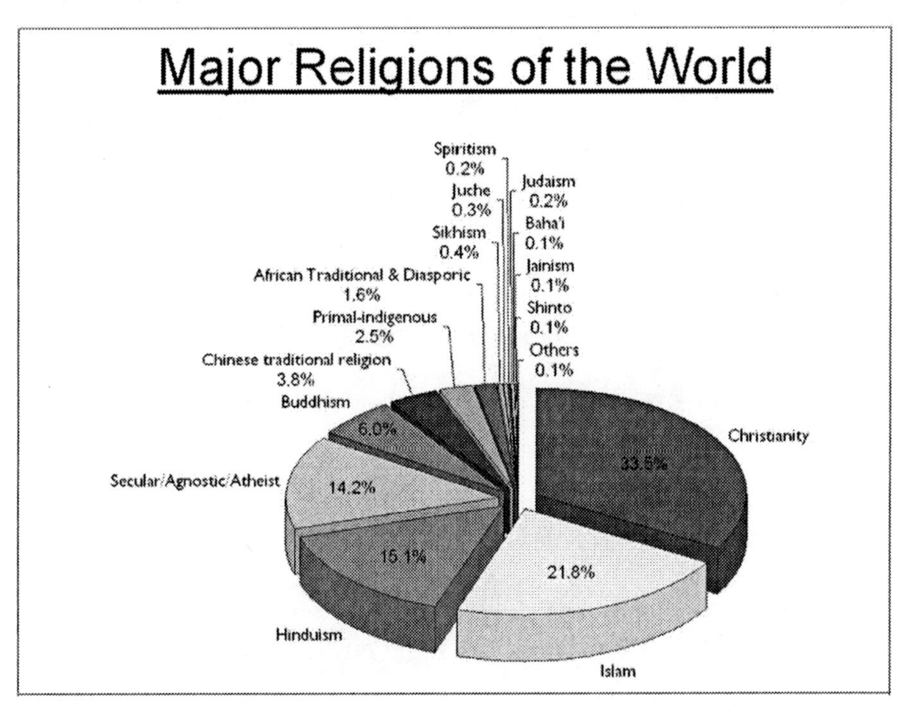

Fig. 10 Graphic of World Religious Identifications (% of population of ca. 6 billion)

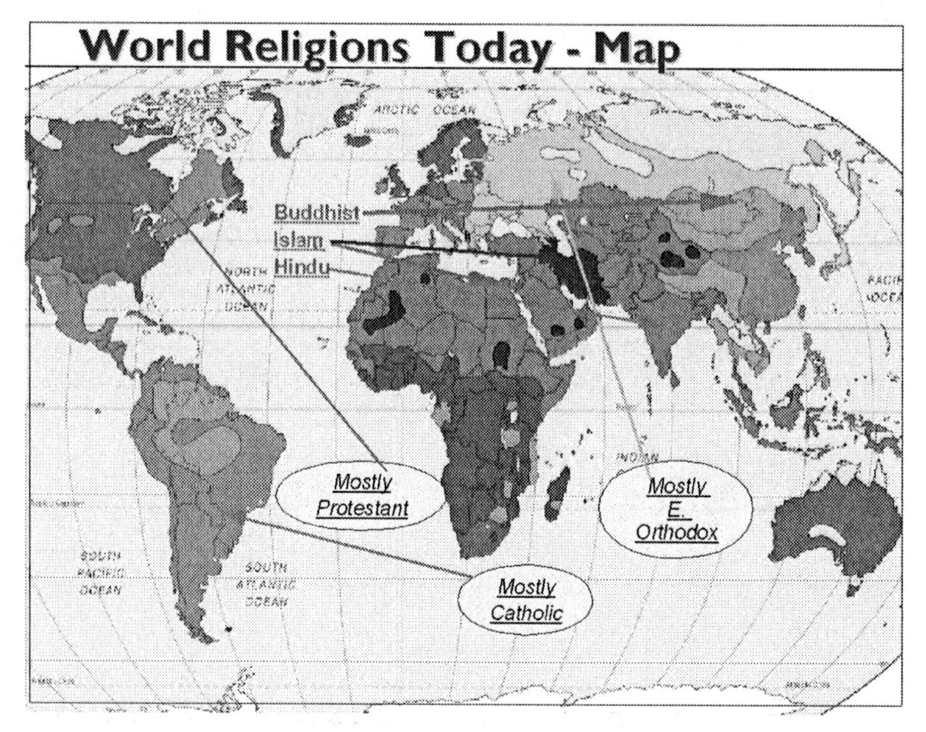

Fig. 11 Geographical Distribution of the Four Largest World Religions

The next two tables (**Fig. 12 and Fig. 13**) show the distribution of Christian factions worldwide:

Major Branches
Liberal and Conservative Denominations

These numbers are approximate and taken from multiple sources (primarily Britannica Almanac 2004), so should be used for rough comparative purposes only.

Major Branches of Christianity—Worldwide

Branch	Number of Adherents
Catholic	1,090,000,000
Protestant	370,000,000
Other Christians*	310,000,000
Orthodox	220,000,000
Anglicans	80,000,000

* Christians outside the above four mainstream labels (e.g., Jehovah's Witnesses, Mormons, New Thought, Friends, Unitarians, Religious Science and many others)

Fig. 12 Major Traditional Branches of Christianity—Worldwide

Liberal and Conservative Branches of Christianity—Worldwide

Denominations are much like contemporary political parties. In the past, we could consider Democrats liberals and Republicans conservatives. Those categories have long since ceased having any meaning, as have the old denominational categories. Now, most Protestant denominations have a liberal wing and a conservative wing, and this is where the real differences appear. Liberal Christians are those who would probably accept the conclusions of modern religious scholarship; however, Conservative Christians would probably not.

Branch	Number (Approx,)
Catholic *	1,090,000,000
Orthodox/Eastern Christian	220,000,000
Conservative Protestant **	200,000,000
Liberal Protestant	170,000,000
African indigenous sects (AICs)	110,000,000
Pentecostal	105,000,000
Anglican *	80,000,000
Jehovah's Witnesses	14,800,000
Latter Day Saints	11,200,000
New Thought (Unity, Christian Science, etc.)	1,500,000
Friends (Quakers)	300,000

* Non-Protestants also have both wings to a greater or lesser degree. ** Born-again, Evangelical, Fundamentalists, Charismatics.

Fig. 13 Liberal and Conservative Christians

United States Religions Today

There are some 600 Million people in the United States. The following tables (both immediately below and in the Appendix for **Fig. 54, Fig. 55** and **Fig. 56**), based mostly on the American Religious Identification Study (ARIS), show the distributions of major branches, denominational families, and denominational bodies in the USA.

The ARIS Study of 2001

The American Religious Identification Survey done in 2001 surveyed adults to determine their purported allegiance to religion.

They asked three questions:

> What is your religion if any?
>
> Do you or a member of your household belong to a religious institution?
>
> In outlook, are you secular or religious?

One of their most interesting findings was that religious identification and institutional membership are two very different things. On average, only 54% of households that claimed religious identity actually had at least one member affiliated with their purported institution. For details of the ARIS study, see the web site: http://www.gc.cuny.edu/studies/key_findings.htm.

Some of the results of that study are reported below (and in the Appendix) in order to assess contemporary religiosity.

Families of Christian Denominations

Today, there are many ways of classifying over 3,000 Christian faith groups in the US and the world.

The following **Fig. 14** describes how many denominations can be sorted into families, according to their historical roots. Notice that of the original four Protestant Families (Lutheran, Anabaptist, Anglican, and Calvinist), the Calvinists have split into the most denominations. Many of today's denominations cannot be identified with one of the originals and, indeed, should not be labeled Protestant at all.

Major Branch	**Major Divisions**	**Next Level Divisions**	**Some Example Denominations**
Roman Catholic	Latin Rite		
	Eastern Rite	National Bodies	Coptic, Ukrainian Chaldean, Marionite, Melkite, Syrian
Orthodox			National Patriarchates
Protestants:			
Lutheran			Evangelical Lutheran Church in America, Lutheran church—Missouri Synod, etc.
Anabaptist	Mennonite	Amish	
Calvinist	Reformed	Presbyterian	Disciples of Christ, Churches of Christ
		Particular Baptist	Northern Baptist, Primitive Baptist, Southern Baptist
		Congregational	
		United Church of Christ	
	Arminian	General Baptist	Free Will
		Methodists	United, AME, Holiness (Church of the Nazarene, Pentecostal—Assemblies of God, Church of God)
Anglican	Church of England		
	Episcopalian		

Major Branch	Major Divisions	Next Level Divisions	Some Example Denominations
Quaker	Friends United		Friends General, Shakers
Mormon	Latter Day Saints		Reorganized LDS
Adventist	Seventh Day		

Fig. 14 Families of Christian Denominations

Contemporary Denominational Families of Christianity and the Year Started

The final statistic in this introduction is that of the founding year of some ancient and contemporary denominational families of Christianity, **Fig. 15**.

Branch or Denominational Family	Approximate Year Started
Jewish Christians	33
Pauline Christians	30's
Gnostic Christians	100's
Orthodoxy	300's
Coptic (non-Chalcedonian)	451
Schism Between Eastern Orthodoxy and Roman Catholicism	1054
Lutherans	1517
Anabaptists	1534
Anglican	1534
Calvinist	1536
Presbyterians	1560
Congregationalists	1582
Baptists	1605
Quakers (Friends)	1654
Amish	1693
Methodists	1744

Branch or Denominational Family	Approximate Year Started
Episcopal	1789
Mormons	1830
Disciples of Christ	1832
Adventists	1846
Christadelphians	1848
Jehovah's Witnesses	1852
Salvation Army	1865
Christian Scientists	1875
Jehovah's Witnesses	1879
Unity	1889
Pentecostals	1901

Fig. 15 Denomination and Year Started (from various sources and very approximate)

Why so Many Variations of Christianity?

When Christianity was virtually a monolithic organization throughout the Middle Ages, there were essentially no variations to the Roman Church in the Western world. To be sure, there were small groups of people who defied the great Church and went their own way. However, they were small underground movements, for when they asserted themselves, they were persecuted and driven back underground. I see the following four major issues that allowed the present day church to splinter into so many variations.

Limited or No Central Control

The most obvious reason is the lack of a centralized controlling organization. With the success of the Protestant Reformation (discussed later), variant groups were now strong enough to assert their right to exist. Still, this alone does not account for the great numbers of the variations. After all, the Lutheran, Reformed and Anabaptist churches could have exerted a controlling force (as had the Roman Catholic Church) that would have limited the variations to just those few in the West.

The deeper answer to the variation problem lies in the heart of the Reformation ideals themselves. In their enthusiasm to return to what they believed were the basic principles that drove the original Christians, the Reformers instituted the following two doctrines that would forever shatter any hope of a return to medieval unity.

Priesthood of All Believers

The first Protestant doctrine was the priesthood of all believers. Human intermediaries between man and God were no longer considered necessary. Each person was to have immediate access to God without going through an intermediary priest. There were many reasons for this doctrine but, perhaps, one stands out as sufficient; that the organization had been corrupted. The intermediaries, from the Pope down, had become involved in the sale of salvation.

Sola Scriptura

The other Protestant doctrine was the belief that one must go directly and only to the scriptures for the truth. Over the centuries, the Church had built an entire theological structure that was independent of the Bible. The churchmen, as we'll see later, had done to the Christian scriptures what the Pharisees of Jesus' time had done to the Torah; they "built a fence" around it in order to address concepts that were handled ambiguously by holy writ. In itself, this could be a good thing unless misused. The Reformers thought that there was misuse and proceeded to strip away most of the accumulated structure to reveal the bare bones of what they believed to be original Christianity.

Ambiguous Interpretations of Scripture

The Church had heretofore appropriated to itself the sole interpretation of the scriptures. When, that central control over Biblical interpretation was gone, everyone was his own priest and the scripture his only guide. If the scriptures were totally straightforward and easy to understand, this might have worked well. Unfortunately, such is not the case. The scriptures are not straightforward, not easy to understand and are, indeed, susceptible to a virtually infinite variety of interpretation. Thus, we have the varieties of contemporary Christianity.

Nevertheless, in spite of this ambiguity, there are certain core doctrines that are adhered to by the majority of Christians. What are those key Christian Doctrines? Are they supported by *sola scriptura*? And, do they really go back to an original Christianity?

Let's look at the Christian doctrines of today.

Christian Doctrines Today

The Fundamentals (1909–1912)

Near the turn of the last century, a group of people was concerned that we may be failing to keep the core doctrines of the Christian faith. Darwinism, secularism, and liberal theology were eroding the traditional faith in doctrines and the Bible. A 12-volume publication (entitled *The Fundamentals*) was created to allay this concern. In it, an attempt was made to settle on the bedrock, key, fundamental doctrines. Without these, there would be no Christian church.

The Fundamentals arrived at five of these *sine qua non* fundamental doctrines:

1. Virgin birth
2. Physical resurrection of Christ
3. Infallibility of the Scriptures
4. Substitutional atonement
5. Physical second coming of Christ

As a result of these volumes, a new word entered the English vocabulary; Fundamentalism.

A Contemporary Conservative View

The Fundamentals is now almost 100 years old. How does it compare to more contemporary Christian views? Unfortunately, it depends! The denomination's dependence on the fundamental doctrines is on the type of Christianity practiced—liberal, conservative, or somewhere in between. The closest to the historical, traditional Christianity of the Reformation are today's religious conservatives. Here is a look at one example of their views.[1]

---

1. For the source, of which this is a paraphrase, see the web site "Basic Christian Doctrine" by Matthew Slick, www.carm.org/grid.htm.

Traditional Conservative Essential Christian Doctrines

The first five doctrines are given as essential to Christian belief and salvation, with the last two being secondarily so.

1. Jesus is both God and man.
2. Jesus rose from the dead physically.
3. Salvation is by grace through faith.
4. The gospel is the death, burial, and resurrection of Jesus.
5. There is only one God.

---

6. God exists as a Trinity of persons: Father, Son, and Holy Spirit.
7. Jesus was born of the Virgin Mary.

Examples of groups that are said to deny these doctrines are:

Mormons—	3, 4, 5, 6, 7
Jehovah's Witnesses—	1, 2, 3, 6
Christian Science—	1, 2, 3, 4
Christadelphians—	1, 3, 6
Oneness Pentecostal—	6

Holding the following doctrines are not considered essential to salvation. However, the denial of them shows a lack of spiritual understanding:

Moral integrity is necessary.
Fidelity in marriage in heterosexual relationships is required.
Homosexuality must be condemned as unacceptable in the church.
The Bible is inerrant.
Baptism is <u>not</u> necessary for salvation.

The following beliefs and practices are not considered essential to salvation. However, denial of these does not show lack of spiritual understanding since these are variously held opinions. These beliefs and practices are most responsible for the multifarious varieties of beliefs:

Predestination, election, limited atonement, and free will;
Communion frequency;

Saturday or Sunday worship;
Pre-, Mid-, Post-Tribulation rapture;
Pre-, A-, Post-Millennialism;
Continuation or cessation of the charismatic gifts;
Baptism for adults or infants.

The following are considered Christian heresies and believing in these errors shows a lack of biblical theological understanding:

Universalism, or the belief that everyone will be saved eventually;
Annihilationism, or the belief that the evil are not eternally damned;
Possession of Christians by demons;
Christians are to be healthy and wealthy by the fact of being Christians;
Women may be allowed to be pastors and elders.

Obviously, this is only one variety of Christianities' opinion. However, it seems to speak for the vast majority of conservative, traditional Christians.

The following are examples of what some Christian sources claim separates true Christianity from the various non-Christian cults. However, many of these alleged "cults" lay claim to being Christian themselves.

1. The Trinity

God is one Being that exists eternally in three persons: the Father, Son, and Holy Spirit. Each person is eternally distinct, eternally coequal, and eternally one God. The word Trinity, although not in the Bible, is used to describe a concept that is in the bible. It describes the relationship of the Father, Son, and the Holy Spirit. Each person is distinct, yet each person is God.

2. Jesus Christ

Jesus is the Son of God and the Second person of the Trinity. He was born of the Virgin Mary and has two natures: divine and human.

3. The Holy Spirit

Third person of the Trinity. The Holy Spirit teaches us, comforts us, directs us, and gives us gifts for the witness of God.

4. God's Attributes & Existence

God is the First person of the Trinity. He is all-knowing (omniscient), all-powerful (omnipotent), everywhere (omnipresent), and exists eternally unchanging.

5. Christ's Resurrection

Christ was resurrected physically (in the same body in which He died) three days after he was crucified.

6. Christ's Second Coming

Christ will return physically to earth and will reign with those who believe in Him.

7. Heaven and Hell

When all are judged, people will either spend eternity in Heaven with God, or they will spend eternity in Hell separated from God. Where you go is determined by your faith or lack of faith in Christ. Heaven is for all those that accept Christ as Lord and Savior. Hell is a literal place of torment for those that don't accept Christ.

8. Salvation

Salvation is a gift from God and comes by faith alone. Out of salvation flows justification and good works; however, good works of themselves can do nothing to save you. All those that accept Christ as Lord and Savior will spend eternity in the presence of the Lord. Historically, those not accepting Jesus would spend eternity in Hell.

9. The Word of God

The Old and New Testaments are the inspired, inerrant Word of God. Nothing shall be added or taken from them.

Each of these doctrines or beliefs has a historical origin that we will examine in the course of reviewing the history and development of Christianity.

RETURN TO THE ONE SINGLE FAITH?

> Now I beseech you…that ye all speak the same thing, and that there be no divisions among you; but that ye be perfectly joined together in the same mind and in the same judgment.
>
> St. Paul, 1 Corinthians 1:10

Ironically, St. Paul was experiencing the same sectarianism that divides Christianity today. There were fewer "denominations" but the ones existent at the time threatened to fragment the unity that Paul beseeched.

With the above doctrinal scenarios in mind, we can ask:

> Can we ever get to a single Christianity?
> Was there ever a single Christianity?

These are some questions we will explore in subsequent chapters.

History and Development Graphics

History Leading to Christianity

As we go through the history of the religions leading to Christianity, the following graphic will be evolved showing the progression of religious thought from ancient Mesopotamia through the birth of Jesus.

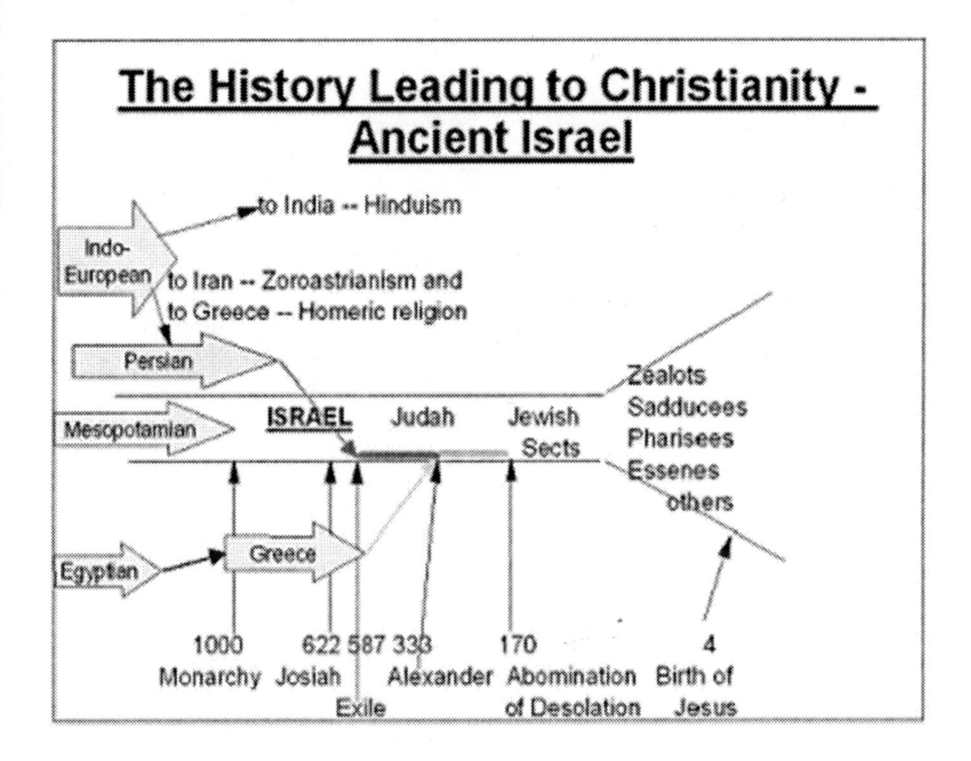

Development of Christianity

The graphic below will be evolved through time from the birth of Jesus, to the institutional church, and finally to the modern ecumenical movement.

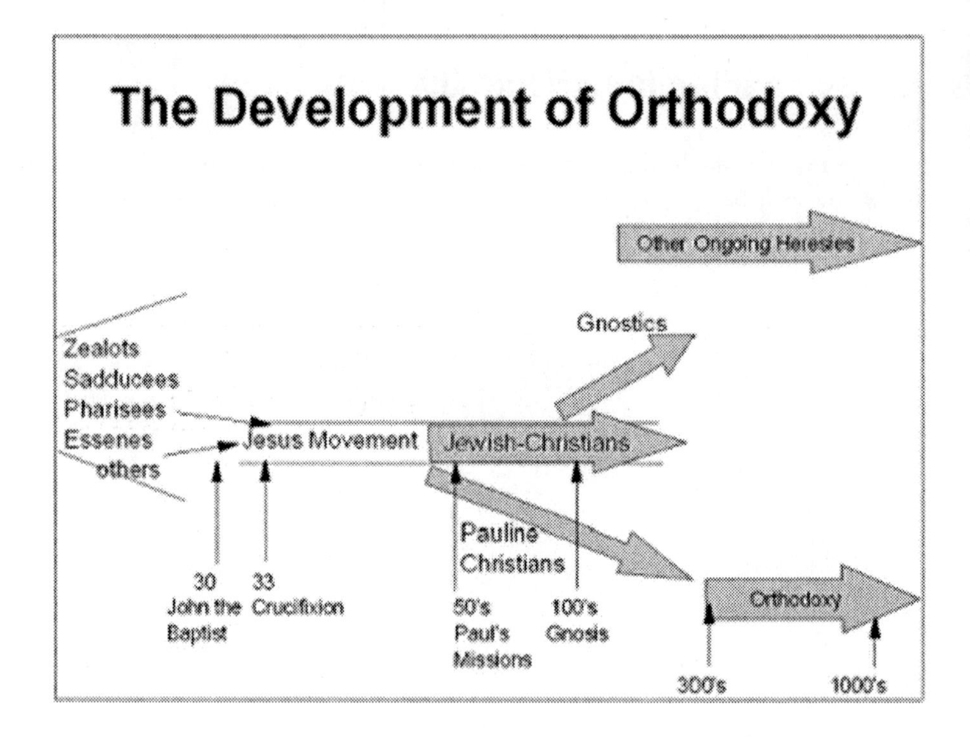

PART II

The History of Christianity

TIMELINES: THE BIG PICTURE (3000–1 BCE)

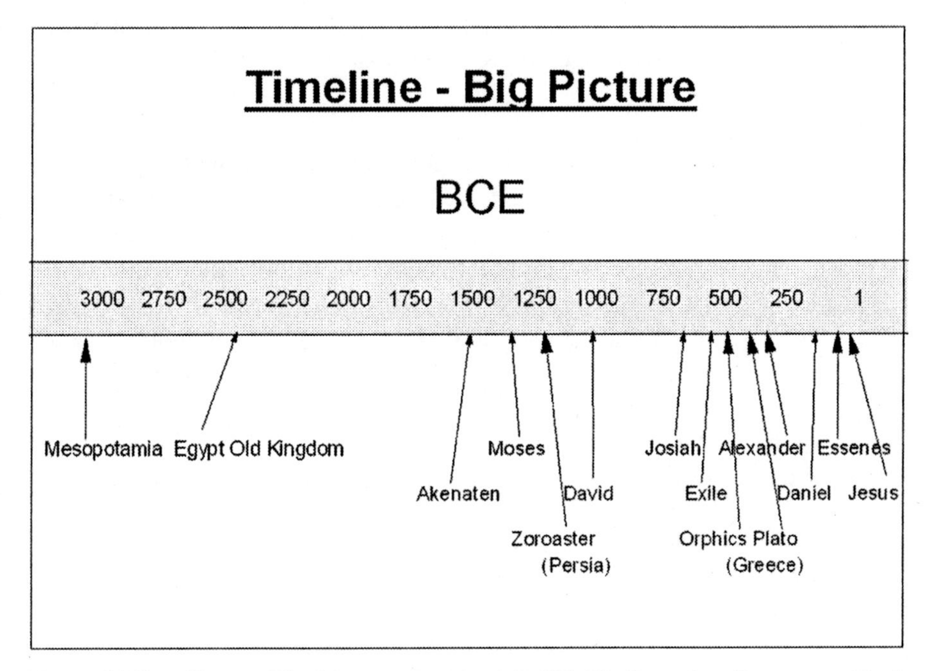

Fig. 16 Timeline—Big Picture 3000–1 BCE (Before the Common Era)
The above figure shows the approximate times of places/people of interest on a linear time scale. "Big Picture" is a very relative term.

A Synopsis of Part II (Encapsulation)

The history of Christianity did not begin with the birth of Jesus. For millennia before his time came a concatenation of events that inexorably led to the founding of a new religion.

All of the action takes place around the Eastern-most part of the Mediterranean Sea and some distance in-land to the East. The center will not be Israel because Israel did not yet exist at the beginning of our journey. At the time we start looking at the events of our story, we find four major civilizations in the entire world: that in what is now Eastern China; Northwestern India; Egypt's Nile River; and Central Iraq. Northwestern India and Eastern China will be developing concurrently with our story and will not affect our tale until many thousands of years have passed.

But, our story begins about 3200 BCE in the Fertile Crescent that lies in the land between two rivers in Mesopotamia (Iraq)—thought by some to be the location of the Garden of Eden. A succession of ancient civilizations will leave their imprint on the region, bequeathing their legends of the search for immortality and their relationship to God to a later people. At the same time, another people living along the river Nile will be creating their own legends that will eventually influence those who live in the Fertile Crescent.

Over a thousand years will pass before we see a stirring of activity in Israel, and after another thousand years pass, we see the religion that will become Judaism begin to take shape. During this long interval, the people of Israel have absorbed the streams of thought coming from Iraq and Egypt. A little later, the two new civilizations of Persia and Greece will insert additional ideas into the emergent matrix.

By the time of the birth of Jesus, a confluence of diverse streams of thought into Israel from Mesopotamia, Egypt, Persia and Greece will have created a religion that we recognize as Judaism. It is into this matrix that Jesus will step and proclaim his good news of the Kingdom of God.

The seed has been planted of what will only later become Christianity.

The Pre-Christian Roots: The Religions of Mesopotamia

Mesopotamia is Greek for "between the rivers" (of the Tigris and Euphrates). Today the nation of Iraq is positioned in the center of that ancient land.

To us in the twentieth century, the civilization of the Greeks seems quite old but when the Greeks named the land between the rivers, its civilization had already been thriving for 3000 years.

Figure, **Fig.** 17, below is intended to show Mesopotamia in relation to its neighbors. In particular, notice the proximity to the city of what will later be Jerusalem to the southwest. Jerusalem will become the great city of David and capital of the united Israelite monarchy 2000 years hence. Then it will become the pawn of one conqueror after another, giving rise to a religion that looks desperately forward to the end of the world and release from oppression.

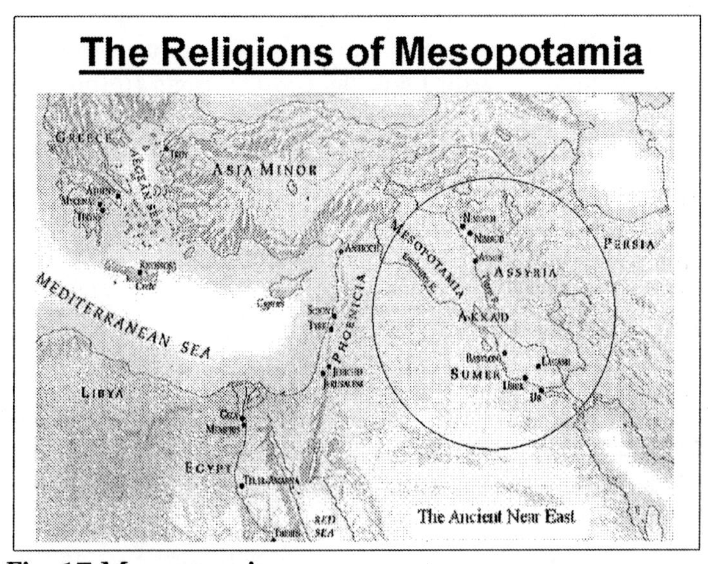

Fig. 17 Mesopotamia

In the third millennium BCE, much of the Near East came under the rule, or at least the influence, of the Sumerians. The Sumerian civilization had flourished for well over a thousand years before Sargon I (ca. 2330–2280) of Akkad founded the great Akkadian (Sumerian) empire, which included Babylonia and Assyria within its borders.

Around 2000 BCE, invasions of nomadic Semitic peoples from the Arabian Desert and other places overwhelmed the non-Semitic Sumerians, allowing the rise of the relatively short-lived Old Babylonian Empire. Old Babylon was to fall within a few hundred years and Assyria was to rule the Near East for almost a thousand years.

Against this historical background, we will see how the religions of Mesopotamia retained its conservative and stable core religious beliefs for over three thousand years.

Sumerian and Akkadian

The Sumerians believed in an array of invisible and immortal beings possessing powers beyond those of mere mortals. These core beliefs were to extend to all of Sumer's succeeding empires. In these beliefs, mankind was held to be powerless against the forces of nature, personified by the gods, and was subject to death.

The original Sumerian pantheon consisted of four major creating gods: An, the god of heaven; Ki, the goddess of earth; Enlil, the god of air and storms; and Enki, the god of water. These gods were, therefore, the rulers of the four substances that comprised the world: heaven, earth, air, and water.

Subordinate to these deities were three astral gods: Nana, the god of the moon, Utu, the god of the sun, and Inanna, the goddess of love and war.

Dying and rising gods

There were many other gods, among the most important being Dumuzi (later to be known as Tammuz). The story of Dumuzi and Inanna is the prototype for later religions' beliefs concerning the cycles of the seasons, the fertility of the land, the death of mortals, and the relationship of the gods to the earthly king.

Planters of the fields noticed that the cycles of nature brought forth new growth from under the earth in the spring of the year and saw it decay into the earth in winter. This cycle of dying and rising needed an explanation and there developed the myths of a god of fertility, who must die for part of the year and then live again in another part. When the god was alive, the fields would flourish with life; when dead, the vegetation would die too.

Story of Dumuzi and Inanna

The story of Dumuzi, which represents the dying and rising god and his power of fertility, generally proceeds thusly.[2]

Dumuzi was a mortal ruler that, through his marriage to the goddess of love, insured the fertility of the land and of the people. The goddess Inanna, his wife, decides to go to the netherworld to visit Ereshkigal, whom she somehow enrages.

> To the Land of no Return, the realm of Ereshkigal, Ishtar [Inanna], the daughter of Sin, set her mind.
> Yea, the daughter of Sin set her mind To the dark house, the abode of Irkalla, To the house which none leave who have entered it, To the road from which there is no way back, To the house wherein the dwellers are bereft of light, Where dust is their fare and clay their food, (Where) they see no light, residing in darkness, (Where) they are clothed like birds, with wings for garments, (And where) over door and bolt is spread dust.[3]

For her effrontery, Inanna is condemned to die and remain in the underworld. Inanna's case is pleaded by her handmaiden and she is revived, but is still not allowed to re-ascend to earth since, "who has ever left the underworld scot-free?" Eventually, she may leave but must provide a substitute for herself, who turns out to be none other than her husband, Dumuzi. It seems that Dumuzi did not lament for his wife while she was trapped in the netherworld, and for this he will pay by being placed there in her stead.

---

2. For more in-depth examination of Mesopotamian religions, see Thorkild Jacobsen, *The Treasures of Darkness,* (New Haven University Press, 1976), 25–73. Also, for texts of Mesopotamia and Egypt, see: James B Pritchard, *The Ancient Near East* Vol 1, (Princeton University Press, 1958).

3. Translation by E. A. Speiser, *Ancient Near Eastern Texts Relating to the Old Testament,* edited by James B. Pritchard (Princeton: Princeton University Press, 1969), 106–109.

In a convoluted mix of myths, Dumuzi's sister exchanges places with him every six months so that Dumuzi may ascend to the surface, once again insuring the fecundity of the land and the people.

The Sumerians celebrated the sacred marriage between Inanna and Dumuzi every year at the autumnal equinox by having their surrogates, the king and the priestess of Inanna, ritually married. These rituals were held in temples that were staffed by religious professionals dedicated to the daily sacrifice to the gods. The religious professionals also performed other practices, such as augury and divination. That these latter practices were very important is shown by the example of Gudea, the ruler of Girsu, who had his dream of building a temple interpreted by an interpreter of dreams, then sought to validate the dreams by auguring the will of the gods in the liver of a goat.

Old Babylonian

The core beliefs of the Sumerians transferred readily to the succeeding Babylonians. However, one major change that took place was the ascension of the god Marduk to the place of preeminence. This transfer of power from the Sumerians to the Babylonians (and from the old gods to the new) is explained in the myth of the Enuma elish.

The assembly of the gods held the ultimate power in the Mesopotamian universe. It was at such an assembly that Marduk was asked to be the champion of the younger gods in a battle against some of the older gods led by Tiamat and Kingu. Marduk defeats the older gods; whereupon, the god of heaven, An, transfers his title as ruler of the gods to Marduk and has all of the gods build him a city which would be called Babylon.

Just like the Sumerians, the Babylonians believed in invisible and powerful gods. Marduk was now the head of the pantheon, but others were also of great importance, including the astral deities: Sin, the god of the moon; Shamash, the god of the sun and of justice; Inanna was now called Ishtar as goddess of love and war; Adad was god of storms; and Ea was the god of wisdom and water. Numerous others filled the sky and the netherworld. So, the essential cosmos of the Sumerians persisted, with only the names changed. With these beliefs, there also persisted the temple, priests, sacrifice, augury, and even the sacred marriage of the goddess and the king at the Akitu festival.

Assyrian

This trend was to continue with the rise of Assyria. The culture and religion of Babylon was taken over fairly intact, with Ashur, a new god, becoming the new ruler of the gods.

The primary god being at the head of the council of gods, of course, argued for the legitimization of the king being Head of the state. The rise of Marduk to being the Head of the Babylonian assembly had served that purpose, as did the primacy of the new god Ashur in promoting the new king of Assyria. One of the major functions of religion would appear to be to provide the divine right or support of the earthly ruler. This function took place in Mesopotamia and Egypt, and would continue by supporting the Israelite monarchy centuries later.

Mesopotamian Religious Literature

Our earliest written history comes from the ancient kingdom of Sumer in Mesopotamia. We have archeological evidence of writing from around 3200 BCE and have a good idea of their civilization from accounts that have been handed down from that era.

The particulars of their religion are well known, especially their concepts of Cosmology and Eschatology. Two stories explain in great detail what these concepts entailed: the Enuma elish and the Epic of Gilgamesh.

Cosmology and the Enuma elish[4]

"When on high" begins the great creation epic. The primordial salt and fresh waters mingle to form all subsequent creation. The waters represent the undifferentiated chaos from which all subsequent elements came and which are always just outside the bounds of our world threatening the dome of the heavens to come crashing in upon us.

---

4. Multiple copies of this story have been found throughout Iraq. This story itself probably dates from well before the time of Hammurabi (ca. 1790–1750 BCE). The edition showing Marduk as the head god was from the Old Babylonian Kingdom (ca. 1830–1530 BCE), and is a political statement concerning the supremacy of Babylon, the city of Marduk.

From Tablet I

> When on high the heaven had not been named,
> Firm ground below had not been called by name,
> Naught but primordial Apsu, their begetter,
> (And) Mummu-Tiamat, she who bore them all,
> Their waters commingling as a single body;
> No reed hut had been matted, no marsh land had appeared,
> When no gods whatever had been brought into being,
> Uncalled by name, their destinies undetermined—
> Then it was that the gods were formed within them.[5]

The story which was written on seven[6] clay tablets continues...

Apsu is the male god of fresh water. Tiamat, his wife, is the goddess of the sea and represents chaos and threat. Tiamat gives birth to the next generation of gods who, in turn, engender the god of the sky, An, who then bears Ea. These later generations of the gods disturb the peace of Apsu who threatens to destroy them. Ea learns of his plan and kills Apsu, which will cause later repercussions from Tiamat, who vows revenge for the murder of her consort. In the Old Babylonian version of the myth, it is Marduk who becomes the hero in the battle against Tiamat, and is given first place as the greatest of the gods. When the Old Babylonians are defeated, its myth is taken over by the Assyrians, and the hero and high god becomes their own god, Ashur.

We learn of the gods and of their dealings with humans, how they created the heavens and the earth and why they created men. Here, we begin to see our ancestors asking the ultimate questions and answering them as best they could through the vehicle of myth.

Of primary importance to us is the Mesopotamian description of the cosmos which was to pervade the consciousness of Middle Eastern cultures for centuries

---

5. Translated by E. A. Speiser, *Ancient Near Eastern Texts*, 60-1. For further information on the Enuma elish see Speiser and also: Thorkild Jacobsen, *The Treasures of Darkness*, (New Haven: Yale University Press, 1976), 167f.

6. The fact of there being seven tablets for this creation story has given rise to a comparison with the seven days of creation in Genesis. Upon further investigation, this comparison is not viable. However, the order of the creation in both stories is essentially identical.

to come. Their world consisted of three tiers: the heavens above; the underworld below; and the habitat of humankind in between. The gods lived in the heavens and the ghosts of the dead dwelled in the underworld called Arallu. See **Fig. 18** for a graphic of their cosmological view.

Humans lived on the earth and differed from the gods in that the gods were immortal while we humans were born and must die and become a wraith-like ghost (having no true life) in the house of darkness under ground. Almost no one hoped for anything better than this present existence except for one man who dared to seek the immortality reserved for the gods.

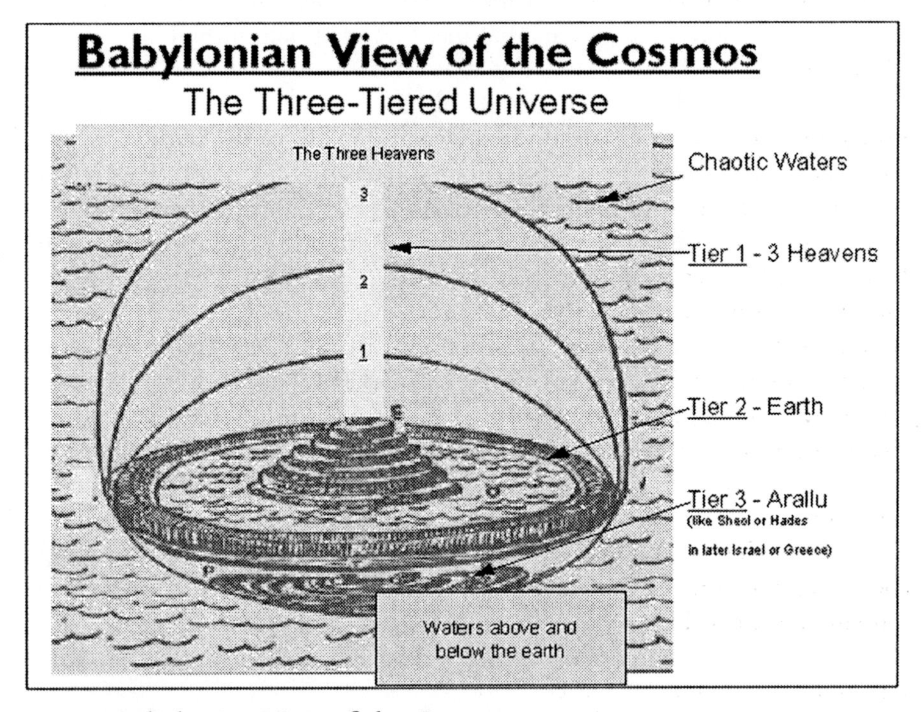

Fig. 18 Babylonian View of the Cosmos

The Mesopotamian worldview would be inherited by the later Israelites and their concept of the afterlife would hold until late into Old Testament times.

Eschatology and the Epic of Gilgamesh

The Epic of Gilgamesh is a very ancient myth originally written in Akkadian, and then translated into several other Near Eastern languages as empire succeeded empire. It concerns the quest for the afterlife and the interaction of the gods with people, briefly rehearsed below:

Gilgamesh's, king of Uruk in Sumer, activities were interfering with the citizenry. They begged the gods for someone to divert Gilgamesh's attention from them. The gods created Enkidu who, after an initial wrestling match with him, became Gilgamesh's fast friend.

They enjoyed many adventures together, one of which was the slaying of the monster Hawawa. Upon returning from that adventure, the goddess Inanna/Ishtar tries to seduce Gilgamesh who rebuffs and insults her. In a rage, she sends the bull of heaven to kill him but the two friends kill the bull instead.

For his part in the killing, the gods now take the life of Enkidu. Gilgamesh, feeling the pains of his friend's death, realizes that this will be his destiny also. The remainder of the story is his search for immortality. His quest takes him to Utnapishtim, the survivor of the great flood, who was granted immortality by the gods. Utnapishtim cannot help him since his immortality was a one-time gift and is not available to other mortals.

As a consolation, Gilgamesh is told of a plant that can renew youth and, therefore, give one a long life. His last adventure is his search for the plant, which he found and was taking back to his city. Exhausted from his quest, he rests and while refreshing himself, a snake swallows the plant and escapes. The snake from then on can be renewed by shedding its skin but Gilgamesh and all humans in addition to being mortal have now lost their chance of even having a long life.

Finally accepting the lot of mankind, Gilgamesh returns to Uruk and rejoices in the mighty works of his hands. The gods may keep immortality to themselves, but we humans have our own rewards.

Below are selected excerpts[7] from the very long poem…

---

7. Translation by E. A. Speiser, *Ancient Near East Texts*, 72–99. Since this is the oldest story of the search for an afterlife, I have reproduced the most interesting parts for our inquiry here.

From Tablet I

Fame haunts the man who visits Hell,
who lives to tell my entire tale identically.
So like a sage, a trickster or saint,
GILGAMESH was a hero who knew secrets
and saw forbidden places,
who could even speak of the time before the
Flood because he lived long, learned much,
and spoke his life to those who first
cut into clay his bird-like words.

He commanded walls for Uruk and for Eanna,
our holy ground,
walls that you can see still; walls where weep
the weary widows of dead soldiers.
Go to them and touch their immovable presence
with gentle fingers to find yourself.
No one else ever built such walls.
Climb Uruk's Tower and walk abut on a
windy night. Look. Touch. Taste. Sense.
What force created such mass?

Open up the special box that's hidden in the wall
and read aloud the story of Gilgamesh's life.
Learn what sorrow taught him; learn of the those
he overcome by wit or force or fear as he,
a town's best child, acted nobly in the way
one should to lead and acted wisely too
as one who sought no fame.

...
He sailed the sea to where Shamash comes,
explored the world, sought life, and came at last
to Utnapishtim far away who did bring
back to life the flooded earth.
Is there anywhere a greater king...

From Tablet X

The girl whose drinks refresh the soul
then said these words to Gilgamesh:
"Is there a simple reason, sir, why you're so sad
or why your face is drawn and thin?
Has chance worn out your youth or did some
wicked sorrow consume you like food?
...
He responded then to her who gives her men
lifesaving drinks:
"Girl, there is no simple reason why I'm so sad
or why my face is drawn and thin.
Chance alone did not wear out my youth. Some
wicked sorrow consumes me like food.
...
because my brother, my only true friend, met death;
he who raced wild horses there,
who caught orange tigers here.
This was Enkidu, my soul's good half,
...

Gilgamesh continued:
"I greatly loved my friend who was always there for me.
I loved Enkidu who was always there for me.
What awaits us all caught him first
and I did thirst for one whole week to
see him once again in splendor until his body decomposed.
Then I wept for my future death
and I fled home for mountaintops to breathe
when my friend's death choked off my wind.
On mountaintops I roamed content to breathe
again when my friend's death choked off my wind.
Walking. Walking. Walking over hills.
Could I sit down to rest?
Could I stop crying then
when my best friend had died
as I will someday do?"
...
The girl whose drinks refresh the soul
then said these words to Gilgamesh:
"Remember always, mighty king,
that gods decreed the fates of all
many years ago. They alone are let
to be eternal, while we frail humans die
as you yourself must someday do.
What is best for us to do
is now to sing and dance.
Relish warm food and cool drinks.
Cherish children to whom your love gives life.
Bathe easily in sweet, refreshing waters.
Play joyfully with your chosen wife."
"It is the will of the gods for you to smile
on simple pleasure in the leisure time of your short days."
...
...my best friend who now is dead.
Mortality reached him first and I am left this week
to weep and wail for his shriveling corpse which scares me.
I roam aloft and alone now, by death enthralled,
and think of nothing but my dear friend.
I roam the lonely path with death upon my mind
and think of nothing but my dear friend.
Over many seas and across many mountains I roam.
I can't stop pacing. I can't stop crying.
My friend has died and half my heart is torn from me.
Won't I soon be like him, stone-cold and dead,
for all the days to come?"

From tablet XI

Then Utnapishtim called out to him:
"Gilgamesh! You labored much to come here.
How can I reward you for traveling back?
May I share a special secret, one
that the gods alone do know?
There is a plant that hides somewhere among the rocks
that thirsts and thrusts itself deep
in the earth, with thistles that sting.
That plant contains eternal life for you."

Immediately, Gilgamesh set out in search.
Weighed down carefully, he dove beneath
the cold, cold waters and saw the plant.
Although it stung him when he grabbed its leaf,
he held it fast as he then slipped off his weights
and soared back to the surface.
Then Gilgamesh said this to Urshanabi, the sailor-god:

"Here is the leaf that begins
all life worth having.
I am bound now for Uruk,
town-so-full-of-shepherds,
and there I'll dare to give
this plant to aged men as food
and they will call it life-giving.
I too intend to eat it
and to be made forever young."
After 10 miles they ate.

After 15 miles they set up camp
where Gilgamesh slipped into a pool;
but in the pool, a cruel snake slithered by
and stole the plant from Gilgamesh
who saw the snake grow young again,
as off it raced with the special, special plant.

Right there and then Gilgamesh began to weep
and, between sobs, said to the sailor-god who held his hand:
"Why do I bother working for nothing?
Who even notices what I do?

I don't value what I did
and now only the snake has won eternal life.
In minutes, swift currents will lose forever
that special sign that god had left for me."
Then they set out again,
this time upon the land.
After 10 miles they stopped to eat.
After 30 miles they set up camp.
Next day they came to Uruk, full of shepherds.

Then Gilgamesh said this to the boatman:
"Rise up now, Urshanabi, and examine
Uruk's wall. Study the base, the brick,
the old design. is it permanent as can be?
Does it look like wisdom designed it?
The house of Ishtar in
Uruk is divided into three parts:
the town itself, the palm grove, and the prairie."

A major function of ancient religion

A major function of Mesopotamian religion was to support the king as head of state. The high gods presumably established the law and any transgression was seen as an offense against them. The ruler, of course, actually established the laws and transgressions were really against him. Enforcement of the ruler's laws was made easier by having a powerful invisible watcher who could mete out punishments. This formulation will factor in all subsequent periods—and places.

As power changed hands, as we saw in the Enuma elish, the religion stayed the same but the name of the high god changed to make his city/state and king the most powerful.

City/State	Approx Dates	High God
Sumeria	3200 BCE	An
Akkadia	2400	Anu
Old Babylonia	2000	Marduk
Assyria	1300	Ashur
Neo Babylonia	612	Marduk
Canaan	1800	El
Israel	1300 (traditional)	Yahweh

Canaanite Religion

The succession of religions in Mesopotamia stayed essentially the same throughout three thousand years of history. The story was the same with only the names of the gods changing as one empire succeeded another. The new empire kept the old religion and simply elevated their own city god to head the pantheon.

In the northwest corner of Mesopotamia, there eventually arose a civilization known as Canaanite. This is one of the places and times for which we actually have archeological evidence that indicates the significant influence that flourished among the various civilizations in the Eastern part of the Mediterranean basin. The Amarna letters from the time of Pharaoh Akhenaten in the 14th century BCE attest to a thriving interaction between Egypt and its neighbors of Babylonia, Assyria, and the region now known as Palestine.

Much of the stable and conservative ancient religion of Sumer and Babylonia shows up again in Canaan. The cosmos is still three-tiered and the afterlife is still bleak. The pantheon still has the astral, chthonic (earth) and netherworld gods, and the ghosts of the dead live on in their tombs where they require help from the living and could, indeed, offer help to the living if treated well.

The Canaanite cult of the dead also resembled the greater Mesopotamian cults. At some time during the third millennium BCE, the idea of the cult of the dead had entered the Near Eastern consciousness. The Mesopotamian ghosts of the dead required help from the living for their needs. If the ghosts were not cared for, they would wander around and haunt the living. The services necessary from the caregivers were: making funerary offerings, pouring water, and calling the name.

This cult was also found among the Western Semitic Canaanites and, later, the Israelites. They believed that the dead do live on in their tombs and are in need of assistance and are capable of helping the living. The Canaanite caretaker was just like his Mesopotamian counterpart; pouring water and setting up ancestral stele, which served the same purpose as calling the name. Both rituals were to keep the name of the person alive; thereby, magically keeping the person himself alive.

Into this cultural matrix, the nation of Israel will evolve. The Hebrew Bible tells the story of Abraham coming to Canaan from the heartland of ancient Sumer, bringing with him the entire panoply of his culture. Only now, as with the successions of other Mesopotamian names of the gods, the name of his high god is no longer An, Marduk, or Ashur—it is El.

Mesopotamian Blends into Israelite

Very ancient Israel will continue adhering to the main worldview of Mesopotamian religion:

Ancient Israel's cosmology remained that of the three-tiered universe, and would remain so for another three thousand years.

Their afterlife beliefs (eschatology) were exactly those of the ghost-like wraiths under the earth, which they now called Sheol.

Their polytheism reflected that of their middle-eastern cousins, and would be the cause of much of the struggle depicted in the Old Testament. An incipient monotheism was being pitted against the entrenched polytheism of past millennia. This struggle would continue down to the time of King Josiah around 620 BCE, when monotheism would finally emerge as the state religion of the southern kingdom of Judah.

The Mesopotamian myths were taken up wholesale by the Canaanites then the Israelites. In the Epic of Gilgamesh was imbedded a subplot that explained how one man's family had survived the great flood of the gods and had received immortality. It was to this flood survivor that Gilgamesh had gone and begged for the secret of everlasting life, only to be told that it was a one-time gift and could not be repeated. This flood myth of the Epic was an all-pervasive story that appeared in many parts of the Mediterranean basin. It was the story that was picked up by the authors of Genesis and used to explain El's destruction of the world that had become evil, and the salvation of one just man's family, that of Noah.

Later in the history of Israel we'll see that the name of the high god will change again—this time from El to Yahweh.

The Religions of Egypt

Evolution of Egyptian Religion

Almost as ancient, the eschatology of the Egyptians could not have been more different from that of Mesopotamia. There, the afterlife was a bleak, barely conscious existence. In Egypt, the afterlife was a glorious immortal existence with the gods in the heavens.

At first, the afterlife was not for everyone. Only the king was considered fit to rule with the high gods, since he was a son of god while on earth. Only gradually did the rest of the Egyptian people acquire the right to a true afterlife.

Historians have divided the Egyptian period into three major kingdoms (see the chart below). The quantum evolution of the afterlife beliefs just happens to fall into those same divisions.

Old Kingdom (ca. 2705–2180 BCE)

Dynasty III (ca, 2705–2640)
Dynasty IV (ca. 2640–2520)
Dynasty V (ca. 2520–2360)
Dynasty VI (ca. 2360–2195)

First Intermediate Period (2180–1987 BCE)

Middle Kingdom (ca. 1987–1640 BCE)

Second Intermediate Period (1640–1530 BCE)

New Kingdom (ca. 1540–1075 BCE)

Dynasty XXXIII (ca. 1540–1292 BCE) [8]

8. Egyptian dates are primarily from Erik Hornung, *Idea into Image: Essays on Ancient Egyptian Thought*, 187–188.

In the Old Kingdom we find the first Egyptian writings concerning the afterlife. They are found inside the pyramids of the 5th Dynasty kings and address the afterlife of the king alone. Because of their origin, they are called the *Pyramid Texts.*

The afterlife they describe is modeled on the resurrection of the god Osiris.[9]

Osiris was the son of the sky goddess, Nut, and the earth god, Geb. He was the twin of Isis and brother to Seth and Nephthys. Osiris became the ruler of Egypt and his brother Seth killed him in a fit of jealousy. His sister-wife, Isis, revived him and they conceived Horus.

Osiris then became ruler of the underworld and, when grown, Horus would revenge Osiris and take back the throne of Egypt; thus we have the son ruling the living and the resurrected Osiris ruling the dead.

Some Old Kingdom texts

<u>The Pyramid Texts</u>

The following are texts found in the pyramids of the kings Unas (5th Dynasty) and Teti and Pepi (6th Dynasty).

<u>Pyramid Text</u> 167:

> Atum, this thy son is here,
> Osiris, whom thou hast preserved alive—he lives!
> He lives—this Unas lives!
> He is not dead, this Unas is not dead:
> he is not gone down, this Unas has not gone down:
> he has not been judged, this Unas has not been judged.
> He judges—this Unas judges![10]

This refrain, a part of Utterance 219, is repeated over several times as addressed to a different god each time. The key phrase is: "he has not been judged."

---

9. For details on the myth of Osiris and Egyptian religion in general, see: Siegfried Morenz, *Egyptian Religion*, (New York: Cornell University Press, 1973).
10. Translated by Alexandre Piankoff, *The Pyramid of Unas* (Princeton: Princeton University Press, 1968), 64.

In this particular spell, the priests of Heliopolis protest against the king having to stand for judgment. This suggests, at least, there would have to have been a judgment for someone—other than the king—in order for such a thought to have arisen. Indeed, the king himself is said to do the judging, rather than being the passive subject of judgment as non-royalty presumably was (or had been) at some earlier time. This and the next text seem to intimate an older belief from when even non-royals had some form of an afterlife.

Pyramid Text 309:

> The King is bound for the sky, on the wind, on the wind! He will not be excluded, and there will be no session on him in the Tribunal of the God, for the King is unique, the eldest of the gods.[11]

This text argues that the King is exempt from the judgment after death. The phrase "there will be no session on him" means that the dead king is not to be judged before the divine tribunal, contrary to the fate of others. Again, the implication is that there must have been such a concept as the judgment of the dead in the Old Kingdom, which was normal for others, but not for the king. On the other hand, see the next spell:

Pyramid Text 316:

> O Geb, Bull of Nut,
> A Horus is Unas, the heir of his father.
> Unas is he who went and came back,
> The fourth of four gods
> Who have brought the water, who have made a purification,
> Who jubilates over the strength of their fathers.
> He wishes to be justified [*maa kheru*][12]
> In what [through that] he has done.
> ...
> And that he should raise himself to what he wanted.[13]

---

11. Faulkner, *The Ancient Egyptian Pyramid Texts*, (Oxford: Clarendon Press, 1969), 68.
12. There is much debate as to what *maa kheru* actually means. An interesting interpretation is discussed in Rudolf Anthes, "The Original Meaning of *ma'a kheru*" *Journal of Near Eastern Studies* 13 (Jan–Oct 1954): 21-51. He interprets spell 316 as meaning "to affirm the rightness (*ma'a*) of an individual by acclaim (*kheru*). The more common translation is "true of voice' or "justified'.
13. Translated by Piankoff, *The Pyramid of Unas*, 36.

Egyptian Pre-History

Some scholars[14] have attempted to discover the origins of Egyptian culture. Their search has led them back to Paleolithic times (before c. 10,000 BCE) when a belief in the afterlife is already indicated.

We see evidence of burials from the Paleolithic period right up to the pre-Dynastic period[15] (before ca. 3000 BCE) when the body has been carefully placed[16] in its tomb and surrounded by articles that would be useful in an after-life. There is evidence that the body was sometimes disassembled with the expectation being that it would be reassembled in the future life. We see echoes of this practice in the *Pyramid Texts*, where the King's body will be reconstituted.[17]

Pyramid Text 2007-9

> You have your water, you have your flood, you have your efflux which issued from Osiris; gather together your bones, make ready your members, throw off your dust, loosen your bonds.[18]

Pyramid Text 738f

> Hail to you, Tait [the Divine weaver]...Guard the King's head, lest it come loose; gather together the King's bones, lest they become loose.

---

14. Some early scholars include: Alexander Moret, *The Nile and Egyptian Civilization* (London: Kegan Paul, Trench, Trubner, 1927), 38ff; W.M. Flinders Petrie, *Religion and Conscience in Ancient Egypt* (1898; reprint, London: Benjamin Bloom, 1972), 11ff. A recent study is John Baines, "Origins of Egyptian Kingship," in *Ancient Egyptian Kingship*, eds. David O'Conner and David P Silverman (Leiden: E.J. Brill, 1995), 95–156.
15. A display of the burial of a man, surrounded by useful grave goods, in the Naqada II period (c. 3650-3300 BCE) is in the Carnegie Museum. James A. Romano, *Death, Burial, and Afterlife in Ancient Egypt* (Pittsburg: The Carnegie Museum of Natural History, 1990), 2; also, Leonard Lesko, "Death and Afterlife in Ancient Egyptian Thought," in *Civilization of the Ancient Near East*, ed. Jack M. Sasson, vol. III (New York: Charles Scribner's Sons, 1995) 1763–1774.
16. Usually in a fetal position and facing West.
17. There are many of these reconstitution texts in the *Pyramid Texts* besides the ones cited here, (e.g., spells 572, 736, 828, 840, 1675, 1685, 1732, 1916, 1981).
18. *Pyramid Texts* are translated, unless otherwise noted, by R.O. Faulkner, *The Ancient Egyptian Pyramid Texts* (Oxford: Clarendon Press, 1969), 289.

Pyramid Text 654

> Oho! Oho! Rise up, O Teti!
> Take your head,
> Collect your bones,
> Shake the earth from your flesh![19]
> Take your bread that rots not,
> Your beer that sours not,
> Stand at the gates that bar the common people!
> ...
> The gatekeeper...
> Sets you before the spirits, the imperishable stars.[20]

The spiritual afterlife

These texts obviously imply the expectation of a bodily restoration even though a much more spiritual concept of the future life is also now propounded in other *Pyramid Texts* where the king's spirit [*akh*] or soul [*ba*] joins the gods in the heavens:

Pyramid Text 152 and 250

> O Re-Atum, this King comes to you, an imperishable spirit [akh]...May you traverse the sky...
> and,

---

19. The texts for this must have come from a time when the dead were still buried in the desert sands and this attests to a far greater age than the 5th Dynasty of many of the spells in the *Pyramid Texts*. Many of these earlier references to "shaking off the earth or dust' appear, (e.g., Spells 645, 736, 748, 1068, 1363, 1732, 1878, 1917, 2008).

20. Translated by Miriam Lichtheim, *Ancient Egyptian Literature* 3 vols. (Berkeley: University of California Press, 1973, 1976, 1980), 1.41f. Not only does this text give evidence for a disassembled corpse but, also more importantly, it suggests that commoners were barred from the king's afterlife, which was still conceived in terms of joining the stars, as opposed to the later solar afterlife. A very good indication that the stellar afterlife was desired appears in the 4th Dynasty Great Pyramid of Cheops where two small passage-ways connect the burial chamber to the outside walls. These passage-ways are aimed directly at the heavenly bodies of Sirius and Orion, which are mentioned in *Pyramid Text* 723 where the king reaches the sky as Orion and his soul is as effective as Sothis (Sirius).

> I come to you, O Nut...I have left Horus behind me, my wings have grown into those of a falcon...my soul [ba] has brought me...[21]

This seeming contradiction between an existence in the tomb and in the heavens is one of many that we see the Egyptians holding, and it makes us wonder how they could simultaneously hold multiple mutually opposed concepts in spite of the logical consequences. A possible explanation of this facet of Egyptian religion might be given by an almost exact analogy from a modern religion, Christianity.

In present day Christianity, the belief in the resurrection of the body is simultaneously held with the belief in the immortality of the soul. These two different beliefs entered Christianity from two diverse places and times. Our later investigation of Plato's immortal soul will explain the origin of the soul idea. The resurrection idea, on the other hand, has Jewish roots, and may have had an even more ancient origin in the Zoroastrianism of the 13th century BCE.

As Christianity spread into the cultural milieu of the Greek world in the second century CE, it encountered Plato's idea of the immortal soul and incorporated it into its developing dogma. Subsequent theologians were able to take these two diametrically opposed concepts and weave them into an integrated whole that has survived to this day.

This is analogous to what happened in ancient Egypt. The pre-Dynastic physical renewal has been skillfully integrated into the Dynastic-era spiritual concepts, such as the king's rising to the sun-god Re.[22] This culminated in the priestly theology of Heliopolis and that integrated material made its way into the *Pyramid Texts* of the late 5th Dynasty.[23]

Somewhere along the way, the human personality became endowed with a multiplicity of spiritual, soul-like, aspects (i.e., the *ba, ka,* and *akh*). Whatever the cause of all of these apparently disparate spiritual ideas, the same kind of theological juggling act (that we have seen being required for integrating the bodily resuscitation and the spiritual rising to the heavens) must have also been at work.

---

21. Faulkner, *The Ancient Egyptian Pyramid Texts*, 44, 58.
22. "I assume my pure seat which is in the bow of the Bark of Re." As referenced above in Spell 710 of the *Pyramid Texts.*
23. Heliopolis, near present day Cairo, was the site of the first developed Egyptian theology.

One conclusion that may be drawn, therefore, is that for centuries prior to Egypt's first religious texts the restoration of the body was one element of the afterlife; and was then combined with the idea of the deceased's spiritual incorporation or union with the stars and the sun.

However the Egyptians' multifaceted physical and spiritual afterlife may actually have developed—whether by a single group or, more likely, by a syncretism from diverse groups—these seemingly conflicting ideas appeared to form a functional system for the ancient Egyptians.[24]

As to why the non-physical concepts of the *ba, ka* and *akh* arose at all is lost in the mists of time. Nevertheless, we can conjecture based on the premise of two facts that clashed—an afterlife was desired and the body did disintegrate after death.

The preservation of the body in the hot, dry sand of the Egyptian desert may have lent credence to the belief in the individual's physical continuity[25] but as sandy graves evolved into more elaborate tombs, the natural bodily preservation no longer sufficed. In spite of efforts to preserve the body, it still decayed, requiring the employment of alternative methods of preservation; hence, the advent of mummification.

Now the fear arose that the mummy itself might be lost, so a duplicate body was prepared in the form of a statue.[26] As the mummified body was ritually revitalized by what became known as "the opening of the mouth" ceremony, the duplicate body, in the form of a statue, might likewise be revitalized. Should the mummy be destroyed, a statue of the person could be ritually transformed[27] and given the same kind of life in the tomb previously enjoyed by the body. The person's statue was filled with the double or *ka* of the deceased person which could move from the statue to the food offerings left by the family and priests.

---

24. Of course, the coherence could have either been syncretized from diverse entries into the *Texts,* or it may have been created *in toto* by the Heliopolitan priests. From our remote frame of reference, we see conflicting ideas that need to be reconciled.
25. Edward F. Wente, "Funerary Beliefs of the Ancient Egyptians," 18-9. Also, James H. Breasted, *Development of Religion and Thought in Ancient Egypt* (London: Charles Scribner's Sons, 1912), 49.
26. Griffiths, *The Origins of Osiris and His Cult,* 72.
27. Transformation of the person into a variety of other things developed greatly in later times.

Also, at this same time, a statue of a god was thought to hold the manifestation of that god called the *ba*. Since the king was also thought to be a god, he and his statue both would have a *ba*; and this entity would be what soared to the heavens to be with the sun god.

Both of these elements now were thought, in the *Pyramid Texts*, to be non-physical[28] elements that duplicated the king. Later theological developments would have them become integrated elements of personhood in general.

The idea of survival in the tomb (possibly associated with Osiris[29]) was still apparently available to other people, as shown by this text that addresses the newly deceased king.

Pyramid Text 251

> Open up your place in the sky among the stars of the sky, for you are the Lone Star, the companion of Hu; look down on Osiris when he governs the spirits, for you [the king] stand far off from him, you are not among them [the other people's spirits] and you shall not be among them.[30]

The king goes to the celestial realm where he will look down on Osiris who rules the other spirits [the *akhs*] in the Netherworld. Thus, it would seem that even the non-royal people had an afterlife, at least as an *akh* in the realm of Osiris.

Post-Old Kingdom Texts

The first intermediate period was one of the decline of the power of the king when the nobility was able to take over the power of the kingdom, and was able to usurp for themselves the former prerogative of the king alone. Now, they laid claim to an afterlife also. We see the evidence of this in the writings that appear on the inside of their coffins. Many of the same concepts (as appeared in the

---

28. There is some indication that these elements or forms were thought to be corporeal rather than spiritual, and "in each of these forms the deceased acts and lives as a full individual…[each form was] considered to be full physical entities and not "spiritual components of a human composite"" (Zabkar, *A Study of the Ba Concept in Ancient Egyptian Text*, 97).
29. Osiris is an ambivalent character. He first appears in the *Pyramid Texts*, here as king of the underworld and only later does he rise to the heavens to be on a par with Re.
30. Faulkner, *The Ancient Egyptian Pyramid Texts*, 58.

Pyramid Texts) now show up in the *Coffin Texts* and the afterlife has become more democratic.

The Coffin Texts.[31]

The following are some representative post-Old Kingdom texts that indicate a developed afterlife attestation for the nobility.

Coffin Text Spell 8, I, 24:

> Hail to you, Tribunal of the God who shall judge me concerning what I have said [and did], I being ignorant at ease and having no care. O you who surround me and stand at my back. May I be vindicated in the presence of Geb, chiefest of the gods. Yonder god shall judge me according to what I know. I have arisen with my plume on my head and my righteousness on my brow, my foes are in sorrow, and I have taken possession of all my property in vindication.[32]

By this time in the development of Egyptian religion, there was a post-mortem council of the gods that judged the non-royal deceased based on what they said and did in life. This text looks very similar to that in Pyramid Text 316 where it is said, "He wishes to be justified in what he has done."[33] Even the non-royal person could now expect to be vindicated of wrongdoing.

Coffin Text Spell 44, I, 181–185:

> The doors of the sky are opened because of your goodness; may you ascend and see Hathor, may your complaint [evil] be removed, may your sin [iniquity] be erased by those who weigh in the balance on the day of reckoning characters.
>
> ...

31. The earliest *Coffin Texts* are usually assigned to the First Intermediate Period. However, a noble named Medunefer of the 6th Dynasty during the reign of Pepy II was buried with texts that had several parallels to and would become part of the *Coffin Texts*. Forman and Quirke, *Hieroglyphs*, 63-4.
32. All *Coffin Texts* translated by R.O. Faulkner, *The Ancient Egyptian Coffin Texts*, 3 vols. (Warminster: Aris & Phillips, 1973), 1.4.
33. So, by analogy, this kind of judgment should apply to the royal also.

> May you sail southward in the Night-bark and northward in the Day-bark; may you recognize your soul [*ba*] in the upper sky, while your flesh, your corpse, is in On.

Here we find the judgment of deceased non-royal persons of the First Intermediate Period associated with the iniquity, evil or goodness of their life. By this time the non-royal person had a ba and the opportunity for a celestial after-life like the king had in the Pyramid Texts before him.

This is one of the first allusions to the balance that will weigh the heart which will become so central to the text and iconography of the much later *Book of the Dead.*

Non-funerary texts of the post-Old Kingdom period

The afterlife also is discussed outside of the burial places. An excellent example of this kind of writing is *The Instruction of Merikare* (ca. 2100 BCE) where we find a king giving advice to his successor. It is perhaps the most prescient text of this period in that it contains the most explicit allusions to the eschatological subjects of the much later *Book of the Dead.*

The Instruction for King Merikare:

> The Court that judges the wretch,
> You know they are not lenient,
> On the day of judging the miserable,
> In the hour of doing their task.
> It is painful when the accuser has knowledge,
> Do not trust in the length of years,
> They [the judges] view a lifetime in an hour!
> When a man remains over after death,
> His deeds[34] are set beside him as treasure,
> And being yonder lasts forever.
> A fool is who does what they reprove!
> He who reaches them without having done wrong
> Will exist there like a god,
> Free-striding like the lords forever!
> ...
> A man should do what profits his *ba*.

34. One's good deeds (works) are a treasure for a favorable judgment.

> ...
> So the *ba* goes to the place it knows.
> ...
> Divine are they who follow the king![35]

The old king here details the duties and behavior of a good king to his successor, King Merikare. He advises that the king must show justice and impartiality in order to succeed in the practical world, as well as in the spiritual world to come. He insists that good conduct and behavior will be seen by the afterlife judges when they review the life deeds of the deceased person. He calls the judges those who see the whole of one's life span (whether the wretch, the miserable, the fool or the non-wrongdoer) as in a single instant.

The Middle and New Kingdoms

The kings regain their power in the Middle Kingdom but the afterlife remains attached to the nobility also. For a second time in history, the monarchy loses power and during this second intermediate period, the afterlife becomes even more democratic. Now, everyone can become an Osiris after death. The writings that show this are no longer found in burial places nor in the philosophies of those of high rank. By around 1600 BCE, they are found everywhere in The Book of the Dead.

Again, the conservative and stable religious environment kept the same personal eschatological concepts going for thousands of years. To be sure, some of the gods rose and fell in stature, and the afterlife was successively opened to more and more of the population. But, the ideas of immortality remained pretty much consistent throughout that time.

Since the gods (as they were in Mesopotamia) were changed in order to support the political faction in power, we see multiple theologies evolved early in the Old Kingdom,. For our purposes, all but one can be glossed over with just a mention.

Egyptian theologies

While Mesopotamia was evolving slowly over time, Egypt was proceeding along its own independent path, in geographic isolation, at the same time that the Mesopotamian empires were rising and falling.

---

35. Translated by Lichtheim, *Ancient Egyptian Literature*, 1.101-2, 1.106-7.

Egypt was mostly able to maintain itself as a political entity for the duration of the multiple empires in Mesopotamia. Thus, the Egyptians did not have a succession of empires that changed the names (and some of the functions) of their gods. They did have, however, a succession of centers of power within Egypt.

The first such center was at Heliopolis (ca. 2600 BCE) where the reigning gods were: Re, ruler and god of the sun; his children Shu and Tefnut, rulers of the air; Geb, ruler of the earth; and Nut, ruler of the sky. Re had four grandchildren: Set, Osiris, Isis, and Nephthys.

These nine gods set the pattern of the Ennead (the nine) for the rest of Egyptian cities. A tenth god, Horus, succeeded his father and mother (Osiris and Isis) as ruler of Egypt—these latter three forming a triad of Father, Son, and Mother.

Osiris was the good god who ruled Egypt, and in a jealous rage his brother Set had killed him. Osiris' wife Isis resurrected him to become the king of the underworld; thus setting the pattern for achieving immortality for the remainder of the Egyptian period.

Subsequent theologies arose with the ascendance to power of other cities. In the Memphite theology (probably the most interesting) which we'll examine more closely later, the triad was Ptah, Sekhet, and Imhotep. Later, in Thebes, the triad became Amon, Mut, and Khonsu. Re appears to have been consistently worshipped and was eventually merged into a single deity as Amon-Re.

A belief in the afterlife was ever the strongest tenet of the Egyptian faith. The Egyptians were convinced that the body and its "soul-like" entities (the *ba* and the *ka*) would continue to live on. Everyone could become an Osiris and be resurrected to eternal life.

This belief was diametrically opposed to the early Mesopotamian belief that humans were simply mortal. But, even in Mesopotamia, we saw that the dead were eventually allowed some form of afterlife; at first a gray shadowy existence in the tomb, and later, a little better existence where the dead were fed and cared for in return for helping the living.

The most advanced early Egyptian religion—Memphite theology

Developed a few centuries after the Heliopolitan, the Memphite (ca. 2400 BCE) theology is based around Ptah, "Creator" or Craftsman, the creator-god of Memphis. The whole Memphite theology is preserved on a slab of basalt, the Shabaka Text. This text is perhaps the earliest record of theistic creation in existence.

As with all the Egyptian theologies, the Memphite religion was also political and Ptah replaced the earlier high god, but it kept all preceding gods in the pantheon. Ptah, the principal god of Memphis, had to be shown to be the great creator-god, and a new myth was developed to show his superiority (just as was done in Mesopotamia). But, it was also important to organize the new cosmogony so that the priests of earlier theologies would not be offended.

Philosophical concepts

Ptah was the great creator-god, but eight other gods were held to be contained within him. Ptah's eight hypostases or "persons" were known as "the Gods who have come into existence in Ptah." The Shabaka Text enumerates Ptah's eight hypostases, as "the *Neterw* who have come into existence in Ptah". Ptah himself emanates these primordial Eight, and then creates the primordial hill from which came all of Egypt.

> He who manifested himself as heart, he who manifested himself as tongue…is Ptah, the very ancient, who gave life to all the Gods.

Ptah conceived the world intellectually (heart) before creating it "by his own word (tongue)'. The above concepts anticipate the much later philosophical and religious ideas of the:

- Creation of the world by the Word	(Israel of ca. 500 BCE)
- Platonic Forms	(Greece of ca. 385 BCE)
- Emanation of the Many from the One	(Neo-Platonism, Gnostic Christians of ca. 2nd & 3rd centuries CE)
- Trinity	(Christianity of ca. 350 CE)

Ptah, as the divine craftsman, also recalls the Judeo-Christian theme of God fashioning the world and making Adam out of clay. In Egyptian iconography, the creation of man is represented by a potter god forming a man and his *ka* from clay on a potter's wheel.

The monotheistic element

In the Memphite Theology it is said of Ptah: "He who made all and created the gods." Ptah is the one who gave birth to the gods, and from whom every thing came forth: foods, provisions, divine offerings, and all good things. Thus, it is recognized and understood that Ptah is the mightiest of the gods.

We have here a strongly developed monotheism[36] well before the time of Akhenaten whom we'll see later!

The Classical Egyptian Judgment of the Dead

As will be seen when we investigate the religious ideas of the Greek Homer, we can also say here of the similar ideas of the Egyptians: 1) there is an afterlife; 2) there is some entity that is experiencing an afterlife; and 3) the afterlife depends on one's conduct and behavior in this life (i.e., a judgment of the dead). These three concepts evolved through time from Egyptian pre-history until the point at which the beliefs have coalesced into the form taken in the *Book of the Dead.*

The *Book of the Dead* is a large corpus of work, but only a few of the spells deal directly with the eschatological judgment itself. Spells 30 and 125 are a representative subset of the whole.[37]

The Book of the Dead

> O my heart which I had from my mother! O my heart which I had from my mother! O my heart of my different ages! Do not stand up as a witness against me, do not be opposed to me in the tribunal, do not be hostile to

36. Since there is more than one god this is technically a henotheism. Unitarian Western religions might well argue that orthodox Christianity is a henothesim by the same criteria.
37. Spells (or sometimes referred to as chapters) 30 and 125 are the major judgment of the dead spells in the *Book of the Dead.*

> me in the presence of the Keeper of the Balance, for you are my ka which was in my body,[38] the protector who made my members hale. Go forth to the happy place whereto we speed;[39] do not make my name stink to the Entourage who make men. Do not tell lies about me in the presence of the god; it is indeed well that you should hear!
> Thus says Thoth, judge of truth, to the Great Ennead which is in the presence of Osiris: Hear this word of very truth. I have judged the heart of the deceased, and his soul stands as a witness for him.
> ...
> Thus says the Great Ennead to Thoth who is in Hermopolis: This utterance of yours is true.
> ...
> Thus says Horus son of Isis: I have come to you, O Wennefer, and I bring [Name] to you. His heart is true, having gone forth from the balance, and he has not sinned against any god or any goddess.
> ...
> Thus says [Name]: Here I am in your presence, O Lord of the West. There is no wrong-doing in my body, I have not wittingly told lies, there has been no second fault. Grant that I may be like the favoured ones who are in your suite, O Osiris...
>
> Book of the Dead—Spell 30B[40]

Spell 30B from the Book of the Dead as quoted above was written after 1500 BCE[41] and stands at the evolutionary end of a long history of religious beliefs. In

38. Interestingly, by this time, the *ka* was believed to be in the body much as Plato's *psyche* also was in the body a thousand years later.
39. The first part of this verse has been found carved on the underside of a heart scarab included in the tomb of the high steward Nebankh of the 13th Dynasty (c. 1730 BCE). It is the earliest known dated reference to the classical Egyptian judgment of the dead. Forman and Quirke, *Hieroglyphics and the Afterlife*, 104.
40. All translations of the *Book of the Dead* are from Faulkner unless otherwise noted. Raymond O. Faulkner, *The Ancient Egyptian Book of the Dead* (Austin: The University of Texas Press, 1993), 27f.
41. Faulkner, *The Ancient Egyptian Book of the Dead*, 11, 14–15. However, as stated in the footnote 39, a form of spell 30 appears on the underside of a heart scarab from the 13th Dynasty (c. 1730 BCE), over 200 years earlier than thought by Faulkner at the time of his publication in 1969.

this spell from the New Kingdom, we see several interesting things concerning the judgment of the dead:

> The dead person begs that his heart not witness against him. He further claims that his heart is his ka, which was in his body and was the protector who made him hale while living. This either equates the heart and the ka or it enfleshes the ka within the body, or both.
>
> Thoth is the judge of truth who weighs the heart in the balance and declares that it is sinless. Next, the Great Ennead[42] says that the vindicated "Osiris [Name]" is to be given a place in the Field of Offerings, instead of being given over to the destroyer Ammit.
>
> Finally, Horus introduces the dead person to his father, Osiris, and claims that he or she should be forever like the Followers of Horus. The dead person then speaks to Osiris and asks that he or she may be vindicated and favored in the house of Osiris.

In this single excerpt from the *Book of the Dead*, which gives an excellent overview of what is involved in the judgment of the dead, we find the fully evolved ideas comprising the judgment of the dead that were to remain important themes throughout subsequent Egyptian history. This spell, along with spell 125, gives us the classical version of the Egyptian judgment. In the *Book of the Dead* there also appeared pictorial scenes or vignettes that illustrated the judgment in great detail, showing the all important scale that weighed the heart against the feather of ma'at (truth, order).

Interestingly, although there is a pronouncement of innocence by a judge, the person's heart is simply weighed in a balance to compare it with the feather of truth (ma'at); if the heart is heavier, the person is annihilated; but if lighter, the person moves on to see Osiris. Here we have an automatic judgment where the

---

42. The Great Ennead was a group of nine gods. In the Heliopolis theology and cosmology, they consisted of: Atum (Re); Shu (air) and Tefnut (moisture); their offspring Geb (earth) and Nut (sky); and their offspring Seth, Osiris, Nephthys, and Isis. Osiris was the ruler of the world but jealous Seth killed him. Isis restored him and Osiris came to rule the realm of the dead. This story of the death of Osiris, and his restoration by Isis, forms the basis of the mythology that undergirds the *Book of the Dead.*

person has already convicted himself by the physical indicators of the kind of life he led. This is analogous to what will happen in Plato's *Gorgias,* where physical scars indicate one's conduct in life, although, there are also judges present.

Akhenaten (ca. 1400 BCE): the First Monotheist?

A brief, abortive attempt at monotheism took place during the 18th Dynasty (ca. 1400 BCE) when pharaoh Amenhotep IV abruptly abolished all worship of any god but Aton. Aton was represented by the solar disc and was proclaimed to be the only god, thereby making this religion the first known true monotheism.[43]

The pharaoh changed his own name to Akhenaton and attempted to purge polytheism from the land. This failed after only one generation, but it is possible that the people who were enslaved in Egypt at that time absorbed the idea and carried it back to Israel.

However, religion is very conservative; people derive solace from believing that they know truth, which for over a thousand years was polytheistic; and the religious leaders have a vested interest in preserving the status quo.

So, did monotheism work? No. It died out in Egypt.

But, according to some hypotheses, it may have been eventually picked up by those who had sojourned there for 400 years. However, the highly developed afterlife concepts were not!

Although, in Egypt, there was considerable thought given to personal eschatology, there was no thought whatever given to what would later be called cosmic eschatology—that would have to wait for a Persian reformer named Zoroaster.

Below, **Fig. 19**, is the first of several evolving graphics that shows the historical relationship between ancient civilizations and later Christianity.

---

43. We will see Zoroaster (ca. 1200 BCE) and Josiah (ca. 620 BCE), in Persia and Israel respectively, abolishing polytheism in preference to monotheism.

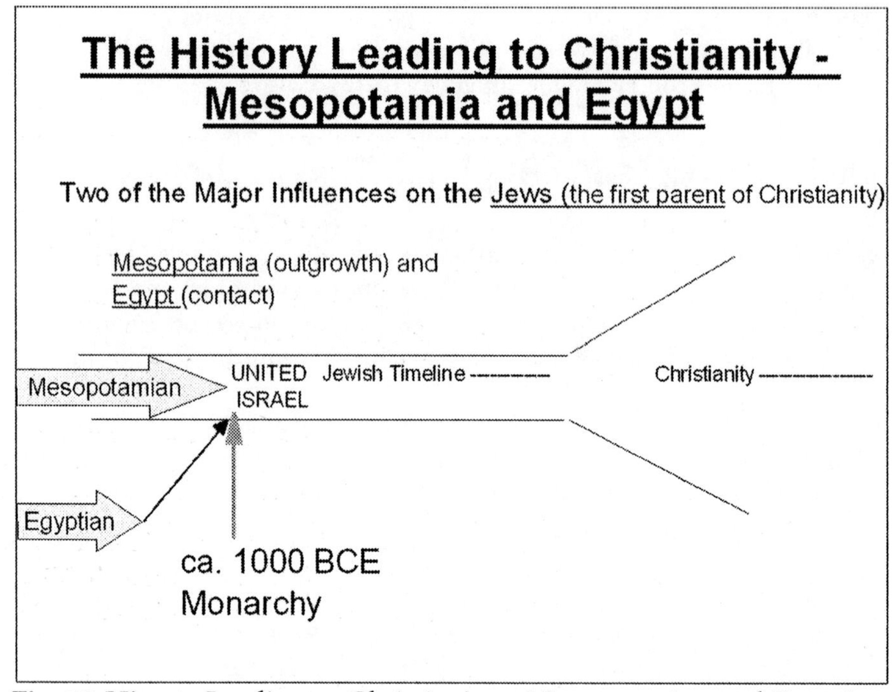

Fig. 19 History Leading to Christianity—Mesopotamian and Egyptian

The Religion of Persia

> Hear the best with your ears and ponder with a bright mind. Then each man and woman, for his or her self, select either of the two. Awaken to this Doctrine of ours before the Great Event of Choice ushers in. Now, the two foremost mentalities, known to be imaginary twins, are the better and the bad in thoughts, words, and deeds. Of these the beneficent choose correctly, but not so the maleficent.
>
> (Gatha: Yasna 30.2–3)

Zoroaster would write his hymns to the good and wise God hundreds of years before there would be a Persian Empire (**Fig. 20**). When the Empire came, it brought with it the religion that Zoroaster had created and spread it almost to Greece in the West. It enveloped the land of what was left of Israel—the tiny kingdom of Judah.

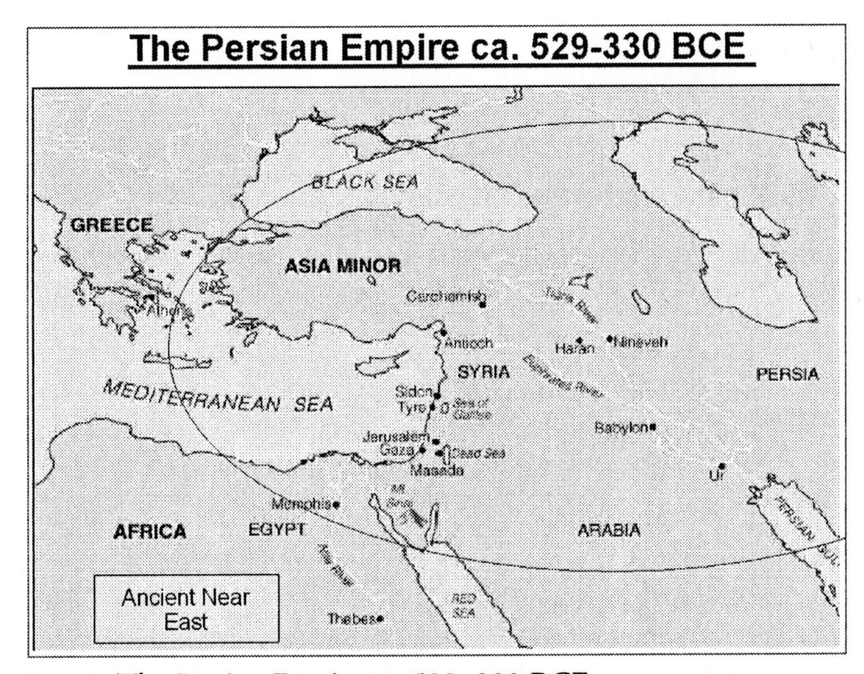

Fig. 20 The Persian Empire ca. 529–330 BCE

Why are we here? Why is there evil? Where did the world come from? Where is it headed? What child has not wondered about these questions? Any religion, if it is to succeed, must answer them, and Zoroaster created a religious story that did so.

Zoroaster wanted to reform the existing religion of the Persians, which was polytheistic (just as was the related religion of the proto-Hindus) and were branches from the same Indo-European tree.

He believed that there was only one supremely good God, but recognized the fact of evil in the world. Faced with this obvious dichotomy, he determined that there must also exist an evil twin of the good God who held an equal or nearly equal place in the cosmos. In order to explain how evil was found in our world, Zoroastrianism posits that before there was a world, only the good God (Ahura Mazda = Wise Lord) and the evil God (Angra Mainyu = Hostile Spirit) existed. Ahura Mazda created this good world as a battleground on which to fight Angra Mainyu. Both gods created other beings to help wage the fight. One set of beings was Mankind who was given a choice to fight the evil ones in the world. If one chose to aid Ahura Mazda in his struggle, one would be rewarded by a resurrection at the end of the physical age.

Zoroastrian Theodicy and Eschatology

The first linear cosmic eschatology.

Zoroaster's **eschatology** explains the **creation of the material world including humans** and the **Theodicy** explains the eschatology; so, let us look at Theodicy[44] first...

Almost every religion must face the problem of evil. This is especially true of the henotheistic and monotheistic religions, since in them there is a high or only god who is assumed to have the best interests of his people in mind. If that is so, whence evil?

---

44. The term "theodicy', meaning justice of God, was introduced by Gottfried Wilhelm Leibniz (1673–1716) in his *Theodicy* (1710), where he claimed that this is the "best of all possible worlds," a phrase made famous by the satire of Voltaire. God's own imposed logical limitations restricted his creation to the one we are in.

This is the classic Theodicy trilemma, which is like a dilemma but with three apexes (see **Fig. 21** below). Assume that God is loving and all-good. Further assume that God is all-powerful as is done in the monotheistic religions of Judaism, Christianity, and Islam. If God allows evil to exist, then He is not all-good. If God cannot stop evil from occurring, then He is not all-powerful. The fact is that evil does exist; therefore, God is either not good or not powerful or not both. Classical Aristotelian logic does not allow for any other conclusions.

Nevertheless, Zoroaster assumed a perfectly good God; therefore, he had to also explain the presence of evil in the world. The main scripture of the Zoroastrians is the Avesta. The Avesta contains the main liturgical texts called the Yasna. The Yasna contains the Gathas, which are hymns composed by Zoroaster and his immediate followers: (Yasna chapters 28-34, 43-51 and 53)

These hymns in the Gathas, written by Zoroaster, explain the dualist concept of the good and the evil forces and the choice humans are given. Three of his Gathas are considered below (emphasis underscored):

Ahunavaiti Gatha Song 3: Good And Evil (Gatha of the Choice)

> Yasna 30
>
> ...
>
> 2. Hear the best with your ears and ponder with a bright mind. Then each man and woman, for his or her self, select either of the two. Awaken to this Doctrine of ours before the Great Event of Choice ushers in.
> 3. Now, the two foremost mentalities, known to be imaginary twins, are the better and the bad in thoughts, words, and deeds. Of these the beneficent choose correctly, but not so the maleficent.
> 4. Now, when the two mentalities first got together, they created "life" and "not-living." Until the end of existence, the worst mind shall be for the wrongful, and the best mind shall be for the righteous.
> 5. Of these two mentalities, the wrongful mentality chose worst actions, and the most progressive mentality, as steadfast as rock, chose righteousness. Therefore, those who would please the Wise God, may do so by choosing true actions.
> 6. Between these two, the seekers of false gods did not decide correctly, because delusion came to them in their deliberations. Therefore, they chose the worst mind, rushed in wrath, and afflicted the human existence.

7. But to the person who chooses correctly, comes endurance of body and steadfast serenity through strength, good mind, and righteousness. Of all these, such a person shall be Yours, because he has come fully out of the fiery test.
8. And when the sinners undergo their punishment, then, O Wise One, the dominion will be realized for them through good mind. God, then they shall be taught how to deliver the wrong into the hands of righteousness.
9. And may we be among those who make this life fresh! You, lords of wisdom, who bring happiness through righteousness, come, let us be single-minded in the realm of inner intellect.
10. Then, indeed, the power of wrong shall be shattered. Then those who strive with good name shall immediately be united in the good abode of good mind and righteousness of the Wise One.
11. If you understand the two principles of prosperity and adversity established by the Wise One, which are a long suffering for the wrongful and a lasting good for the righteous; you shall, then, enjoy radiant happiness.

Ahunavaiti Gatha Song 4: Guidance (second Gatha of the Choice)

Yasna 31

1. Keeping the two principles of Yours in mind, we shall teach the hitherto unheard words to those who destroy the righteous world by their wrongful doctrines. No doubt, the two principles will prove the best for those who are devoted to the Wise One.
2. Since it is not easy for the soul to find the better course, I, whom the Wise Lord knows, come to you all as the leader of the two parties, so that we may all live in accordance with righteousness
3. The happiness You grant, has been promised to the two parties through Your mental fire and righteousness. It is a matter of principle for the discerning. O Wise One, for our knowledge, speak with the very words of Your mouth. It will help me guide all the living to choose aright.
...
11. O Wise One, at the beginning, You, through Your mind, fashioned for us the living world, conceptions and intellects, put life in the physical frame, and gave deeds and words, so that one makes his choice through free will.
...

> 20. Whoever goes over to the righteous, enjoys a bright future. But the wrongful lives a long life of darkness, evil splendor and woeful words, because it is on account of his deeds, that his conscience leads him to it.
> 21. God Wise grants wholeness, immortality, abundance of righteousness, independence in dominion, and a lasting good mind to him, who is His friend in mind and action....

Perhaps the clearest explanation of Zoroaster's dualistic teaching is in Yasna 45, verse 2:

Ushtavaiti Gatha Song 10: Proclamation (the Two Spirits)

> Yasna 45
>
> 1. Now, I shall proclaim, hear and listen, you who have come from near and far as seekers. Now, clearly bear these in mind. Let not the evil teacher, the wrongful, with his evil choice and perverted tongue, destroy life for a second time.
> 2. Now, I shall proclaim the two foremost mentalities of life. Of these, the more progressive one told the retarding one thus: Neither our thoughts, nor teachings, nor intellects, nor choices, nor words, nor deeds, nor consciences, nor souls agree.
> ...
> 9. I shall seek to please Him for us with good mind, for He has granted us the will to choose between progress and retrogress. May the Wise God, through His sovereignty, grant us the exercise to promote our cattle and men with the cooperation of good mind through righteousness.
> 10. I shall seek to exalt Him for us with praises of serenity, Who, by a new name, is known as the Wise God. He grants, through righteousness and good mind, wholeness and immortality in His dominion. May He grant us steadfast strength and endurance....[45]

As with the Bible, these verses attest to great spiritual teachings. Also as with the Bible, there is great ambiguity and room for multiple interpretations. How should one interpret the dualistic doctrines found here?

Zoroastrian's themselves have historically had two main interpretations: the ethical and the cosmic. The question, as Zoroastrians debated it, was whether Zoroaster's

45. Gathas translated by Ali A. Jafarey. *The Gathas Our Guide*. Ushta Publications. 1989.

dual spirits were real cosmic beings or simply the two natures found interior to the person—a higher nature and a baser nature. I will not attempt to solve that 3500 year old issue here, rather I will allow, as did later Zoroastrianism, that there is a cosmic explanation which is reflected in the dual nature of mankind itself.

Later followers would notice some inconsistencies in Zoroaster's original dualist scenario; and realize that if there were twin Gods, then they must have had a common source. This common source they named Zurvan (Time), which they believed fixed the flaw in the original dualistic concept. To the true Zoroastrian, Zurvanism was a heresy that eliminated the possibility of a totally good supreme god. Now if Zurvan were supreme, why did he allow evil? No, the only solution was the original one of a totally good supreme god and a totally evil nearly supreme god.

Humanity now had a reason for existing—to help Ahura Mazda fight evil; evil had a reason to exist—the result of Angra Mainyu. The world is here to provide a battleground on which to fight, and when the fight is won, the world will cease to exist in time and humanity will live on through eternity. Zoroaster had answered all of the ultimate questions.

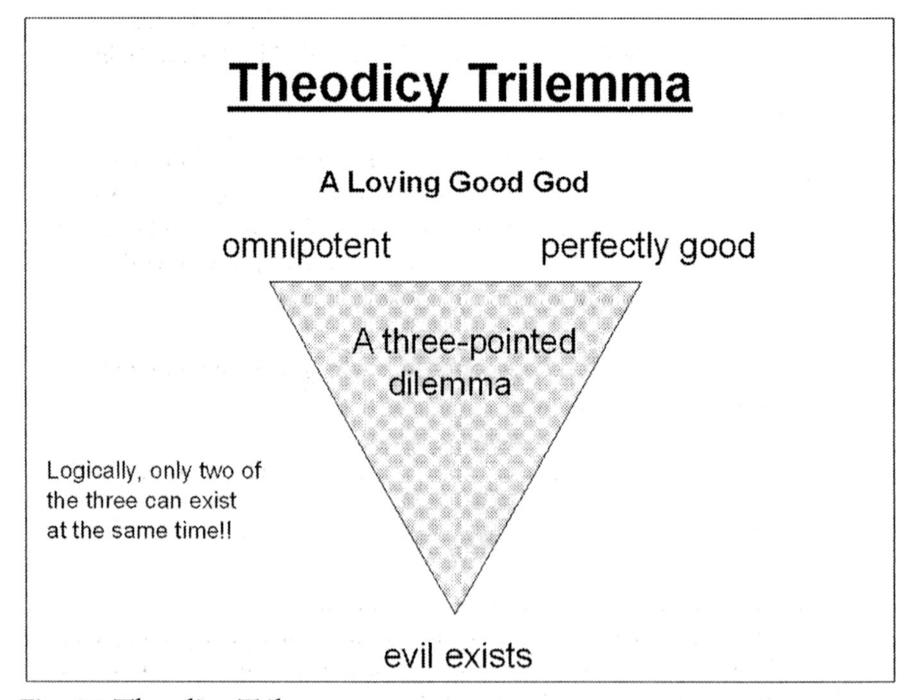

Fig. 21 Theodicy Trilemma

An introduction to some general solutions to the theodicy problem

The Theodicy problem has created many atheists,[46] for how could there even be a God if he allows horrible things to happen to his creatures? Most people can understand that, if we assume the will of man is free; then the actions of evil people will logically result in the harm of innocents. That is the unfortunate outcome of human freedom. But, why allow so-called "acts-of-God" types of evil? A god of earthquakes and pestilence must be evil himself, unable to stop such evil, or not exist at all. In order to combat the tendency toward atheism, many religions have offered the following various solutions to the Theodicy problem:

1. Deny God. Deny the very existence of God or deny some of his attributes.

2. Dualism. Assert that there is a duality in the cosmos between spirit and matter (flesh) or between good and evil.

3. We are guilty. We all sin of our own free will and all are guilty and deserving of suffering. Human guilt (original sin) is blamed on the Fall in Eden by St. Augustine (354–430 CE). Theologian Alvin Plantinga is a modern proponent of Augustine's theory.

4. Means to an end. Suffering serves the purpose of "soul-making" by providing a means of spiritual development. Pain causes us to recognize our need for God. This solution was first suggested by St. Irenaeus (130–202 CE) and again in the twentieth century by theologian John Hick.

5. Only temporary. This earthly life is short and there will be an afterlife to make up for our suffering.

6. Illusionary. This world is not real and suffering is an illusion.

---

46. In the 20th century the French Existentialists (the most famous being John Paul Sartre) claimed that if God is good, then evil cannot exist, but evil obviously does exist; therefore, the good God does not exist.

7. Time and Chance. Suffering or reward is not dependent on one's deeds but on the vagaries of time and chance as explained in Ecclesiastes 9:11 and alluded to in Luke 13:4.

Zoroaster's solution to the theodicy problem

Zoroaster's solution to the Theodicy problem used numbers one and two in the general solutions chart above.

1—Zoroaster's primary solution was to posit two nearly equal Gods; however, if they were totally equal, there would be an infinite impasse. So, Angra Mainyu lacked one of the attributes of Ahura Mazda; namely foresight. It was foresight that enabled him to see that he would win the battle by following his plan of creation and challenging Angra Mainyu to wage a war with him. The evil God lacked foresight and was thus ultimately vulnerable.

This dualism was between good and evil and not, as later religions would have it, between flesh and spirit.

2—His second solution was to deny some attributes of God. The good God could not be all-powerful and the evil god also had to lack some capability, namely foresight. Diminished attributes in both Gods explained the problem of evil; yet, still allowed for a totally good creator of the world and humankind.

Zoroaster's theodicy would make its way into later religions and form the basis of their solutions to the problem of evil in the world.

The Religion of Zoroaster

Having examined Zoroastrian theodicy and eschatology, let us now look generally at the religion of the Persians.

As stated above, the founder of the reformed Persian religion was Zarathustra (Zoroaster), ca. 1200 BCE who was said to be conceived by a shaft of light and born of a virgin. He reformed the more ancient Persian religion from polytheism to monotheism.

God is Ahura Mazda (Wise Lord), but he is opposed by the creator of the evil daivas, Angra Mainyu (Destructive or Hostile Spirit). God is the sole creator of our completely good spiritual and material world, which exists as a battleground for good to conquer evil.

Main doctrines of Zoroastrianism

> Eschatology—judgment of soul at death and resurrection at the end times.
>
> Dualism—principle of evil vs. good.
>
> Freewill—created humans have a choice to fight evil.
>
> Cosmology—the four ages of the world.

Eschatology

Which of the two afterlife options (resurrection or soul judgment) came first is lost in the mists of time. There are good arguments for both positions. What is known for certain is that they both became Zoroastrian doctrines.

This text of later Zoroastrianism explains what happens after a person's death:

> (71) Put not your trust in life, for at the last death must overtake you;
> (72) and dog and bird will rend your corpse and your bones will be tumbled on the earth.
> (73) For three days and nights the soul sits beside the pillow of the body.
> (74) And on the fourth day at dawn (the soul)…(will reach) the lofty and awful Bridge of the Requiter to which every man whose soul is saved and every man whose soul is damned must come.
> …and will (needs submit) to the weighing (of his deeds) by the righteous Rashn who lets the scales of the spiritual gods incline to neither side, neither for the saved nor yet for the damned, nor yet for kings and princes:
> (77) not so much as a hair's breadth does he allow (the scales) to tip, and he is no respecter (of persons),
> (78) for he deals out impartial justice both to kings and princes and to the humblest of men.
> (79) And when the soul of the saved passes over that bridge, the breadth of the bridge appears to be one parasang broad.
> (80) And the soul of the saved passes on accompanied by the blessed Srosh.

(81) And his own good deeds come to meet him in the form of a young girl, more beautiful and fair than any girl on earth.
(82) And the soul of the saved says, "Who art thou, for I have never seen a young girl on earth more beautiful or fair than thee."
(83) In answer the form of the young girl replies, "I am no girl but thy own good deeds, 0 young man whose thoughts and words, deeds and religion were good:....
(89) I am thy good thoughts, good words, and good deeds which thou didst think and say and do....'
(91) And when the soul departs from thence, then is a fragrant breeze wafted towards him, (a breeze) more fragrant than any perfume.
(92) Then does the soul of the saved ask Srosh saying, "What breeze is this, the like of which in fragrance I never smelt on earth?'(93) Then does the blessed Srosh make answer to the soul of the saved, saying, "This is a wind (wafted) from Heaven; hence is it so fragrant.'
(94) Then with his first step he bestrides (the heaven of) good thoughts, with his second (the heaven of) good words, and with his third (the heaven of) good deeds, and with his fourth step he reaches the Endless Light where is all bliss.
....
(l00) And for ever and ever he dwells with the spiritual gods in all bliss for evermore.
(101) But when the man who is damned dies, for three days and nights does his soul hover near his head and weeps, saying, "Whither shall I go and in whom shall I now take refuge?"...
[the soul is dragged] off to the Bridge of the Requiter.
...
(108) Then a young girl who yet has no semblance of a young girl, comes to meet him.
(109) And the soul of the damned says to that ill-favoured wench, "Who art thou? for I have never seen all ill-favoured wench on earth more ill-favoured and hideous than thee.
(110) And in reply that ill-favoured wench says to him, "I am no wench, but I am thy deeds,-hideous deeds,-evil thoughts, evil words, evil deeds, and an evil religion.
...
(116) Then with his first step he goes to (the hell of) evil thoughts, with his second to (the hell of) evil words, and with his third to (the hell of) evil deeds. And with his fourth step he lurches into the presence of the accursed Destructive Spirit and the other demons.

...

(118) And the Destructive Spirit cries out to the demons, saying, "Ask not concerning him, for he has been separated from his beloved body, and has come through that most evil passage-way;

(119) but serve him (rather) with the filthiest and most foul food that Hell can produce.'

(120) Then they bring him poison and venom, snakes and scorpions and other noxious reptiles (that flourish) in Hell, and they serve him with these to eat.

(121) And until the Resurrection and the Final Body he must remain in Hell, suffering much torment and many kinds of chastisement.

(122) And the food that he must for the most part eat there is all, as it were, putrid and like unto blood.

Menok i Khrat, I, 71–124[47]

Dualism

This is Zoroaster's primary solution to the Theodicy problem, where he says in the Gathas:

> Truly there are two primal spirits, twins renowned to be in conflict.
> In thought and word, in act they are two: the better and the bad.
>
> Neither our thoughts nor teachings nor wills, neither our choices
> nor words nor acts, nor our inner selves nor our souls agree.

Avesta: Gathas, Yasnas 30.3, 45.2

Freewill

Humans are created to fight evil. Nevertheless, they are given the option to decline the battle of their own free will. Lines from Yasnas 30 and 31 show this choice:

> Let each one choose his creed with that freedom of choice each must have
> at great events.

47. Translation by R. C. Zaehner, *The Teachings of the Magi*, (New York, McMillan Company, 1956), 133-8.

> And by Thy Thought gave our selves the power of thought, word, and deed. Thus leaving us free to choose our faith at our own will.

Cosmology

In the Bundahishn (meaning Creation), we see the Zoroastrian conception of the four ages of the world, each of which will last for 3000 years.

1. Spiritual creation—menog (good and evil are separate), Angels—(Amesha Spentas) are the beneficent immortals, evil starts the struggle.

2. Material creation—getig (world is created perfect, mingling of good and evil). Six stages of creation: sky, water, earth, plants, animals, and humans.
Humans asked to take part in battle of their own free will. Their eternal fate will depend on their choice.

3. Struggle between good and evil—evil attacked the good creation.

4. Zoroaster appears—proclaims the good religion.
In the final 1000 years (millennium) the Savior (Saoshyant) will come to usher in the Frashokereti, which is the transfiguration, renewal of all,[48] and the Kingdom of God will be established on Earth.

In later years, the list of doctrines below would be absorbed by subjects of the Persian empire and eventually provide for the foundational beliefs of Christianity:

> Resurrection of the Dead
> Last Judgment
> Savior
> Apocalyptic
> Angels
> Devils
> Satan

---

48. One of the things promised in the end-of-the-world renewal is that the metal in the hills will be melted, and they would be made low and the valleys will fill up, causing the restored world to be smooth as it was in the beginning. An interesting verse in Isaiah 40:3 says: "Every valley shall be filled [lifted up], and every mountain and hill [shall] be made low; the uneven ground shall become level, and the rough places a plain." This verse is used in Luke 3:5 to usher in the Kingdom of God at the end of the world. Of course, it could just mean roadwork.

Dualism (Light vs. Darkness, Good vs. Evil)
Hell
Six days of creation
Garden of Eden (paradise, *pairidaiza* = the Persian King's enclosed forest/garden)

A leading scholar on Zoroastrianism has this to say about the ancient religion's influence on Christianity:

> So it was out of a Judaism enriched by five centuries of contact with Zoroastrianism that Christianity arose in the Parthian period, a new religion with roots thus in two ancient faiths, one Semitic, the other Iranian.[49]

Thus, we come to the second historical graphic, **Fig. 22**:

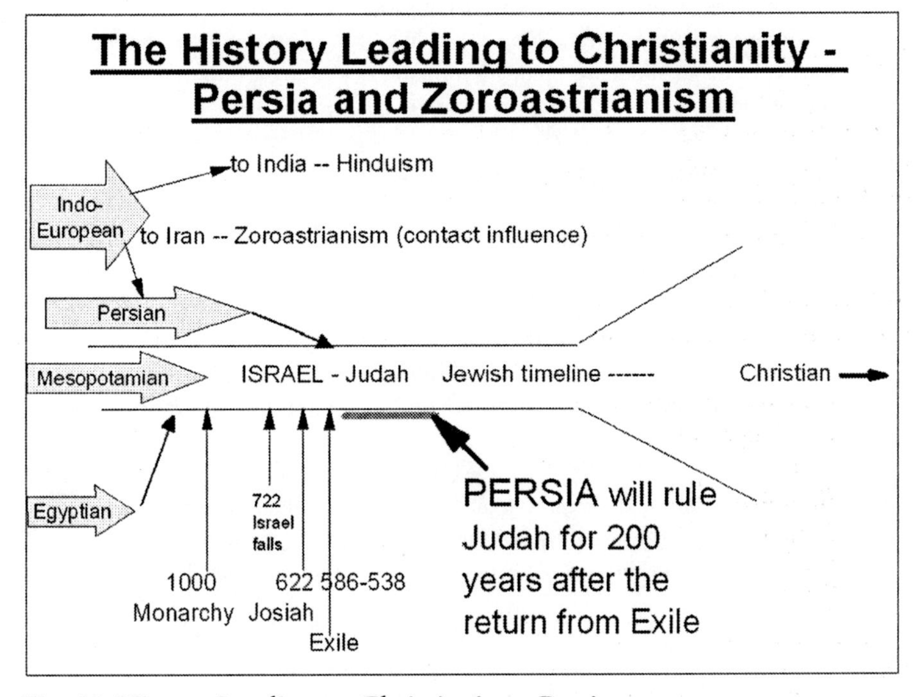

Fig. 22 History Leading to Christianity—Persia

49. Mary Boyce, *Zoroastrians: Their Religious Beliefs and Practices* (London: Routledge & Kegan Paul. 1979), 99.) Many scholars agree with Boyce on this assumption, but not all. See Yamauchi. *Persia and the Bible*. 1990. for contrary opinions. Both Boyce and Zaehner are excellent sources for additional information on Zoroastrianism.

The Zoroastrian Noah?

As a life-destroying winter is approaching. Yima, the first man and first king, is told to build an enclosure (vara) in which he is to keep the best of every kind of animal and plant.

> (46) And Ahura Mazda spake unto Yima, saying:
>
> 'O fair Yima, son of Vîvanghat! Upon the material world the fatal winters are going to fall, that shall bring the fierce, foul frost; upon the material world the fatal winters are going to fall, that shall make snow-flakes fall thick, even an aredvî deep on the highest tops of mountains.
>
> (61) Therefore make thee a Vara [enclosure], long as a riding-ground on every side of the square, and thither bring the seeds of sheep and oxen, of men, of dogs, of birds, and of red blazing fires.
> Therefore make thee a Vara, long as a riding-ground on every side of the square, to be an abode for men; a Vara, long as a riding-ground on every side of the square, to be a fold for flocks.
>
> (65) There thou shalt make waters flow in a bed a hâthra long; there thou shalt settle birds, by the ever-green banks that bear never-failing food. There thou shalt establish dwelling places, consisting of a house with a balcony, a courtyard, and a gallery.
>
> (70) Thither thou shalt bring the seeds of men and women, of the greatest, best, and finest kinds on this earth; thither thou shalt bring the seeds of every kind of cattle, of the greatest, best, and finest kinds on this earth.
>
> (74) Thither thou shalt bring the seeds of every kind of tree, of the greatest, best, and finest kinds on this earth; thither thou shalt bring the seeds of every kind of fruit, the fullest of food and sweetest of odour. All those seeds shalt thou bring, two of every, kind, to be kept inexhaustible there, so long as those men shall stay in the Vara.
>
> 'Vivavdat,' Fargard II[50]

The story is of a similar type to the flood myths. God is going to have a disaster kill all life except that which is saved by the builder of an enclosure.

---

50. Translation by James Darmesteter, *The Zend-Avesta* part 1, in *Sacred Books of the East, IV* (2nd ed.; Oxford: Claredon Press 1895), 15–18.

THE RELIGIONS OF THE GREEKS: FROM ZEUS TO THE MYSTERIES

Greece will be a nest of warring city-states for most of its existence, but, for one shining moment, they came together to battle against a common foe. As we've seen, Persia had established a great empire throughout the Middle East, Asia Minor, and Northern Africa. In 492 BCE, they pressed westward to capture the Greek mainland but were repeatedly turned back. This left the way open for the development of philosophy under the Greek trinity of Socrates, Plato, and Aristotle. Aristotle was to tutor a young and promising prince from Macedonia to the north of Greece.

This young prince was to sweep down from the North, take control of all Greece and continue eastward conquering the entire empire of the Persians. By 332 BCE, Greece was included within the great empire, but it was now called the Empire of Alexander the Great, **Fig. 23**.

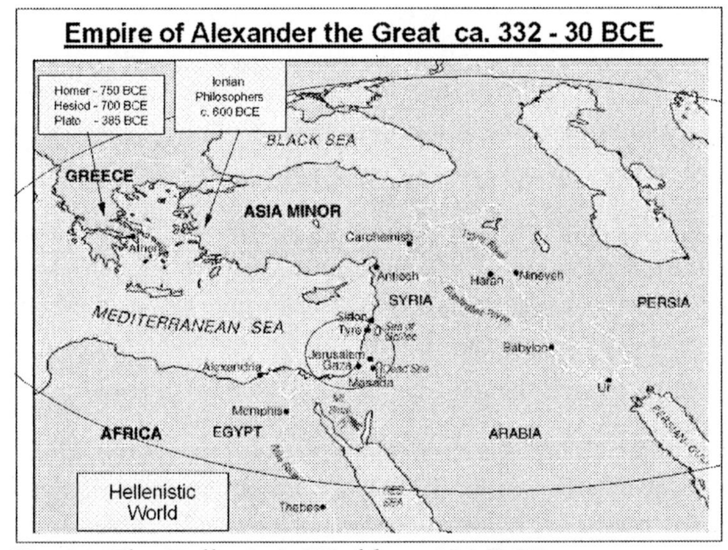

Fig. 23 The Hellenistic World ca. 332 BCE

A Comparison of Eschatological Concepts in Ancient Egypt and Ancient Greece

αἰθὴρ μὲν ψυχὰς ὑπεδέξατο σώματα δὲ χθών.

For the fallen at Potidaea,
Greece 432 BCE[51]

My Ba (soul) in heaven, my corpse in the graveyard.

Hepusonb,
New Kingdom ca. 1400 BCE

May you recognize your soul in the upper sky, while your flesh, your corpse, is in On.

Coffin Texts 44, I, 181f,
Middle Kingdom ca. 2000 BCE

The Akh (spirit) belongs to heaven, the corpse belongs to the earth.

Pyramid Texts,
Old Kingdom ca. 2300 BCE[52]

A possible cultural transmission

Are the quotations above merely coincidental or can we see a cultural transmission of the religious idea of the soul belonging to heaven and the body belonging to the earth. The idea spans the entire history of Egypt and then appears again in fifth century Greece.

Although the conclusions of this book do not depend on a theory of any kind of a cultural transmission between the two societies of ancient Egypt and Greece, I would be remiss if I did not investigate such possible interconnections. However, keeping in mind the admonitions of Jonathan Z. Smith, concerning the perils of

51. The air (ether) has received their souls (psyches), the earth their bodies (CIA i.442). Cf. Euripides "let soul release to air, body to earth" (*Suppliants* 533), "The mind of the dead does not live, yet it has eternal thought as it falls into eternal ether" (*Helen* 1014–16).

52. Heaven (ethereal realm) has the spirit, the earth has the body. *Pyramid Text* 474, in Spell 305.

comparative religion, one must be careful in making too much of perceived similarities.[53] There are, as we will see, some very interesting similarities that may imply a causal relationship; nevertheless, for our purpose here, the evolution of the Egyptian and Greek religious beliefs may just as satisfactorily be treated as independent and parallel developments.

Our investigation of ancient Greece opens with the writings of Homer and Hesiod (ca. 800–700 BCE). By this time the Egyptian Book of the Dead had been in existence for at least 700 years and the Pyramid Texts for at least 1500 years. The civilizations of palatial Minoan Crete and Mycenae had come and gone respectively during ca. 2000–1470 BCE and ca. 1450–1200. Greece had been influenced by the successive invasions of northern Indo-European-speakers from 2000 BCE on and then influenced by the Minoan civilization from around 1500 BCE.

The ancient religion of the Cretans and Mycenaeans (with their cults of the dead) had been drastically changed by various societal destructions and no longer reflected the common views of the early Eastern Mediterranean civilizations. A key change that appears in Homer was the practice of cremation instead of the normal inhumation of the Cretans, Mycenaeans, and Egyptians. The subterranean afterlife where one could still benefit by one's grave goods had disappeared, and Homer tends to ignore the indigenous agricultural and chthonic gods in favor of the Indo-European ones.

There was still an afterlife, but it was that of a "thoughtless or powerless head'[54]—a mere shadow of the formerly living person that now existed in an undifferentiated region that held king and commoner, good and bad alike. Status and conduct in one's life no longer mattered. This situation could have reflected the beliefs of nearby Semitic cultures or the northern invaders or, perhaps, both.

---

53. Jonathan Z. Smith, *Map is not Territory* (Leiden: E.J. Brill, 1978), 240–264; *Imagining Religion* (Chicago: University of Chicago Press, 1982), 19–35.

54. When the soul leaves the body it becomes an ἀμενηνός κάρηνον or strengthless head (Od. 10.520, 535, 11.29, 49), while the body becomes κωφὴ γαῖα or, literally, "dumb earth" (Il. 24.54). Achilles is mistreating the body of Hector and the gods are angry with him for dishonoring his remains, metaphorically, "mindless dirt".

However, even in Homer, we see glimpses of a residual religious belief that was inherited from the earliest inhabitants of what was to become the Hellenic homeland. Some of these residual beliefs are thought to have been inherited from Egypt by way of Crete and Mycenae.[55]

Evolution of the Greek Religions

Greek religion went through at least three major phases. The first phase was the chthonic religion of the pre-Aryan conquest period. The second phase was that of the familiar Olympian religion in which all of the gods (we learned of in elementary school) held places of honor. This was a syncretism of the pre-conquest and the Aryan gods of the invaders of Greece. The third phase is the most important one for the purpose of studying the roots of Christianity. This phase includes the various Mystery religions that operated beneath the surface of the primary belief in the gods of Olympus. We know that all three religious phases operated side by side throughout much of Greek history.

The Olympic religion was the religion of the ancient writers Homer and Hesiod. Although there were never any books that would be considered canonical scripture in Greece, the works of the 8th century poets were tantamount to scripture. Hesiod described the creation of the cosmos, and Homer insured the continued existence of the immortal gods in the minds of Greeks, then Romans, for centuries to come.

However, it is the Mysteries that captured the souls of the Greeks. Never as popular in the literary works as the Olympians, the gods of the Mysteries assured the salvation of the souls of their adherents, as the gods of Olympus never could. It is the Mysteries that brought about the development of the soul and became the religion of individual salvation. The chart, **Fig. 24** below, cryptically shows the evolution of the religious outlook of Greece

55. See Martin P. Nilsson, *The Minoan-Mycenaean Religion and its Survival in Greek Religion.* (Lund: C.W.K. Gleerup, 1950), 625, passim.

Philosophy/religion	Flourished	Key Event or Result
Aryan	ca. 2000	syncretized chthonic and Aryan gods
Homer	750	Olympian gods, fates
Hesiod	700	the ages of man
Orphic poetry	550	immortality and divinity of the soul (inscriptions)
Pythagoras	540	immortal soul, reincarnation
Heraclitus	490	all is flux—becoming
Parmenides	480	all is One—being
Democritus	420	atoms—determinism
Plato	365	soul, Forms, cosmic dualism
Aristotle	335	countered Idealism of Plato, teacher of Alexander the Great
Zeno/Stoic	310	fate rules, God is immanent and providential
Epicurus	310	swerve of atoms—fate does not rule

Fig. 24 Evolution of Greek Thought

Homer (ca. 750): the descent into Hades

The bedrock statement of the general belief in the Homeric corpus (concerning man's common lot in the afterlife) can be succinctly summed up in Sarpedon's speech to Glaucus and the story of his death in the Iliad:

> Man, supposing you and I, escaping this battle, would be able to live on forever, ageless, immortal, so neither would I myself go on fighting in the foremost nor would I urge you into the fighting where men win glory. But now, seeing that the spirits of death stand close about us in their thousands, no man can turn aside nor escape them, let us go on and win glory for ourselves, or yield it to others (Il. 12.322–28).

Sarpedon would avoid the fight and the attendant glory if only he were immortal. Since he is not, he must gain some portion of immortality the only way the Homeric Hero can—by glorious remembrance.

Later Sarpedon is faced with imminent death at the hands of Patroclus. His father, Zeus, wants to save him from death; but he is dissuaded from doing so by the goddess, Hera, who claims that if Zeus saves his son, all of the other gods would want to do likewise. Rather "bury [him] with a grave and a marker. This is the lot of mortals" (Il. 16.430–65). Here, Homer is saying that even the son of a god is mortal. Even Sarpedon must accept the fate of all lesser mortals, which is the finality of death where the immortal fame of the dead survives only in the memory of future generations. Sarpedon and, in these passages presumably Homer, accept the belief that without the immortal fame acquired by heroic deeds, the person at the end of his life is truly dead.

The *Odyssey*, book eleven, recounts when Hades was thought to be a place where virtually all humans went after death. It was a form of an afterlife existence in which almost all people suffered the same fate—to barely exist as a shadowy, wan, and ghostly shade of one's former self. There were very few exceptions. For a few heroes, there was the Elysian Fields; and for the vilest of people, there was Tartaros where they were judged by Minos to endure horrible eternal punishments. Much later, this would change with the Mystery religions and Plato.

Ambivalence about the afterlife in Homer

No culture appears to be immune from ambivalent thinking about the possibilities of an afterlife. We saw Gilgamesh's final acceptance that there was none; yet, we also saw their cult of the dead. Granted, it's not much of an afterlife compared to that of modern Christianity or Islam, but enough to be indicative of ambivalence.

The Greeks also had ambiguous and unclear thinking on the subject as witnessed by the excerpts from Homer below:

Iliad 3.276

Father Zeus…and you who under the earth take vengeance on dead men, whoever among them has sworn to falsehood, you shall be witnesses, to guard the oaths of fidelity.

Iliad 13.415

Asios lies not now all unavenged. I think rather as he goes down to Hades of the Gates, the strong one, he will be cheerful at heart, since I have sent him an escort.

Iliad 19.256

Let Zeus first be my witness…and Earth, and Helios the Sun, and the Furies, who underground avenge dead men, when any man has sworn to falsehood.

Iliad 23.100
Even in the house of Hades there is left something, a soul and an image, but there is no real heart of life in it.

Iliad 23.178
Good-bye, Patroklos. I hail you even in the house of the death god.

Odyssey 4.561
[Menelaus is to be sent to Elysium, a rare gift for a very few].

Odyssey 11.90
Now came the soul of Tiresias the Theban, holding a staff of gold, and he knew who I was, and spoke to me.

Odyssey 11.300
Kastor, breaker of horses, and the strong boxer, Polydeukes. The life-giving earth holds both of them, yet they are still living, and, even underneath the earth, enjoying the honor of Zeus, they live still every other day; on the next day they are dead, but they are given honor even as the gods are. [also see Il. 3.235].

Odyssey 11.476
To Hades place, where the senseless dead men dwell, mere imitations of perished mortals.

Odyssey 11.488
Do not speak soothingly to me of death, glorious Odysseus. I should choose to serve as the hireling of another, rather than to be lord over the dead that have perished. [The shade of Achilles speaking to Odysseus.]

Odyssey 11.576
[Tityos, Tantalus and Sisyphus suffering in Tartaros, the lowest place in Hades from which there is no escape].

Odyssey 11.601
[Heracles' phantom in Hades, himself among the immortal gods. He was split between Hades and the abode of the gods].

Odyssey 24.4
[Hermes leads the spirits of the dead suitors of Penelope, they follow gibbering].

Odyssey 23.333
Kalypso…would make him ageless all his days, and immortal.

Odyssey 24.98
Now as the spirits were conversing thus with each other, there came approaching them [Achilles and Agamemnon] the courier Argeiphontes, leading down the souls of the suitors killed by Odysseus. These two in wonderment went up to them as they saw them.

Hesiod's (ca. 700 BCE): five ages of man

Hesiod looked at the world and saw the terrible shape it was in and wondered if he was living in a degraded age. Surely, there was a time when the world was a loftier place, and civilization must have since devolved into the present state of affairs.

With these thoughts in mind, he looked backward to an age that was golden and far superior to ours. Could mankind have fallen so abruptly, or did it descend by stages? It must have gone down by stages because he could see back to a recent heroic age when men like Achilles and Hector walked the earth performing great deeds beyond the scope of today's men.

Yet, even these great men died only to subsist as wraiths in the underworld called Hades. There must have been heroes that fared better in a more perfect world of longer ago. There must have been a golden age where all was heroic and men lived forever.

Many religions look back to the beginning when all was fresh and new and long to re-create that sacred time and place. Hesiod said there was such a place where men of gold lived.

There is an afterlife in Hesiod where the "golden" race "in the time of Kronos…[after they died] they have been divine spirits…watchers over mortal men" (*Works* 110ff). The next race of silver, when they had died "have been called the mortal blessed below" (*Works* 142f). These races did nothing in the way of conduct or behavior to deserve their reward. Indeed, those of the silver race were witless, committed crimes, and dishonored the gods; but still they had a blessed afterlife.

The next race, that of the bronze, deserved punishment for their crimes and did suffer the more traditional Homeric common fate of going down "to chill Hades" house of decay leaving no names" (*Works* 153f). As we saw earlier, the members of the fourth race of the Heroes were the first to be rewarded for their conduct. Although some of them died and suffered the traditional fate, Zeus allowed some to be rewarded for their heroism and be sent alive to the Isles of the Blest.[56]

Hesiod's fourth and fifth races of men

Works and Days 166

> After the earth covered up this race too, Zeus son of Kronos made yet a fourth one upon the rich-pastured earth, a more righteous and noble one, the godly race of the heroes who are called demigods, our predecessors on the boundless earth. And as for them, ugly war and fearful fighting destroyed them, some before seven-gated Thebes, in the Cadmean country, as they battled for the flocks of Oedipus; and others [war] led in ships over the great abyss of the sea to Troy on account of lovely-haired Helen. There some of them were engulfeded by the consummation of death, but to some Zeus the father, son of Kronos, granted a life and home apart from men, and settled them at the ends of the earth. These dwell with carefree heart in the Isles of the Blessed Ones, beside deep-swirling Oceanos: fortunate Heroes, for whom the grain-giving soil bears its honey-sweet fruits thrice a year.
>
> Would that I were not then among the fifth men, but either dead earlier or born later! For now it was a race of iron; and they will never cease from toil and misery by day or night, in constant distress, and the gods will give them harsh troubles. [57]

Lastly, Zeus made yet another generation, the fifth, of men of iron. Hesiod, and mankind today, belong to his fifth race and can be rewarded by the gods for conduct and behavior, but never in a personal afterlife. In fact, a final cataclysm will eventually descend on this race, and even the gods will abandon mortals to defenselessness against evil (*Works* 175ff). We poor mortals are given to die but the gods retain immortality for themselves.

---

56. The heroes in Homer were translated to Elysium due to some relationship with the gods, but in Hesiod Works (156ff) it is justice and nobility that wins a reward for the fourth race of humans in the Isles of the Blest.

57. Translated by M. L. West, *Hesiod: Theogony and Works and Days,* (Oxford University Press, 1988), 41-2.

The Peasant Bard, Hesiod, seems to have no conception of a blessed afterlife for the people of his and our race. If Hesiod did not know of such an afterlife, could the earlier Homer have known? Could the foregoing observation be cited as an indication that the afterlife sections of the even earlier Homer are actually later non-Homeric interpolations? Perhaps it could, but this small observation will not resolve that great scholarly question. For, it is just as likely that it could also simply show that the non-aristocratic Hesiod reflected the more popularly accepted belief of the common lot for all in Hades, that of being a mindless shadow of the person that is hardly a life at all.[58]

Mankind did not devolve all at once, but went through stages: first gold, then silver, and bronze before coming to the heroes; then us.

This was the legacy of the poets, Homer and Hesiod; that we all die with no hope of a beneficent afterlife.

Pythagoras (ca. 540) and the Greek Mysteries

It seems that the vast majority of Greeks accepted this state of affairs for most of Greek history, but not all of them would. Sometime before the sixth century, an eschatological hope was born—mankind must have a greater purpose and destiny than to be born, suffer and cease to exist. With these thoughts came the birth of the soul and the Greek religion of the individual's salvation—the Mysteries.

The Mysteries opposed the Olympic religion of Homer and Hesiod's pessimistic afterlife, and offered people hope beyond the miseries of this world and the annihilation in the next. The Eleusinian mysteries (based on the myth of the goddess, Demeter, and her daughter Persephone) are believed to be the first of these religions.

The myth of Demeter and Persephone is quite beautiful. It tells of a mother's love for her daughter—a love that is directed totally toward finding her daughter after she had been abducted by Hades, the god of the underworld, who takes her as his wife. In a tale similar to that of the Mesopotamian Dumuzi and Inanna, Demeter completely abandons her beneficent duties toward the earth and all things cease to bloom.

58. We should also consider that just because a belief appears at any given time (Homer), it is not necessary that subsequent people (Hesiod) have to continue adherence to it.

Eventually, she frees her daughter from Hades, but Persephone must return there for three months of each year to be with her husband.

In what is clearly a vegetation myth, this is the story of the seed that is buried in silos during the hot summer months; then planted and sprout when the rains come. However, it is also, obviously, an allegory of the human condition. One must be buried in order to fully reap the blessedness awaiting us in the future.

The final lines of the *Hymn to Demeter* assures us of the blessedness to come:

> Happy is he among men upon earth who has seen these mysteries; but he who is uninitiate and who has no part in them, never has lot of like good things once he is dead, down in the darkness and gloom.

The Orphics (ca. 550)

Βίος Θάνατος Βίος "αλήθεια..."Ορφιχόι (life death true life...from Orpheus)

Orpheus was a man, the son of a god, who possessed such artistry that his singing could move the underworld gods to tears. In the myth of Orpheus and Eurydice, he ventured into Hades to retrieve his lover who had died from snakebite. By his song he persuaded Hades and his wife, Persephone, to grant him his wish to take Eurydice back to the world of the living. One caution was that he not look back as he exited. Almost freed from Hades, he glanced back to see if she were still following him and she disappeared back into hell.

This myth is pervasive in the ancient world. It teaches a lesson that once commanded by god to go forward at his behest, one must never look back in distrust of the word of god. We see a similar story in the Hebrew Bible where Lot had been given the chance to save his wife from the destruction of Sodom. It is the wife that failed to keep faith with God and is immediately punished. Jesus would say a similar thing to those who would follow him:

> No one who puts his hand to the plow and looks back to the things behind is fit for the kingdom of God.
>
> Luke 9:62

Overwhelmed with grief, Orpheus retired to the mountains where he rebuffed and offended some female followers of the god Dionysus—the Maenads. Feeling slighted by Orpheus, they tore him to pieces. The Muses gathered up the pieces and buried them all except the head, which was still singing, and it was carried into a river.

Orpheus became renowned for his excellence, and his myths were worked into a religion by intellectuals like Pythagoras, in which he became the chief priest of Dionysus.

Once again, we have to ask the questions of why we are here, where did we come from, and where are we going? The Orphics answered these questions by an appeal to the cosmogonic myth, involving the god Dionysus.

Zeus ruled the world as the supreme god along with his brothers and the rest of the Olympian gods. Zeus wanted a son to some day rule in his place and begot Dionysus with one of the Olympian goddesses.

One wonders why he would risk such an endeavor since he came to power by eliminating his own father, the Titan Cronus (just as his father, Uranus, had done to his grandfather). Apparently head gods have a short memory. Regardless, Dionysus was born and was well loved by Zeus who placed the scepter in his hand and told the gods that Dionysus would rule them all.

Hera, Zeus' main wife, was not the mother of Dionysus and became enraged that he would rule. She incited the Titans, who had been earlier overthrown by Zeus, to kill the infant Dionysus. They were happy to oblige and lured him from safety with child's toys. Too late, Dionysus realized his danger and was torn to pieces and devoured by the Titans.

Athena managed to save his heart, which she kept alive and gave to her father Zeus. From the heart, Dionysus would be resurrected. Now, Zeus was enraged and destroyed the Titans with his lightning bolt and burned them to ashes. It was from these ashes that humans arose.

Enter the first dualism of the flesh versus the spirit—the two natures of man. Man's body is of the Titans but also contains a divine part that comes from the devoured infant Dionysus. Thus, we are a mixture of good and evil. In the myths Orpheus suffered the same fate as the infant and, therefore, he was linked to the mystery of the Dionysic religion.

Somehow we know that we have a part of us that does not belong here. There is that divine part that wants to return to the world of the gods. The Orphic initiate could discover this mysterious part of himself and, by proper living, could escape from this mortal world into that one above.

In Orphism, God created the entire cosmos and human beings. Humans have a dual nature and contain a spark of divinity. They say that *soma sema* (the body is the tomb of the soul), the material world is illusory and evil; and our real home is elsewhere. The beautiful poems below reflect that belief.

Orphic Gold Tablets (c. 325–275 BCE)

On the famous gold tablets found in Petelia and Thurii in southern Italy we find some very interesting inscriptions which have usually been considered as reflecting Orphic beliefs in the afterlife. Two of these tablets, from Petelia and Thurii respectively, are partially cited here:[59]

Plate from Petelia, South Italy, fourth-third century BCE:

> Thou shalt find to the left of the House of Hades a spring,
> And by the side thereof standing a white cypress.
> To this spring approach not near.
> But thou shalt find another, from the Lake of Memory
> Cold water flowing forth, and there are guardians before it.
> Say,
>
> > I am a child of Earth and starry Heaven;
> > But my race is of Heaven alone.
> > This ye know yourselves.
> > But I am parched with thirst and I perish.
> > Give me quickly the cold water flowing
> > forth from the Lake of Memory.[60]

---

59. Both translated by W.K.C. Guthrie, *Orpheus and Greek Religion* (London: Methuen, 1935), 171-5.

60. The Petelia tablet reflects the belief that humans are fallen gods who return to their heavenly home after a sojourn in the flesh on earth. This mirrors the inscription on the fifth century bone tablet of Olbia on which we find the words, "life-death-life;' a reference to one's multiple existences. One originally lives in the divine world, suffers death in the flesh; then returns to the divine world.

> And of themselves they will give thee to drink of the holy spring,
> And thereafter among the other heroes thou shalt have lordship.

Also, from Thurii, South Italy, fourth century BCE:

> I come from the pure, pure Queen of those below...
> For I also avow that I am of your blessed race.
> And I have paid the penalty for deeds unrighteous...
> I have flown out of the sorrowful, weary circle...
> And now I come as a suppliant to holy Persephoneia...
> Happy and blessed one, thou shalt be a god instead of mortal.[61]

The fact that a "weary circle" is mentioned would lead one to believe that the inscriber was referring to cyclic transmigration of souls and that therefore metempsychosis is an Orphic doctrine since these tablets are described as being Orphic. The reason they are so described is because they look like the similar material in Plato. Of course, the reason that Plato is linked to Orphic doctrine is that it is generally believed that some of his ideas came from them. Here we have a unbridled circular argument that neither shows that the tablets were Orphic nor that Plato based his dialogs on Orphic beliefs.

In the two tablets shown above we have a possibility of two different doctrines: one having—and one not having—multiple incarnations. Are both Orphic?[62] I will argue that there is at least one variant of the Orphic/Pythagorean tradition that holds to no doctrine of metempsychosis at all. This will be based on the evidence of silence from the Petelia tablet[63] and more scientifically on the positive

---

61. The Thurii tablet expresses essentially the same thing as the Petelia tablet, but adds two issues: a judgment penalty for unrighteous deeds, and an allusion to a cycle of incarnations, whereas, a single incarnation would suffice in the former tablet.
62. Walter Burkert, for example, says that there are traditions of both the Orphic and Pythagorean doctrines of metempsychosis. Burkert, *Greek Religion* trans. John Ruffan (Cambridge: Harvard University Press, 1987), 298–301.
63. Also, similarly in the more recently discovered Pelinna lamellae dated to the late fourth century. See Fritz Graf, "Dionysian and Orphic Eschatology: New Texts and Old Questions," in Thomas H. Carpenter and Christopher A. Faraone, *Masks of Dionysus* (Ithaca: Cornell University Press, 1993), 240.

statement on the bone tablet found at Olbia in 1978 that states simply: βίος θάνατος βίος and a word indicating Orpheus ὀρφιχοί or ὀρφιχων.[64]

This has been taken to show that the Orphic belief was in a cyclic rebirth where "temporary death is replaced with a new birth."[65] My contention is that no cycle of life—temporary death—then reincarnation is implied here. Rather this indicates that these Orphics believed in an original life in the divine realm, followed by a death into the earthly flesh, followed by rebirth into true life as a divine being once more. Furthermore, the fragments of Heraclitus do not require multiple incarnations, although, those of Empedocles and Pindar do. Interestingly, Plato's first eschatological myth in the *Gorgias* contains no reincarnation doctrine. That was to come later, in the *Phaedo*, after his visit to Sicily and his indoctrination into Pythagoreanism.

For these reasons, I am persuaded that the Pythagoreans believed in metempsychosis but the earlier Orphics did not.[66]

Plato (ca. 365 BCE)

Theology was never to be the same after Plato. While it is true that he stood on the shoulders of his predecessors, such as the Orphics and Pythagoras, for some of his ideas on the soul, he alone is responsible for developing the consistent philosophy of religion that affected almost all subsequent theologies.

---

64. These bone tablets are dated to the later fifth century BCE. Zhmud' says that one of the three plates of "Orphic graffiti from Olbia (Vth century B.C.)" has the phrase "βίος θάνατος βίος ἀλήθεια Διονύσω ὀρφιχοί" which proves that there was an organized Orphic community in the fifth century. He also claims that they believed in metempsychosis because one of the plates had ψυχή and σῶμα on the recto (Leonid Zhmud', "Orphism and grafitti from Olbia," *Hermes* 120 [1992]: 159–168). His first claim may be true; however, I disagree with the latter claim and contend that the phrases are better interpreted as: life—death—true life, to Dionysus from Orphics. They did indeed believe that the soul (ψυχή) was fallen into a body (σῶμα), but that it could return to true life once again.

65. Zhmud', "Orphism and grafitti from Olbia," 168.

66. For more on Orphic and Egyptian eschatology in greater depth see: Gary A. Stilwell, *Conduct and Behavior as Determinants for the Afterlife: A Comparison of the Judgments of the Dead in Ancient Egypt and Ancient Greece*, 2000.

The biggest impact of Platonism, other than on his own school, was the thinking of the Jewish philosopher, Philo, the Neo-Platonists, the Gnostics, and the Christian Fathers. Even the cult of Mithras[67] shows signs of Platonic influence with Plato's astral immortality and the Diotima-like flight of the soul.

Plato had developed a spiritual hierarchy headed by the highest Idea of the Good. Below this, there were the highest Forms of Truth, Beauty, and Symmetry, and below these were such Forms as wisdom, courage, justice, and the mathematical functions. The world was not created by the highest Good, but rather by a lower Demiurge, who used the Forms as templates to make the world of our perceptions.

A human consisted of a body and a tripartite soul; rational, spirited, and acquisitive (Republic 434e–442d). The highest aspiration for a person was to liberate one's soul from the material world and the flesh of the body in order to rise to behold the One Form of the Good.

In these few ideas lay the foundation for the subsequent theological developments of later religions and philosophies—as we shall see in Part III, the Development of Christianity.

The afterlife as described in Plato's Myth of Er

In the *Republic*, the Myth of Er intensifies Plato's argument that the unjust (or unrighteous) become less fit to live in the ideal world and more fit to live in the present world with their own kind of people. The total separation in the afterlife (of the unrighteous from the righteous) expresses a truth that mere dialectic cannot. Each will go to one's own place: the better to the better, and the worse to the worse.[68]

The Myth of Er (Republic 614b–621b).

> Once upon a time he [Er, son of Armenius] died in war; and...as he was lying on the pyre, he came back to life, and...told what he saw in the other world (614b).

---

67. The religion of Mithraism competed with Christianity in the Roman Empire. See Plato's *Symposium* for his discussion of Diotima and the flight of the soul.

68. Cf. *Rep*. 442a, 472e, 519ab, 571b, 609e.

At Republic 10.614c, Plato's Er describes the site of the judgment. There are two openings side by side in the earth, and two openings in the heaven, with judges sitting between them who judge the newly dead. The just are sent to the right and up through heaven and the unjust to the left and down. All are wearing tokens, presumably to indicate their degree of goodness or badness.[69] The other two openings have souls coming back from a long stay in heaven, or under the earth where they have been rewarded or punished ten-fold for their former behavior. This arrangement denies any once-for-all judgment since all those dead for a thousand years—except the incurably wicked—are brought back to be reborn.

The newly brought back are allowed to choose a new lot in life and are reincarnated. However, the choice is almost entirely based on one's previous existence on earth and in the afterlife.[70] Reincarnation is now a continuous cycle (617d) and all good or curable people are reborn, including the philosopher. This raises the question: Is reincarnation a further punishment after one has already paid the price, as in the *Phaedo*, or (worse yet) after one had already reaped the reward of one's past life only to have it taken away?[71]

Punishments in the afterlife are said by some to be purgatorial, rather than vindictive; although, the "incurables" still remain forever in Tartarus.[72] All other souls will continue to be reincarnated.

---

69. Rep. 614cd. The tokens are reminiscent of the Orphic tablets, and the Egyptian *Book of the Dead* texts that were buried with the corpse to mark their way through the underworld. Four hundred years later "to the right and to the left" will be associated with the sheep and the goats in the Gospel of Matthew.

70. Rep. 620a, 617e. Plato attempts to offer free will to the souls in order that the blame for any future failure not be on god, since he insists "god is never in any way unrighteous" (*Theatetus* 176). His attempt at Theodicy fails because the choice is not really free. It is tied to the success or failure of a previous existence over which the reincarnated person has no control and maybe even no memory.

71. Rep. 619bc has one soul who had spent a thousand years in heaven now choosing a lot that will almost surely send it to Tartarus at its next death. Conversely, one who had been in Tartarus chooses a lot that will assist it to achieve heaven. Regardless, even the best souls of philosophers are condemned to the punishment of again being placed into a body. They can avoid future hells, but not future incarnations.

72. *Rep.* 615a–616a. (cf. *Phaedo* 113e; *Gorgias.* 525b-d; *Protagoras* 234b). Eternal punishment of the incurables runs counter to Plato's claim that punishment will cure wickedness. To many, eternal punishment for finite crimes seems quite vindictive and won't cure anything.

In spite of the significant changes in afterlife beliefs from Homer to Plato, this myth appears to represent a regression back to Homer, where all souls ended up alike in Hades whether they were good or bad.[73] Only with Plato, it is not in Hades, but there in the "other world', that all alike end up. Some may be treated better than others, but all are threatened with the same punishment: to be placed once more in a body.[74] The religions of India had (by this time in history) figured a way out of this continuous cycle of birth and rebirth;[75] but this possibility does not appear in the Myth of Er, or indeed, anywhere in the rest of the *Republic.* What is needed is a way to accumulate wisdom throughout all reincarnations and then use that wisdom to finally break the cycle.[76]

The soul concept in Egypt and Greece

A cursory look has the "soul" in Egypt and Greece appearing to be quite similar. In both, it is the entity or entities that complete the human personality. It is that element which achieves immortality and, in some cases (the king in the *Pyramid Texts* and everyone in Plato), is pre-existent to the body.

---

73. Note that Homer's main description of the undifferentiated dead is that of a "strengthless head' (*Od.* 11.29, 476) in Hades having no true life at all (*Il.* 23.100 ff).

74. It is possible for the eternal soul to achieve a never-ending series of heavenly blissful stays without ever going "underground" (619e). Even with this possibility, the soul's justice may still seem somewhat abrogated because it must also endure an endless series of incarnations, with a concomitant chance for failure to achieve the next scheduled bliss.

75. For a Hindu parallel compare *Bhagavad-Gita* 14.2 where it is stated "by becoming fixed in this knowledge, one can attain to the transcendental nature, like my own, and not be born at the time of creation or disturbed at the time of dissolution" (A.C. Bhaktivedanta Swami, *Bhagavad-Gita: As It Is* [Los Angeles: Bhativedanta Book Trust, 1977], 220). In his later myths, Plato would come to this same conclusion; that pre-natal knowledge (i.e., recollection) of the Forms would eventually allow cessation from the cycle of rebirth.

76. The Hindus, Buddhists, the Greek Empedocles and even the later Plato would solve this problem for the individual soul. Plato's doctrine of recollection does not help, because it is not explicitly noted in the Er myth nor in the entire *Republic.* However, *Rep.* 621a, concerning the measure of water drunk from the River of Forgetfulness, may have implications as to the soul's recollection in the next incarnation. It is this recollection that solves the problem of breaking the cycle of reincarnation.

In both, there is a celestial or ethereal afterlife and both have instances of the soul going to reside among the stars. There the similarities end.

The Pythagorean/Orphic/Platonic soul has fallen from a lofty height, and is condemned to live in the flesh due to some original sin.[77] This concept of the body being the tomb of the soul would have been abhorrent to the Egyptians (who loved life in the flesh and expected the body to live eternally with the souls).

In Egypt, all of the non-physical elements of the personality (*ba, ka, akh*), along with the body lives on; whereas, in early Greece, only the psyche does so; and the body souls (*thymos, nous, menos*) cease to exist.[78] With Plato, the immortal psyche becomes the tripartite soul (rational, appetitive, and spirited), and assumes all of the functions of the other body souls and later, with Aristotle, only the highest of the three (the rational) would attain immortality.

In Platonic thought, the soul would endure a purgation period before returning once more to a body, unless that soul had achieved the highest reward or punishment. In Egypt there was only bliss or oblivion and no place of purgation for a return, nor was there a place of punishment until much later in their history.[79]

---

77. Plato explains the original sin at *Laws* 854b where he says, the impulse to evil "is a sort of frenzied goad, innate in mankind as a result of crimes of long ago that remain unexpiated." In *Laws* 701c, Plato had explained the origin of the crimes of long ago as being revealed by having people "reincarnated in themselves, the character of the ancient Titan (Τιτανικὴν) of the story…and thanks to getting into the same position as the Titans did, they live a wretched life of endless misery." Of course, Empedocles had alluded to this idea much earlier.

78. The Greeks had no resurrection of the body, but the Egyptians expected a reconstitution of the body like that of Osiris. The Homeric Greeks certainly had non-material elements of the personality called *thumos, nous, and menos*. Homer even had *psyche* (breath) but none of these survived death. However, due to ambiguity, something ghost-like did survive in Hades.

79. Herodotus (2.123) had claimed that the Egyptians invented the transmigration of souls. He probably mistook their transformations for reincarnation. They indeed metamorphosed into other creatures and even into their gods, but not for a return to the flesh. Later in the New Kingdom, the Egyptians eventually would also develop a concept of hell as a punishment for misdeeds, instead of simple oblivion.

Pre-Platonic Writer's Influence on Plato

Introduction

An investigation into earlier writers would show that the literature of much of the Greek world was expounding on concepts, such as the immortal soul (the soul's rebirth through cyclic lives and an afterlife consequence for one's conduct while alive). At this same time, the Mainland Greek writers were still holding on to the predominant Homeric idea—that of no beneficial afterlife.

The Sophistic movement was creating a morally relativistic society where the laws were being questioned as having no support other than the conventions of the majority.[80] Into this societal breakdown came Socrates with his ideas of respect for the virtues and the laws. Plato followed through with support beyond mere convention—explaining in his dialogues and myths—that the virtues were based in a much deeper reality.

However, Plato did not create these great dialogues and myths in a vacuum. Many earlier Greek writers helped set the stage for what he was later able to accomplish—some with ideas in eschatology and some in ethics.

Eschatology

Olympiodorus in his *On the Phaedo* has said that Plato paraphrases Orpheus everywhere.[81] Perhaps that is a bit strong, but Plato certainly used the material that, in the *Gorgias* 493a, he attributes to certain wise men from "perhaps some inhabitant in Sicily or Italy."[82] As we've seen, these can only be the Pythagoreans and/or Orphics who were the forerunners of eschatological writers: Heraclitus, Pindar, and Empedocles.

---

80. Plato discusses Sophistic opinion in his dialogues against Callicles and Thrasymachus in the *Gorgias* 481ff and the *Republic* book I.

81. Plato mentions Orpheus many times: *Crat.* 400c; *Gorgias.* 493a; *Rep.* 364b; *Symp.* 179c; *Euthyd.* 277d; *Meno* 81a and *Laws* 715e.

82. Also in *Gorgias* 493a: "Sages say that we are now dead and the body (σῶμα) is our tomb (σῆμα)."

In the *Meno* 81b, Plato is supposed to have summarized the Orphic eschatology,[83] where he writes:

> MENO: What was it, and who were they?
> SOCRATES: Those who tell it are priests and priestesses of the sort who make it their business to be able to account for the functions which they perform. Pindar speaks of it too, and many another of the poets who are divinely inspired. What they say is this—see whether you think they are speaking the truth.
>
> They say that the soul of man is immortal. At one time it comes to an end-that which is called death—and at another is born again, but is never finally exterminated.
>
> On these grounds a man must live all his days as righteously as possible. For those from whom Persephone receives requital for ancient doom, In the ninth year she restores again their souls to the sun above.
> From whom rise noble kings and the swift in strength and greatest in wisdom, And for the rest of time they are called heroes and sanctified by men. Thus the soul, since it is immortal and has been born many times, and has seen all things both here and in the other world, has learned everything that is.[84]

"They say a man's soul is immortal, sometimes it ends its existence which is called death and sometimes it comes into being again." Did Plato really get that from the Orphics? They had only contended, somewhat differently from Pythagoras,[85] that a human being contained a divine spark that was punished by being entombed in the flesh.[86] The Orphic goal was to return to whence one came in a "life in the divine world—death in the body—back to life" scenario. This fits

---

83. Socrates tells of what he has heard from wise men and women (priests and priestesses) and from Pindar whose fragment 133 he quotes. I believe that the first part (*Gorgias*. 493a) cited above is Orphic, but that Pindar's quote (at *Meno* 81b) allowed Plato to say that the soul "has been born many times." Cf. Heraclitus frag 63, Pindar frag 133, Empedocles frag 146 and Plato *Meno* 81bc.

84. Translated by W. K. C. Guthrie, in Hamilton and Caims (ed.), *Plato.—The Collected Dialogues* (New York: Bollingen Series LXXI, 1961), 364.

85. Pythagoras is supposed to have claimed that the soul wanders through countless lives, as humans, plants, and animals.

86. Socrates equates this doctrine with "the Orphic poets" at *Cratylus* 400c.

with what both Heraclitus and Empedocles (except for his multiple lives) had to say on the subject. It also fits with the bone tablets of Olbia where we see the inscription: *bios—thanatos—bios*. Therefore, the lines in *Meno* 81b also fit the Orphics, but Plato will put a cyclic rebirth spin on it just as did Pindar.[87]

Pythagoras is supposed to have claimed that a person passed through several lifetimes, and Empedocles echoes this claim with his statement that he has passed through many types of existence.

Nevertheless, the mechanics of their reincarnation theory is unclear. The Orphic material that we have is late and Pythagoras did not write anything down, therefore, we do not know for sure what they said happens after one's death and before another rebirth. Most of the popular concepts we have of the Pythagoreans and Orphics have been filtered through the gauze of Platonic myth thus it is difficult to tell what they really believed as opposed to what Plato embellished. Even so, it seems that we can take the testimony of Pindar and Empedocles as attesting to the metempsychosis theory of Pythagoras,[88] and the Heraclitean and "bone tablets" as attesting to the life-death-life concept of the Orphics.[89] It remains to further examine both of these cases to determine if an afterlife judgment makes any sense.

---

87. As with everything else where the facts are sparse, there is a scholarly debate over whether the Orphics taught the doctrine of metempsychosis. Rohde and Dodds hold that they did. Rohde says, "Least of all did they [Orphics] need to derive the doctrine of the migration of souls and its application from this source [Pythagoreans]," therefore, it was their own. Later he says that, "The Orphics retained, in spite of everything, the doctrine of transmigration" (Rohde, *Psyche*, 336–342, 346; Dodds, *Greeks and the Irrational*, 149, 170 n. 94). And, Dodds allows that the Orphics did believe that the body was the prison of the soul where it is punished for past sins, and that this doctrine is supported by the belief "in a preexistent detachable soul." I maintain that the Orphics did not necessarily hold to the doctrine of metempsychosis since the pre-existent soul need only support the life-death-life scenario.

88. Xenophanes' (560-470) frag 7 is an early attestation of the reincarnation belief of Pythagoras where he orders the maltreatment of a dog to stop because the dog is the soul of a friend.

89. Heraclitus disagreed with Pythagoras at frags 40, 81, 120, 129. His statements that, "mortals are immortals and immortals are mortals" implies a life from death and a death from life, but not necessarily a cyclic reincarnation. Heraclitus' statement is closer to the inscription on the bone tablet of Olbia than to the doctrine of metempsychosis taught by Pythagoras.

Does the Pythagorean believe that one reincarnates immediately at death? In that case, there is no need for any place like a Hades in which to be judged. Or, do they spend an interval between incarnations, in which case there certainly is a requirement for such a holding place.

Does reincarnation allow or even require a judgment for one's living conduct? I would have to say yes to both (allowing and requiring some form of judgment) since in all cases, one's ultimate destination depends on what one has done in past lives.

Plato is very clear about his belief, excepting the earlier *Gorgias* which posits no reincarnation, in that he holds to an interval between incarnations and specifies that one will be judged each time one dies. Nevertheless, his judgment scenes evolve over time, ranging from the final judgment found in the Gorgias where actual judges examine the scars left by bad conduct, to his later myths where the judgment becomes more automatic and, finally, in the *Phaedrus*, where there are no judges at all. Pythagorean reincarnation is not the same thing as an afterlife judgment; although, Plato will combine these two concepts very effectively.

Pindar is the first major poet to speak of a judge below the earth who passes sentence on wrongdoers. He also allows that those who abstain from wrongdoing through three lifetimes are destined for the Isle of the Blessed. There is no need for a judge below the earth for either Pythagoras or the Orphics;, and Pindar's story might be seen as a syncretism of the afterlife punishments found in Homer, added to the rebirth ideas of Pythagoras.

Now, does the Orphic believe that he or she experiences a reincarnation after death? We do not really have enough facts to know the answer. However, since the punishment for the Orphic is the fall into flesh for a perceived original sin, there is no reason to necessarily posit a rebirth doctrine in their eschatology. As to a judgment, we may ask why did one receive the punishment of being incarnated if some form of a judgment had not already taken place? If the bone tablet scenario accurately describes Orphic beliefs, then this judgment must take place in the first life as a divine or semi-divine being. There must be an implicit judgment for some primordial sin that condemns one to an incarnation.

This incarnation concept does not match that of the *Gorgias* myth, but the "life-death-life" scenario is exactly what is happening in the *Phaedrus*. The evolution of the idea is that, instead of a single life-death-life, Plato has incorporated the

Pindaric (and therefore Pythagorean and Empedoclean) concept of multiple reincarnations.

We might ask, if the Orphic's punishment was to be born into the flesh, why does Plato speak of other punishments like "the barbaric slough of the Orphic myth" (*Rep*. 533d, cf. 363d). This "everflowing dung" type of punishment also showed up in an earlier play, *Frogs*. But was it Orphic? Possibly, but it was most certainly Eleusinian and, therefore, associated with the presumed "founder" of the Mysteries—Orpheus.

By the time of Plato's *Republic*, some Orphics, who by now must have been practicing a disreputable form of Orphism, were being condemned for their "babble of books." Nevertheless, the "barbaric slough" and the "everflowing dung" seem to have no place in the eschatology of the gold leaves and the bone tablets.

It is most unfortunate that these "Orphic myth" punishments, instead of the optimistic beauty of the Orphic gold leaves, were to influence the eschatology of later Christian doctrine.

Plato's Idealism

Plato's, as opposed to subsequent philosophies, was not materialistic. He needed something to refute the epistemological relativism and skepticism of the earlier Sophists and Skeptics. The latter had denied the possibility of objective knowledge, and Plato believed that if all was material and subject to the human senses, that they might be correct. However, he claimed that objective knowledge was possible because all true and real knowledge is based on non-material, pre-existing, immutable and eternal models—the Ideas (or Forms), which are otherworldly archetypes of the material objects that we perceive in our world of the natural senses (*Republic*, 506d–521).

Calling on Pythagorean and Orphic traditions, he used their concepts of metempsychosis, immortality, and recollection to explain how we are able to know reality. The body is the tomb of the soul and the soul's real home is in the celestial realm where it knows the Ideal Forms. Periodically, it leaves its celestial home to inhabit an earthly body. Unfortunately, it forgets the Ideas and only a few philosophers are able to re-acquire them through hard work. All die and the soul is released only to complete the cycle again and again until such time as philosophical works free it from the bondage of the material world (*Republic*, 614a–621d).

The material world of Becoming is opposed to the unchanging Ideal world of Being in an irreconcilable dualism. The pure soul once freed from the corporeal world "goes away to a place that is...unseen world...into the presence of the good and wise God" (*Phaedo*, 80d). Plato's worldview is ambiguous, as is his view of the god(s). He holds to the geocentric cosmology, but the place of the afterlife varies from the earth's surface of Er to the "true Hades" of the world of Ideas. Plato's gods exist, sometimes as the God of the *Phaedo* (67a), sometimes as the Demiurge of the *Timaeus* and sometimes as the gods of the popular religion.

Plato's later influence

When Christianity needed a philosophical basis for its Hebraic thinking in a Hellenistic world, it would turn to Plato. It would be Plato's eschatology that reigned supreme for over a thousand years, displacing or modifying original Christian concepts, such as the millennial Kingdom, in which all of the righteous resurrected dead would participate on the earth.

Stoics and Epicureans (ca. 310 BCE)

The Fates were the personification of one's inevitable destiny in the Homeric religion, and even Zeus' son could not escape his fated death. The Greek tragedians built their stories on the fact that one's destiny was foreordained. Being possessed of virtue (*arête*) and heroism would not divert Oedipus from his fate, regardless of his attempts to outguess the predictions of the gods.

The Mysteries were to give one a way out of his fate with an appeal to gods who were greater than the controllers of fate. However, the Mysteries appealed only to a minority and the incipient scientific explanations of the universe produced a need for less magical methods.

In the scientific philosophies, fate (also called determinism) had to be explained rationally. Two such philosophies attempted to do just that—coming down on opposite sides of the solution.

The Stoics were exemplars of determinism. Built on the atomism of Democritus, their cosmos was fated to repeat cyclically. Since one's fate was determined, the Stoics prized the attributes of indifference (things are neither good nor bad in themselves) and apathy (reason dominates emotion). Therefore, one must "go with the flow".[90] These attributes would also be prized by the early Church Fathers, until Platonic philosophy came to dominate Christian thinking and free choice trumped fate.

Their concept of the *Logos*[91] (the overall plan of all things and events as contained in the divine mind—the pattern for all creation and history) would greatly influence later Gospel of John, neo-Platonism and the Christian Fathers.

The Epicureans took the other side and claimed that fate did not exist. They denied the Stoics claim of fate and exemplified the concept of indeterminism.

The Stoics and Epicureans versus Plato

In the seventeenth century CE, Sir Isaac Newton formulated the theory of gravity, and set the stage for a mechanistic view of the universe. With John Dalton's rediscovery of the atom in the nineteenth century, the Universe was now seen to be a swarm of moving particles whose trajectories could theoretically be calculated. Indeed, if it were not for the fact of there being so many of these material objects, one would be able to predict, from any given starting point, their positions into the indefinite future, making all future events knowable and, thus, already determined. The nineteenth century universe was seen to be totally materialistic and determinant.

With these discoveries, the world-view of the ancient Stoics was revived and was thought to have been proven by modern science.

In what turns out to be quite ironic, Stoicism claimed to be a counter to the misguided philosophy of the Epicurean's world-view of luck and chance. For the Epicureans, the world consisted of an earth surrounded by the heavenly spheres. And, all was composed of Democritus' atoms. There were innumerable worlds since there was an infinity of atoms, in a void, that existed for all eternity (letter to Herodotus 41; and Pythocles 89).

90. This non-academic phrase exemplifies Stoic thought—as does *Star Trek's* Vulcans.

91. Heraclitus (ca. 500 BCE) originally used the term *Logos* to express parallelism of structure between the actual cosmos and our own thinking about it. The cosmos is the divine's spoken word. The belief that the world was rationally ordered gives credence to the idea that it is not accidental and must, therefore, be designed by a maker.

The Epicureans realized that, if indeed, all things were composed of atoms moving on their own calculatable trajectories, then there could be no such thing as human free will. Since there did appear to be free will, they needed a means to allow for indetermination. It was for this purpose that they imparted a "swerve" to the atoms. This swerve allowed for chance collisions and, therefore, a possibility for choice and free will.

For the Epicureans, choice and free will were doctrines that, combined with their ideas of the complete non-involvement of the gods in the affairs of humans, gave humans the complete freedom to live as they might. All was material, all was chance, and nothing was directly controlled by the gods—the human soul was a combination of atoms that disintegrated upon death, so there was no fear of punishment in an after-life (Epicurus' letters to Herodotus and to Menoeceous).

Nevertheless, the gods do exist, as they have been perceived through dreams; but they do not directly interfere in the lives of humans, rather they are "left free from duties and in perfect blessedness" (Epicurus' letter to Pythocles).

How then could an individual be happy? Only by attaining the highest good in life; that is, the absence of pain and the maximum of pleasure.

As suggested above, the Stoics opposed the Epicureans and said that God exists, does care for human things, and was indeed responsible for the creation of the world; and that his divine spark of fire caused the seminal reason (*logos spermaticos*) to be born. Humans arise from this same divine action and, therefore, partake of this same *logos*. But, God initiated the world and determined that it would follow his pre-ordained path for the duration of this current world and all the world's cycles to come (*Meditations* II: 11–14, XII: 26). This eliminated the possibility of chance or free will.

Thus the Stoics banished the Epicurean "swerve." The only hope for the individual was to play his apportioned part in the cosmos. This meant recognizing that all are essentially of one divine essence and that the virtue of following the divine will, and doing one's pre-ordained duty, in this best of all possible worlds, was the only way to happiness. The Stoic philosophy was to influence the Christian religion for many centuries, while the philosophy of Epicurus would be condemned.

Interestingly, in the early part of the twentieth century, the "swerve" was rediscovered. It appears that the trajectories of the atoms might not be pre-ordained after all. The Copenhagen interpretation of quantum mechanics rests on two pillars of scientific observation: Niels Bohr's Principle of Complementarity exemplified by the wave/particle dualism of light; and the Heisenberg Uncertainty Principle that the position and momentum of bodies can be physically traded off (as can energy/time and other complementary dualisms).[92] Thus, any object (including Democritus' atoms) can instantaneously alter their positions of their own volition—the Epicurean "swerve.'

So it seems, at least by our current stage of modern science, that the Epicurean's view on chance and free will has won out after over 2000 years of being denied first by the Stoics, then by others—among them the sixteenth and seventeenth century versions of religion and science.

The cosmologies of both schools were materialist, but the implications for the afterlife were very different. The Epicurean allowed for no continuation after death of the body; the soul being made of material atoms simply disintegrated. The soul of the Stoics, however, was reunited after death with Providence or their Principle that controls everything, the Logos. "Re-absorption" may be the more appropriate description for the reunion of the human soul with the pantheistic God, allowing it to reappear in subsequent world cycles of fiery destruction and re-birth.

Neither of these schools of philosophy allowed for a personal continuation of life after death. That option had already been put forward by their predecessors, the Orphics, Pythagoras and, most of all, Plato.

The materialism of Epicurus and Zeno the Stoic was destined to be extinguished for centuries, while the idealism of Plato was to live on in the great philosophies and religions of the West. With the Enlightenment, materialism revived only to be partially extinguished again by the scientific revolution of the twentieth century.

---

92. For those who would question this oversimplification, I offer this more detailed explanation: Heisenberg actually claimed that the position and the momentum of an object cannot be exactly determined (still, but less so, an oversimplification). The more exact you get one attribute, the less exact is the other. This is not just a measurement problem; the indeterminacy actually exists in nature. The reality of our universe is that there are complementary attributes of material objects that can be traded off in the manner suggested by measuring position and momentum. Time and energy are also complementary attributes in that time can be traded for energy. This allows for the existence of virtual particles that spontaneously appear; essentially borrowing mass/energy from time. Such a spontaneous creation is responsible for the evaporation of black holes and, quite possibly, for the very existence of our observable universe.

A summary of three Greek philosophies

For Plato, the world was a dualism of the material and the Ideal Forms; the god(s) exist both as the highest Good and in the world of human beings; the afterlife contains reward, punishment, and rebirth for the masses.

For Epicurus, the world was all eternal material atoms in the void; the gods were aloof from humans and dwelt blissfully between the worlds; the afterlife was not possible since all souls disintegrated at death, so the threats of post-mortem punishments were false.

For the Stoics, the world was a monistic living organism made of matter that cyclically was destroyed and re-created. The one God (although there were lesser others) was responsible for strictly determining the fate of all, which was repeated identically in all cycles; the afterlife was non-personal with the soul reabsorbed into the Logos to be reborn in subsequent world cycles.

Christianity, especially the early Fathers, would embrace much of Stoicism's immanent and providential God, its rationally created order, and its anthropology and ethics, but would reject the philosophy of Epicurus. Plato is so important for the understanding of later Christianity that, at the appropriate time in "Part III—the Development of Christianity," we will examine the impact of Platonism on all subsequent religious thought.

A counterfactual historical footnote

Or, what might have been…

The Greeks and the Persians are both extremely important to the history of Christianity. It is interesting that they battled each other for supremacy in the Mediterranean world. Had the Persians won, Greece would have come under the control of the Persian Empire and subsequent history would have been altered.

Would Christianity have even arisen if that scenario had occurred? We will never know, but consider this:

- Socrates and Plato probably would have spoken Persian.
- Their philosophy would never have taken place.
- Aristotle would not have taught Alexander the Great.
- Alexander would never have conquered the Persian empire.

- The world would not have been Hellenized.
- Zoroastrian monotheism would have remained strong.

Since Israel had enjoyed the benevolent rule of Persia:

- Judah would not have fought the Maccabean wars.
- Jewish sects would not have been born.
- There would have been no Essenes.
- The Jews would not have been oppressed by the Romans.
- There would have been no apocalyptic eschatology.
- John the Baptist would not have been preaching the end of the world.
- The Temple would not have been destroyed.
- There would have been no reason to preach the "good news."

However, if Jesus still had initiated his movement:

- It would have had to compete with an established monotheism instead of Greek/Roman polytheism.
- Greek Platonism would not have influenced the later development of the Church.
- The Mysteries would not have influenced the later development of the Church.

Therefore, Christianity and Western Civilization, as we know it, would not have developed.

We owe a huge debt of gratitude for the valiant Greeks, and their leader Miltiades, who defeated the Persians at the battle of Marathon. As a footnote to history, the hero of Marathon, Miltiades, was tried for failing to be successful in a later battle. He was fined and, unable to pay the fine, was left in prison to die.

Such is the order of the cosmos that one incident, or one man, can alter the fate of the future. However, like Miltiades, most such heroes have not been rewarded for their pivotal roles in shaping the world in which we live.

Figure **Fig. 25** indicates the historical involvement of Greece in the evolution of Western religious thought.

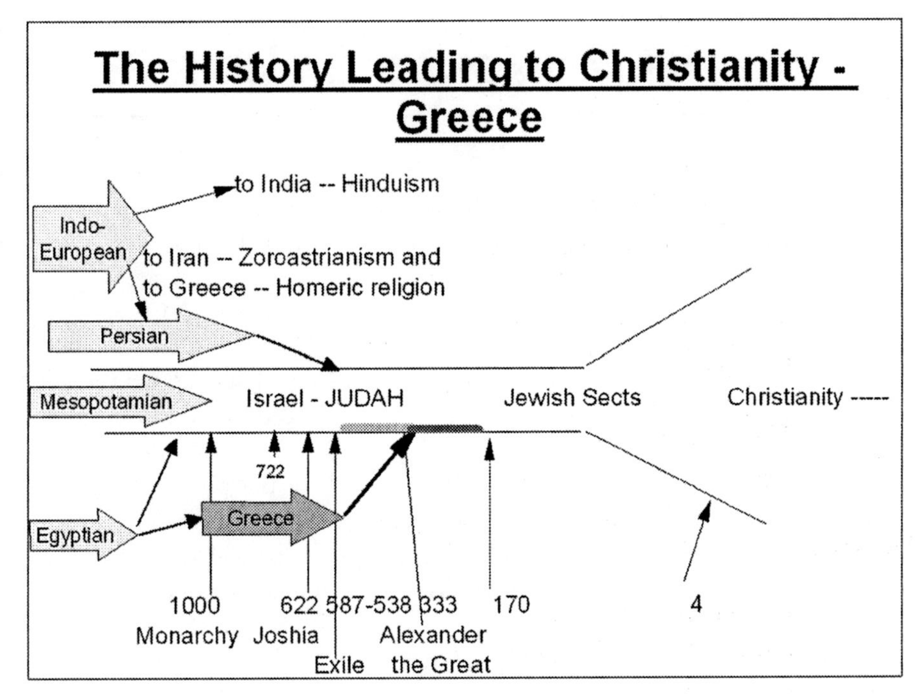

Fig. 25 History Leading to Christianity—Greece

The Religions of Ancient Israel

For the fate of the sons of men and the fate of the beasts is the same; as one dies, so does the other.... All go to the same place; all are from the dust, and all turn to dust again.

Eccl. 3:19–20.

Although Israel has a long history in its own right, the fact that it sits between the two greatest powers of the ancient world has contributed to the inculcation of a multitude of foreign ideas. The northern kingdom was erased and the southern kingdom strove to continue on. However, it too fell to Babylon and was then saved and subjected by a benevolent Persia. Two hundred years later, it became part of the Hellenized world (first under Egyptian, then Syrian rulers). Less than 300 years later, when Jesus is born, it will have fallen under the Romans.

But, let's start at Israel's beginning, **Fig. 26**.

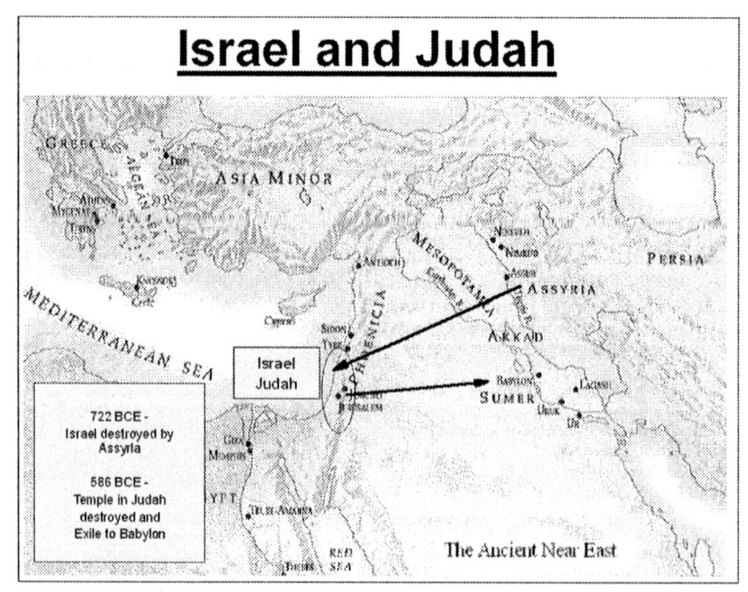

Fig. 26 The Land of Israel and Judah

A Brief History of Judaism (Encapsulation)

There are at least two traditional[93] invasions of the Hebrews into Palestine. The first was thought to have taken place around 1800 BCE when Abraham came into Canaan from Mesopotamia. The second took place around 1300 BCE when Moses led the Israelites back into Canaan from their captivity in Egypt.

I say these are traditional advisedly, since they are not well attested in the archeological evidence or in any documentation from the Egyptian New Kingdom. For our purposes here, the historical accuracy of these events does not really matter to the history of Christianity. We do know that the Mesopotamian religion greatly influenced the Canaanites, who in turn influenced the Israelites. As to Egyptian influence, we know that there was ample opportunity for cultural interchange between the two peoples, as attested by the Amarna documents of 14th century BCE Egypt.

There are two ancient sources for the personal God of Israel. From Northern Mesopotamia we get El-Shaddai (god of the mountain), and the very name of the god is included in the name of the country, Isra-el. From the Southern mountains of Sinai or Horeb, we get Yahweh (I will be what I will be), and that name appears in personal names such as Yehoshua (Joshua).

A syncretism with the indigenous religion of Canaan (Palestine) with its Baals, asherahs (stones and poles), and nature worship gradually developed into the religion of the Israelites. The Yahweh religion would eventually win out, but the indigenous religion operated side by side with the incipient monotheism until the reforms of King Josiah (c. 620 BCE), which would give birth to true Jewish monotheism.

Persistence and commonality of myth

Several myths have great staying power. The pervasive myth of the Flood is a case in point. There was apparently a devastating flood in Mesopotamia early in, or before the time of Sumer. This event entered the consciousness of the Sumerians as a punishment from the gods.

---

93. There are other non-traditional theories, such as: they were already Canaanites who rebelled against stronger masters; they were refugees from the coast which was invaded by the Sea Peoples; and they were desert nomads who infiltrated the land.

In the Sumerian myth of the flood, the king of Shuruppak rode out the flood in a boat. In the later Akkadian story of Atrahasis, the gods had fashioned men to do their work. The human population grew and their noise irritated Enlil, who planned to eliminate them. Enki warned Atrahasis of Enlil's coming flood, and he built a boat and saved his family and animals of all kinds.

Even later, in the late Akkadian and Old Babylonian story of Gilgamesh, the hero Utnapishtim was saved from the flood by Ea, when he built an ark and saved pairs of all animals and his family. For this, he was granted immortality, a boon denied to all later human beings.

Finally, in the late Biblical story of Yahweh's flood, Noah is saved because of his righteousness. In an ark of his own building, he saved his family and pairs of all animals in order to re-populate the world.

So, it can be seen that the concepts in this, and other, myths were shared in common in the Middle East[94] from the time of Sumer until the time of Israel and beyond.

Monarchical Israel

As we've seen in earlier periods, dynasty and the national deity are mutually beneficial. At the time of the Davidic monarchy (ca. 1000 BCE), Israel was still polytheistic and, as yet, had no personal or cosmic eschatology. That polytheism would gradually change as a belief in Yahweh supported the well being of the state and king; and the king would, in turn, guarantee a national cult to Yahweh and his priests. Centralization of government (under a united kingship and centralization of national worship) encouraged a single national deity at the expense of all other local deities—a state of affairs which would eventually lead to monotheism.

As the protector of the monarchy, Yahweh supported Israel in international conflicts; and then when Israel was successful against her enemies, Yahweh became the sovereign power over, Israel, as well as all the nations. Subsequently, the

94. The Flood story is ubiquitous; it shows up everywhere. In addition to those places described above, we have a similar story among the Persians (deadly winter, not water) and the Greeks. This pervasiveness lends much enforcement to the fact of a real wide-spread flood in pre-historic times.

erosion of a personal eschatology will be linked to the advance of this Yahweh-only monotheism in an inverse relationship; the stronger the Yahweh-only cult grew, the weaker a personal afterlife belief became.

Yahweh's sovereignty over other nations led to the condemnation of the foreign nations and many of their religious practices. By this time, Canaan had long been divorced from Israel and, thus, was now considered foreign. The cult of Baal, the cult of the dead, and other practices formerly incorporated into, or tolerated by the cult of Yahweh, were now despised as foreign.

The monarchy had split in 925 BCE into Israel in the North and Judah in the South. Israel was destroyed in 722 BCE by the Assyrians and its people scattered from their land, giving rise to the myth of the ten lost tribes of Israel. Judah, escaping that fate, became a vassal state to Assyria, but gained temporary independence ca. 612 BCE. This independence allowed a new king the latitude to solidify the position of the Yahweh-only cult.

The reforms of Josiah—Deuteronomist history

Josiah flourished as king of Judah ca. 620 BCE (2 Kings 22 & 23). During his reign, a book was discovered that contained a restatement of the Law. This book was most likely the second Law, literally in Greek called Deuteronomy. Josiah used the occasion of the discovery to call for religious reform, especially for the centralization of all religious practice in the Temple at Jerusalem. He further banned various religious practices, such as belief in other gods (i.e., YHWH only), idolatry, and the high places used for sacrificial offerings to false gods. Furthermore, many of the priests of the high places were slaughtered and burned on their own altars.

Still, the Lord remained angered at Judah because of the provocations of the earlier king, Josiah's grandfather, Manasseh, and resolved that Judah would be removed from out of His sight, as had Israel. But, because Josiah was humble before the Lord, he was promised to "be gathered to your grave in peace" before the coming disaster. The instrument of Josiah's death was Pharaoh Necho, who was coming to the aid of Assyria in the war against Babylon. Necho killed Josiah in 609 at Megiddo, a place that strikes fear into one's heart even today as the hill of Megiddo—Armageddon.

The first short-lived disaster was that Judah now became a vassal to Egypt only to fall within a dozen years to the conqueror of Assyria, King Nebuchadnezzar of

Babylon. Assyria, even with the help of their ally Egypt, had been defeated by Babylonia in 612. Egypt retreated back to their homeland and Assyria fell, never to rise again. The greatest disaster was that Judah was defeated, and its most important people taken into exile in Babylon. The Exiles occurred in 597 and 587 BCE and would last for fifty years until the Persians, in turn, defeated Babylon.

Beginning with the Exile, we see the first unambiguous attestation to true monotheism. Until that time, even counter to the exhortations of the pre-Exilic prophets and kings, the Israelites were still accepting of other cult practices. They were never to do so again.

Post-Exilic Judaism

The Temple cult had grown as a result of Josiah's reforms, and had devolved in short order into the usual religious bureaucracy of lesser men. The prophet Jeremiah arose to claim that Yahweh would reject his people and that the Temple would be destroyed, which it was in the Exile (Babylonian Captivity) of 587/6 BCE.

Cyrus the Great of Persia, now proclaimed the messiah in Isaiah,[95] would free the Israelites to return home and help them rebuild the Temple. He also ushered in a benevolent rule over Judah that was to last for 200 years.

This post-exile Persian rule helped introduce these, among others, new concepts from Persian Zoroastrianism:

> The principle of evil (Satan). In the early Bible texts, God is the maker of both good and evil, whereas in the Biblical texts written after ca. 300 BCE, God is wholly good and Satan is responsible for evil.
>
> Apocalyptic, Last Judgment, Last Days. Apocalypse means an "unveiling" or "revelation", a pulling back of the curtain of illusion to reveal ultimate reality.
>
> The Resurrection at the end of time. This concept is definitely first noted in the book of Daniel ca. 165 BCE.

---

95. Isaiah 45:1 calls Cyrus the Messiah for delivering them from exile. He is the only non-Israelite to ever be called by that title in the Hebrew Bible.

The post-exile Persian period (Cyrus 539 BCE) marks the beginning of the second Temple period and likely marks the beginning of Judaism.

The Greek period, after the conquests of Alexander the Great (post 332 BCE) introduced Greek ideas into Judaism; the main one being Plato's concept of the immortal soul, which was incorporated in the *Wisdom of Solomon* (ca. 25 BCE).

Philo of Alexandria (ca. 10 BCE–45 CE) was the first major Jewish writer to attempt to reconcile Judaism with Greek philosophy. Philo built on Platonic dualism, but with the intention of proving the priority of the Hebrew scriptures; thus, placing the Hebrew creator, God, in the place of Plato's creative principle, as he had posited in the *Timaeus*.

Philo was to have a great influence on the development of later Christianity.

The Sects of the First Century BCE

Pharisees and Sadducees

Sects arose in mid-second century BCE as a response to Hellenism. Under the Maccabean successor, John Hyrcanus (ca. 134–104 BCE), these opposing factions came into being.

The Pharisees were the "middle class" lay teachers who rejected Hellenism and accepted the doctrines of: the last judgment, resurrection, angels, heaven, and hell.

The Sadducees were rich and highborn who wanted to accept Hellenism and who rejected the Pharisee concepts as un-Biblical.

The Essenes (the pious)

The Essenes were one of the four sects named by Josephus in his *Jewish War* and *Antiquities of the Jews* (written ca. 75 and 94 CE). We've already seen the first two. The fourth he called simply the fourth philosophy, which probably referred to the Zealots, who wanted to violently overthrow Rome.

As opposed to the others, the Essenes are never mentioned in the Bible. They emerged during the second century BCE (ca. before 110 BCE), and are thought to be the sect of the Dead Sea Scrolls of Qumran.

They had much in common with early Christianity: expectation of the Kingdom of Yahweh, baptism, sacred meals, a Messiah figure, an apocalyptic day of judgment with rewards and penalties, the final victory of good (light) over evil (darkness), angelology and demonology, poverty and, like Jesus, they denied divorce. The doctrines that provide the surest link from Zoroaster through Judaism to Christianity are:

Apocalyptic eschatology
Dualism

The Eschatological War will be fought between the Sons of Light and the Sons of Darkness that reflects the dualism of Zoroaster's description of good and evil. That dualism comes through in their document known as the *War Scroll.*

War Scroll 1:5–15

> The dominion of the Kittim shall come to an end and iniquity shall be vanquished, leaving no remnant; for the sons of darkness there shall be no escape. The sons of righteousness shall shine over all the ends of the earth; they shall go on shining until all the seasons of darkness are consumed and, at the season appointed by God, His exalted greatness shall shine eternally to the peace, blessing, glory, joy, and long life of all sons of light.
>
> On the day when the Kittim fall, there shall be battle and terrible carnage before the God of Israel, for that shall be the day appointed from ancient times for the battle of destruction of the sons of darkness. At that time the assembly of the gods and the hosts of men shall battle, causing great carnage; on the day of calamity the sons of light shall battle with the company of darkness amid the shouts of a mighty multitude and the clamor of gods and men to make manifest the might of God. And it shall be a time of great tribulation for the people which God shall redeem; of all its afflictions none shall be as this, from its sudden beginning until its end in eternal redemption.
>
> On the day of their battle against the Kittim they shall set out for carnage. In three lots shall the sons of light brace themselves in battle to strike down iniquity...the mighty hand of God shall bring down the army of

> Belial, and all the angels of his kingdom, and all the members of his company in everlasting destruction...[96]

Another Essene document that links them to Zoroastrianism is the *Community Rule* that, in the excerpts below, practically quote the Gathas.

Community Rule 3:17–30

> He has created man to govern the world, and has appointed for him two spirits in which to walk until the time of his visitation: the spirits of truth and injustice. Those born of truth spring from a fountain of light, but those born of injustice spring from a source of darkness. All the children of righteousness are ruled by the **Prince of Light** and walk in all the ways of light, but all the children of injustice are ruled by the **Angel of Darkness** and walk in the ways of darkness. The Angel of Darkness leads all the children of righteousness astray, and until the end, all their sin, iniquities, wickedness, and all their unlawful deeds are caused by his dominion in accordance with the mysteries of God...But the God of Israel and His Angel of Truth will succor all the sons of light. For it is He who created the spirits of Light and Darkness and founded every action upon them and established every deed upon their ways.

Community Rule 4:15–25

> The nature of all children of men is to be ruled by these two spirits, and during their life all the hosts of men have a portion of their divisions and walk in both their ways. And the whole reward for their deeds shall be, for everlasting ages, according to whether each man's portion in their two divisions is great or small. For God has established the spirits in equal measure until the final age, and has set everlasting hatred between their divisions. Truth abhors the works of injustice, and injustice hates all the ways of truth. And their struggle is fierce in all their arguments for they do not walk together. But in the mysteries of His understanding, and in His glorious wisdom, God has ordained an end to injustice, and at the time of the visitation He will destroy it forever.
>
> ...

96. Translated by Geza Vermes, *The Complete Dead Sea Scrolls in English*, (New York: Penguin Press, 1997), 163-4.

> Until now the spirits of truth and injustice struggle in the hearts of men and they walk in both wisdom and folly...For God has established the two spirits in equal measure until the determined end, and until the Renewal, and He knows the reward of their deeds from all eternity. He has allotted them to the children of men that they may know good and evil, and that the destiny of all the living may be according to the spirit within them at the time of the visitation.[97]

The Scrolls of Qumran on the Dead Sea

Until very recently, in modern times, we had little information about the third Jewish sect. We knew a fair amount about the Pharisees and Sadducees but almost nothing about the Essenes. The Jewish historians,[98] Philo and Josephus, had written somewhat on them; but they did not always agree on the facts. Then in 1947, the great and accidental discovery of the Qumran scrolls was made that would bring to light the religion of the Essenes by way of their own original 2000-year old writings.

We have already looked at some excerpts that showed their relationship and possible dependence on the writings of Zoroaster. Now, we will look at one that connects the Essenes with Christianity.

The resurrection of the dead was a doctrine that was developing among some Jewish sects in the second century BCE.

One of the Dead Sea Scrolls has this amazing correlation with the teachings of Jesus:

> ...the heavens and the earth will listen to His Messiah, and none therein will stray from the commandments of the holy ones.
>
> ...
>
> Over the poor His spirit will hover and renew the faithful with His power. And He will glorify the pious on the throne of the eternal Kingdom.
>
> ...
>
> And the Lord will accomplish glorious things which have never been as...

---

97. Translated by: Geza Vermes. *The Complete Dead Sea Scrolls in English.* 101-3.
98. Judaeus Philo (30 B.C.–50 A.D.), Jewish philosopher and historian, a native of Alexandria, Egypt. Flavius Josephus (37–100 A.D.), a Jewish writer and historian.

> For he will heal the wounded, and revive the dead and bring good news to the poor.[99]

This scroll fragment (Scroll 4Q521 dated to ca. 90 BCE) is called the Messianic Apocalypse. It refers to the expected Messiah at the end of days who would do great things for those righteous and faithful to him. One of the great things was to resurrect the dead. Some of this text appears in Isaiah 61:1 and is quoted in Matt 11:4–5 and Luke 7:22–23.

However, in spite of all the similarities to Christianity, there are also significant major differences:

> The Essenes were exclusive and secretive.
>
> They believed in the Platonic immortal soul and, as Josephus would have us believe, its pre-existence. Josephus even claims that they believed in an afterlife, as did "the sons of Greece." That they believed in an immortal soul is unquestioned. As to a belief in the soul's pre-existence, that is unproven.
>
> The Essenes were sticklers for the Law, where concerning the Sabbath, they said:
>
>> No man shall assist a beast to give birth on the Sabbath day. And if it should fall into a...pit, he shall not lift it out on the Sabbath.
>> Damascus11: 12
>
> Compare Jesus on the subject of the Sabbath:
>
>> What man of you having one sheep, if it should fall into a pit on the Sabbath day, would not lay hands upon it and lift it out.
>> Matt 12:10–11

So, can we say that Christianity developed out of Esseneism? Certainly not, based on the above example; although, they perhaps did share some other common

99. Translated by: Geza Vermes. *The Complete Dead Sea Scrolls in English.* 391-2.

values and doctrines. I would even say that developing Christianity[100] was a continuation of the trends of post-Exilic Judaism, that both the Essenes and later Christians would accept, but the later Pharisees and Sadducees would reject. An indication that this is so can be shown by the results of post-destruction (ca. 70 CE) Judaism; the Pharisees went on to develop rabbinic Judaism, while the Christians went on with a continuation of apocalyptic that had been rejected by the Pharisee mainstream.

The Making of the Hebrew Bible—Old Testament (Encapsulation)

In 1611, King James of England requested that a group of scholars compile an English version of the Bible based on the best available ancient language manuscripts. This effort resulted in the much beloved text containing the now archaic English we have come to associate with the language of religion.

In the Old Testament, the list of accepted books follows that of the Hebrew canon (i.e., standard or rule), namely: the five books of the Law; the 21 books of the Prophets; and the 13 books of the Writings. Whereas, the New Testament has: the four Gospels; the seven General epistles; the 14 epistles of Paul; Acts of the Apostles; and Revelations.

The King James arrangement of the Old Testament, of course leaves out many other books, which earlier were considered authentic scripture for many centuries by the Church Fathers and Councils. Most of these latter books are still held to be authentic by both the Roman Catholic and Eastern Orthodox churches; although, they remain absent from the Jewish Bible.

How did we arrive at this construction of the present day Bible? In order to answer that, we must look into the earliest development of the Hebrew Scriptures, which will take us back, at least, to the monarchy in 1000 BCE when they were first evolving.

---

100. I also maintain that proto-orthodox Christianity and the early Jesus Movement held different views on those trends, in that proto-orthodox Christianity was definitely apocalyptic.

We know that the earliest portions of the Law (also called Torah or Pentateuch) were written in both the Northern kingdom of Israel and the Southern kingdom of Judah; then, subsequently, combined along with other material, attaining their final form during, or just after the return from, the Babylonian exile around 500 BCE. The book that closed the Hebrew canon (with the single exception of the much later Daniel (ca. 165 BCE)), was Ezra, written around 400 BCE.

Following the Exile, The Jews became widely dispersed over the next few centuries; and found themselves living throughout the Hellenistic world that had been created by Alexander the Great in the fourth century BCE. These Diaspora Jews had become Greek speakers and desiring to read their scriptures in Greek, they created a translation around 200 BCE that became known as the Septuagint. These were the scriptures, later called the Old Testament, that were used by the early Christian Church.

The Documentary Hypothesis

Scholars have come to the conclusion that the Hebrew Bible evolved over time, and that we can clearly see traces of this evolution. The most obvious of the traces can be seen in the contradictory stories that appear in the first two chapters of Genesis. Consider the flow of the two creation stories:

Genesis 2:4–3:24 (first to be written)

God is called Yahweh in this story
Creation events:
The creation of earth/heaven
The creation of man, then garden, trees, beasts, birds, and woman
The fall of Man
The expulsion from the garden

Genesis 1:1–2:3

God is called Elohim in this story
Creation events:
The creation of the Cosmos in four days—light, sky, dry land, seas, plants, sun/moon/stars,
The creation of life and people in two days—water animals/birds, land animals/man
Rest on the seventh day

There has been a long history of Biblical criticism:

11th century—Isaac the Blunderer noticed that there were anachronisms in the Torah, such as the Edomite Kings. He told an incredulous audience that Edom did not exist at the time of Moses, hence, his nickname.

In the eighteenth century many doublets, such as the two creation stories above, were identified along with some others of note:

- covenant with Abraham
- naming of Isaac
- renaming of Jacob
- Ten Commandments
- Moses striking a rock

In the nineteenth century, triplets were identified. The triplets and doublets contradicted each other, so some one or more of them could not be inerrant. Gradually, a consensus developed that there were at least four writers and two redactors (editors) who created the Pentateuch.

During the twentieth century, Bible scholars continued to refine what had become the Documentary Hypothesis.

One of the first clues of multiple authors was the difference in Genesis for the name of God. The first called him Elohim and that writer from the Northern kingdom of Israel was dubbed "E'. The second called him Yahweh (Jehovah in German) and that writer from the Southern kingdom of Judah was designated "J'. Two other writers were also later identified and were called Deuteronomist (D) and Priestly (P). It was the P writer that wrote the beautiful story of Genesis 1 and combined it with the existing J and E version. Finally, there were at least two editing's of these various texts.

The Genesis "J" story was written sometime after the time of Solomon (ca. 850 BCE); whereas, the Genesis "P" story was written after the Babylonian Exile (ca. 500 to 400 BCE).

Schematically, in **Fig.** 27, the Documentary Hypothesis looks like this.

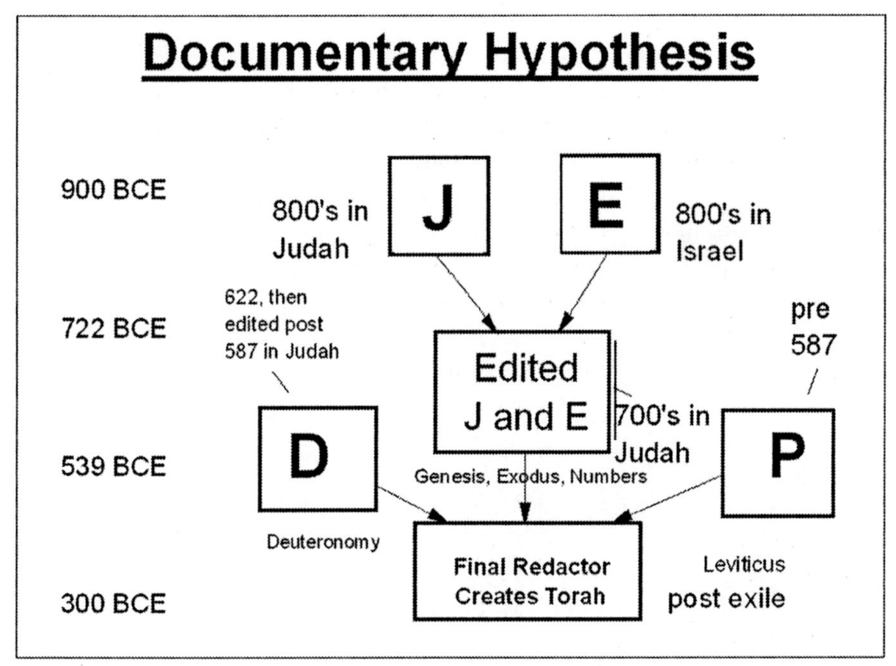

Fig. 27 Creation of the Torah—Documentary Hypothesis

Some dates of the Books of the Hebrew Canon[101]—TANAKH

<u>The Pentateuch</u>	(Torah): ca. 10th to 4th century BCE
The 1st five books: Genesis, Exodus, Leviticus, Numbers, Deuteronomy	
<u>The Prophets</u>	(Neviim):
Joshua	ca. 10 to 7th century BCE
Judges	8–7th
Ruth	5–4th

101. The term canon is a Greek word, meaning rule. Hence, a canon of law or a canon of books is that which conforms to the proper rule. TANAKH is an acronym for: <u>T</u>orah<u>N</u>eviim<u>K</u>etuvim.

1&2 Samuel	560
1&2 Kings	580
Isaiah	700, 550, 520, 200 [102]
Jeremiah	610, 530
Ezekiel	570, 300
12 Minor-	
Hosea thru Malachi	8–5th
The Writings	Ketuvim:
Psalms	prior to 586 BCE
Proverbs	9–4th
Job	6th
Song of Solomon	wide range
Ruth	5th
Lamentations	550
Ecclesiastes	3rd
Daniel	165
Esther	125
Ezra-Nehemiah	5–3rd
1&2 Chronicles	5–4th
The Apocrypha	Was in the Septuagint (LXX)[103], but failed to make it into the Hebrew canon that was set ca. 90 CE at Jamnia by the proto-Rabbinical Pharisees
Tobit	225–175 BCE
Judith	120
Esther+	between 114 BCE–93 CE
Wisdom of Solomon	30 BCE
Ecclesiasticus	190–130
Baruch	170

102. Multiple dates indicate multiple authors at different times created the book as we have it today (i.e., Isaiah would be called 1st, 2nd, 3rd and 4th Isaiah).

103. The Septuagint (named for the traditional seventy independent translators) was translated from Hebrew into Greek ca. 272–100 BCE at Alexandria by Hellenistic Jews.

Letter of Jeremiah	4–2nd
Daniel+	2nd
1&2 Maccabees	100–63

Additional Books in Greek and Slavonic Bibles, not in the Catholic and Protestant Bibles:

1 Esdras	150 BCE
Prayer of Manasseh	30
Psalm 151	unknown
3 Maccabees	between 100 BCE–70 CE
2 Esdras	10 BCE, 50 CE, 150 CE
4 Maccabees	between 63 BCE–70 CE

The Evolution of General Religious Ideas in Early Judaism

In order to explore religious evolution into the first century, and to find the roots of later Jewish religious thinking, we must return to some ancient places and religions already examined in order.

As we've seen, early Judaism appears to be very much like the Mesopotamian religion via the Canaanites, since the culture of Canaan cannot be separated from that of Israel. In fact, written script, language, material artifacts, and burial methods attest to the continuity of what later became two peoples during the late Bronze and early Iron ages (1500–1000 BCE).

By 1200 BCE, Israel was recognized as a separate political entity; but its culture and religion had not yet begun to diverge from the surrounding environment. The appearance of a unique Israelite religion was starting at about this time. The original god of early Israel was named El. This supposition is supported by the Bible in Exodus 6:2–3, where Yahweh appears to Moses and tells him that his name is Yahweh, and that he had appeared to the patriarchs as El, but did not make himself known to them as Yahweh. By the time of the Judges (1200–1000 BCE), the Canaanite god, El, had been identified with Yahweh, who takes on El's attributes in a syncretistic manner—reminiscent of the progressions in Mesopotamia where Marduk assumes An's place, then Ashur assumes Marduk's.

During the time of the Judges, there seems to be no conflict among El, Baal, Asherah and Yahweh cults in Israel. That came only in the tenth century with the appearance of the monarchy.

With the spread of the cult of Baal by King Ahab and Jezebel (primarily in the Northern kingdom) and with Jezebel persecuting the prophets of Yahweh, a break came. Before that time, we see no indication that the cults were in competition. During the later monarchy, the Israelite pantheon did increase with the importation of foreign cults and astral gods; but they were not assimilated into the Yahweh cult.

Formerly acceptable practices in the periods of the Judges and the early monarchy were now being stripped away from the central religion of the Israelites. The asherah and the high places where the people sacrificed to the deities were at first supported. Practices concerning the dead were also supported down to the seventh century (except necromancy because it conflicted with prophecy). Feeding, mourning, sacrificing to and seeking the aid from the dead were all part of Canaanite religion that was blending into Israelite religion.

The goddess Asherah is mentioned only once in the Bible; however, her symbol, the asherah, is referenced several times. The asherah is a wooden pole (probably a tree that devolved into a simple symbol). It was allowed as part of the cult of Yahweh, but fell out of favor later when its purported abilities to help perform divination competed with prophecy. There is some consideration that Asherah was an Israelite goddess and the consort of Yahweh. In Canaan she was the consort of El, and since El was now identified with Yahweh, she could now be Yahweh's consort. Indeed, a Hebrew inscription found in Judah from around 700 BCE reads "Yahweh and his Asherah".

The practice of child sacrifice is, perhaps, the most objectionable (to the modern sensibility) practice that carried over from Canaanite and other Near Eastern cults into the early Israelite religion. That the Israelites practiced it in the early period is attested to by Ezekiel 20: 25–26—"And I defiled them through their very gifts, in their offering up all their firstborn, in order that I might horrify them"; possibly Isaiah 30: 27–33, where Yahweh is a devouring fire; and possibly Genesis 22: 2–13—"Take your only son Isaac whom you love and go into the district of Moria, and there offer him as a holocaust on the hill". These verses indicate that it was possibly part of the Yahweh cult until the seventh century BCE, even though later more humane redactions attempt to purge this from the record.

Hebrew Bible eschatology

Apocalyptic eschatology came late to the Jews.

Ezekiel (ca. 560 BCE) had prophesied a reconstituted nation for exiles, and Second Isaiah (ca.540) had prophesied transformation of the world with Yahweh as its king.

But, the first true apocalypses are in Daniel (ca. 165 BCE)—due to the horrors of the Maccabean War with Syria—where we find a personal bodily resurrection, a final judgment, and reward or punishment.

Only the Essenes would make apocalyptic eschatology central to their beliefs before the advent of the Christian Movement.

Evolution of Jewish eschatology: a recapitulation with Biblical examples (essay)

Ancient Judaism professed neither a resurrection, a post-mortem judgment, nor an immortality of the individual beyond that of being a mere shadow of ones former self. This shadow existed in the netherworld of Sheol, where the good and the bad shared the same undifferentiated fate. Even at that time, God was a judge of the living, not the dead.[104]

In the early Hebrew Bible, God would judge individuals according to their works; how they interacted with their families, their nation and their God.[105] This judgment may be delayed until succeeding generations, but it was always a judgment upon the living. Through a person's righteousness, he or she could be rewarded with children, wealth, and long life. Or, they could be punished by the loss of such things. The reverse of this expected fortune is told in the poignant story of Job, where a righteous man is given the opposite of what he should have received—had the system worked.

It was not until around 200 BCE that Jewish thought developed the idea that man was not just doomed to non-existence or shadow-hood; but, rather, that there was hope for a resurrection in the Day of the Lord. How this came about is the subject of this section.

---

104. We have seen this scenario in the Homeric Hades, where there are no determinants for the shadows of the dead to obtain a differentiated fate.

105. See Eccl. 12:14; also Ezek. 30:1-19 for Judgment Day.

Death and the Afterlife in the Ancient Near East

In ancient Mesopotamia, the ideas of a pre-existent soul or a bodily resurrection never took hold. Nevertheless, they wondered at the existence of death.

One Sumerian cosmological (cosmogonic) myth, the Enuma elish, is an early attempt to explain the question of why there is death. First, it says, that humans were made in order to do the work formerly done by the gods. Second, the myth says that the gods were playing a game at which they made "freaks" to see if they could fit into the human social structure. Finally, the god, Enki, makes misshapen and diseased people, who once made cannot be unmade. Thus, disease and death are made part of the human condition.

Another Mesopotamian myth, that of the Epic of Gilgamesh, explains human mortality in the most direct terms. The epic, anticipating Homer[106] by over a thousand years, claims that the gods created man to die, while keeping eternal life to themselves.

As we've seen, the Egyptians had very early come to the conclusion that man was indeed immortal; and that by proper application of religious rites, could insure eternal life. However, many of the peoples of Mesopotamia did not arrive at that conclusion; but accepted their fate as transient beings, as exemplified by the Enuma elish and the Epic of Gilgamesh. Even in these stories, immortality was thought to exist, but only as the purview of the gods and those whom they chose to offer it (e.g., Utnapishtim, the survivor of the great flood).

Other Mesopotamian myths suggest that, perhaps, humans were originally offered immortality, but, through hubris or fault, lost it. Thus runs the Akkadian myth of Adapa, who lost the opportunity to gain immortality because of the treachery of his patron deity, Enki. The sky-god, Anu, had offered man, through Adapa, the gift of "life', but because Enki had told him that this gift would kill him, Adapa refused—thus lost the chance of immortality for all humankind.[107]

---

106. Homer, *The Iliad*, trans. Robert Fagles (New York: Penguin Books, 1990), 605-6. "So the immortals spun our lives that we, we wretched men live on to bear such torments—the gods live free of sorrows…Grief for your son will do no good at all. You will never bring him back to life" (Il. 611, 646).

107. Thorkild Jacobsen, *The Treasures of Darkness* (New Haven: Yale University Press, 1976), 115f.

The Ugaritic myth of Aqhat says: "In his arrogant rejection of Anath's offer of immortality...describes the fate that awaits him and mankind generally at death...[glaze] will be poured on [my] head, a groove [will be made] on the top of my pate."[108] Aquat even calls the goddess a liar for making the offer.

Even the Sumerian (Akkadian) Gilgamesh was offered marriage by the immortal goddess Ishtar at a time when he was not ready to think of such things and, through his youthful pride and ignorance, lost what he later tried so hard to get. Of course, marriage to an immortal would not necessarily have given him immortality. He also lost a good substitute—eternal youth—which would have sufficed. If not arrogance, then poor choices lost immortality for humans.

The Egyptians had their solution to immortality but the solution came harder in Mesopotamia,. Despite the fact that many had intellectually accepted the mortal nature of man, they still could not really believe in their own total extinction. This was not necessarily a much better thing, because they also came to believe that what survives the physical death was a terrible gray, almost lifeless sojourn in an underworld. It is very easy to see how these ideas could develop. Since the gods had immortality, the concept of immortality was considered a fact. And, since it is virtually impossible for a person to conceive of his or her own non-being, it would be reasonable to conjecture that something of one's self could survive the physical death.

Many "western" peoples have held such a survival concept in the form of a place of shadows, where the person was a shadow of one's former self. In later Greek thinking, with Homer, this place would be Hades. In earlier Israelite thought, it was Sheol and in even earlier Mesopotamian thought, it was a "house of darkness'.

At some time during the third millennium BCE, the idea of the cult of the dead had entered the Near Eastern consciousness. In order to meet their needs, the Mesopotamian ghosts of the dead required help from the living. If the ghost were not cared for, it would wander around and haunt the living. "The person responsible for the care of a ghost was known as a paqidu."[109] The services necessary

---

108. Baruch Margalit, "Death and Dying in the Ugaritic Epics," in Bendt Alister, ed., *Death in Mesopotamia* (Copenhagen: Akademisk Forlag, 1980), 251.

109. Miranda Bayliss, "The Cult of Dead Kin in Assyria and Babylonia," *Iraq* 35, no. 2 (autumn 1973): 116.

from the paqidu were: "making funerary offerings', "pouring water" and "calling the name'.[110]

This cult, definitely spread among the later Western Semitic Canaanites and the Israelites. They also believed that the dead live on in their tombs, are in need of assistance, and are capable of helping the living. At Ugarit, "the living king had only a low-grade divinization and did not include any notion of immortality…even…El's son, must die like a mortal."[111] However, upon his death, he achieved a type of transcendent character where "the deceased entered into the revered company of the [long deceased] and continued to exist in the underworld. They certainly were not cut off from any relation to the living and could…be beseeched to grant favors"[112] This was not restricted only to royalty. The Ugarit caretaker performed similar duties as the Mesopotamian paqidu, "pouring water" and "setting up the ancestral stela" (similar to calling the name).[113]

Again, this is not a very happy [to us] solution to the fact of death, but it does offer some consolation to one who wants to continue some type of individual existence.

Ancient Near Eastern influence on Israel

The myths. R. J. Clifford says, "scholars are agreed that Mesopotamian traditions have influenced the creation stories in Genesis 1–11. The material is diverse: theogonies…allusions to creation in rituals and prayers, and…cosmogonies, such as *Enuma elish* and *Atrahasis.*"[114] The Near Eastern physical cosmos was a disk of earth with water below, separated from the water above by the dome of the firmament. The gods populated the sky; the earth was populated with people; and under the earth was the place to which the cosmic bodies would descend. The underworld was also the place of the chthonic gods and the dead. Like the story

110. Bayliss, "The Cult of Dead Kin in Assyria and Babylonia," 116.

111. Theodore .J. Lewis, *Cult of the Dead in Ancient Israel and Ugarit* (Atlanta: Scholars Press, 1989), 49.

112. Lewis, *Cult of the Dead in Ancient Israel and Ugarit*, 50.

113. Lewis, *Cult of the Dead in Ancient Israel and Ugarit*, 96.

114. R. J. Clifford, "Creation in the Hebrew Bible," in *Physics, Philosophy, and Theology: A Common Quest for Understanding*, eds. Robert J. Russell, William R. Stoeger and George V. Coyne (Vatican City State: Vatican Observatory, 1988), 151.

in Genesis (in the beginning), there is only undifferentiated and unlimited waters in the Enuma elish:

> When above the heaven had not (yet) been named,
> (And) below the earth had not (yet) been called by a name;
> (When) Apsu primeval, their begetter,
> Mummu, (and) Tiamat, she who gave birth to them all,
> (Still) mingled their waters together,
>
> ...
>
> (At that time) were the gods created within them.[115]

In the Atrahasis cosmogony we find parallels to Genesis 2–9: creation of humans to maintain the universe, human proliferation and fault, the decision to destroy humanity in a great flood and the saving of a pair to repopulate the world.[116]

In the Canaanite (Ugaritic) texts known as the "Baal Cycle', we find correspondences to "biblical texts, such as Psalms 74:12–17, 77:12–21, 89:10–15 and 93, Second Isaiah, and Exodus 15...use vocabulary and traditions"[117] which show cosmological similarities, like the creation of the world from the dragon Leviathan, or the waters of chaos.

One scholar claims that in the ancient Near East:

> Concern with death and the afterlife was an integral part of daily life [but]...not the slightest trace of the Egyptian...or the Mesopotamian tragic heroism can be found in the Hebrew Bible of ancient Israel.[118]

To some degree, this is probably true. However, I would suggest that the reason for this is that the early prophets, and in 623 BCE, the Yahwist-only reforms of Josiah purged the influence of the ancient Near East from the earlier Biblical

---

115.Alexander Heidel, *The Babylonian Genesis* (Chicago: University of Chicago Press, 1951), 18.

116.Clifford, "Creation in the Hebrew Bible," 154.

117.Clifford, "Creation in the Hebrew Bible," 154-5.

118.Nico van Uchelen, "Death and the Afterlife in the Hebrew Bible of Ancient Israel," in *Hidden Futures: Death and Immortality in Ancient Egypt, Anatolia, the Classical, Biblical and Arabic-Islamic World*, eds. J. M. Bremer et al (Amsterdam: Amsterdam University Press, 1994), 78-9.

texts. Thus, the early texts do tend to reveal a lack of belief in an afterlife, which we will discuss after a comment on the cult of the dead.

The cult of the dead. The dead under the earth were formerly seen as powerful ancestors with god-like powers to help the living. Like the Egyptian cult of the dead, this cult would also have "the concept that the family was not simply an association of its living members but a corporation of the living and the dead."[119] Even though expunged from most of the Scriptures, some indication of the early Israelite's adherence to their neighbor's (both East and West) cults of the dead still show through in these older texts, although, mostly in anti-cult polemic:

1 Sam 28:13

"The king said to her, "Have no fear; what do you see?" The woman said to Saul, "I see a divine being [elohim] coming up out of the ground'." This recalls the age when the dead were like "gods'.

2 Sam 18:18

"Now Absalom…said, "I have no son to keep my name in remembrance'; he called the pillar by his own name." This is like "calling the name" in Mesopotamia and Canaan.

2 Kings 13:21

"As a man was being buried…was thrown into the grave of Elisha; as soon as the man touched the bones of Elisha, he came to life and stood on his feet." Here is an indication that the dead were still powerful (although, in this instance, the credit was directed to Yahweh).

Isaiah 8:19

"Consult the ghosts and the familiar spirits that chip and mutter; should not a people consult their gods, the dead on behalf of the living…" The answer is no; this practice is condemned by the Yahweh-only cult.

---

119. Alan B. Lloyd, "Psychology and Society in the Ancient Egyptian Cult of the Dead," in *Religion and Philosophy in Ancient Egypt*, ed. William Kelly Simpson (New Haven: Yale University Press, 1989), 130.

Death and the Afterlife in Early and Post-Reform Israel

The Genesis story of the Fall is said to explain why man dies. We need to look at the early Hebrew myth of the Garden of Eden to see that man was, indeed, created immortal.[120] but chose to throw it away by disobedience. Yahweh had created all things perfect and had made the first humans perfect and immortal. Unfortunately, like the treachery of the Mesopotamian Enki (the serpent in the story) advises that Yahweh was keeping the tree of the knowledge of good and evil to himself and that if the man and woman ate of it, they, too, would become like Yahweh. They accepted the advice of the serpent and ate; whereupon, Yahweh drove them from the garden and condemned them and all their offspring to suffer and die.

Very few people would be willing to accept the fact that man is created mortal, or to accept that he lost his chance to become immortal, or to accept that he was already immortal and lost it. Which brings us to the question of immortality: "is there life after death'?

In a strong reaction to the Canaanite and early Israelite beliefs in the cult of the dead, the Yahwists had condemned the cult practice and, thereby, left the Israelites without much hope of an afterlife (except the devalued shades in Sheol who no longer spoke to gods nor to the living).

In the process of history, Yahwists were concerned with the sovereignty of God; therefore, they had suppressed "the mortuary cults [that facilitated a belief in] a post mortem existence—[and championed the belief in] the creation of man from the clay of the ground animated by the breath of life but destined to return to dust from which he was fashioned."[121] In fact, the idea of the afterlife is denied at least three times in Job 14:12:

> And man lies down and never rises...
> They wake not till the heavens decay...
> They rouse not from their sleep...

---

120. Actually, the story in Genesis does not claim that Adam was immortal, but the statement "you shall die" has been taken to mean that you will lose immortality by some exegetes.

121. E.O. James, "Professor Brandon's Contribution to Scholarship," in *Man and his salvation*, eds. Eric J. Sharpe and John R. Hinnells (Manchester: Manchester University Press, 1973), 14.

Nevertheless, vestiges of death cult practices are attested to in the Books of Samuel and Kings (Saul and the witch of Endor, David's Ritual Descent, Absalom's Monument, Jezebel's Burial, and Elisha's' Bones).[122] Feeding, mourning, sacrificing to, and seeking aid from the dead were all part of the Canaanite religion that was blended into the religion of Israel.

From the time of Josiah's reforms (when the cult of the dead was practically eliminated, to the time of Daniel),[123] in the second century BCE, the Israelites were without a belief in any real form of human immortality.

By the time of Daniel (ca. 165 BCE, contemporaneous with the Maccabees), this understanding had progressed to the status of fact for some Jewish sects, such as the Pharisees. The issue of reward for living a good life—and especially dying for God—finally required justice in an afterlife, since it was all too obviously not forthcoming in the present one.

Post Josiah Reforms (the Elimination of Foreign Influence)

Josiah's reforms (ca. 623 BCE), in 2 Kings 23:24, eliminated the cult of the dead and replaced it with nothing for the afterlife, causing the focus of religion to be on the rewards and punishments of this world. The dead ancestors under the earth were no longer god-like but were, at best, mere shadows of their former selves. They no longer served any purpose for the living, so they were truly dead. From the early monarchy and before the exile (ca. 900–600), we have these Biblical texts:

Deut 32:39

> "See now that I, even I, am he; there is no god besides me. I kill and I make alive." This stresses the Yahweh-only cult; the dead cannot function as god-like figures.

---

122. Lewis, *Cult of the Dead in Ancient Israel and Ugarit*, 125. See 1 Sam 28; 2 Sam 12:15–24; 2 Sam 18:18; 2 Kings 9:34–37; and 2 Kings 13:20–21.

123. Daniel 12:2. "those who sleep in the dust of the earth shall awake".

Gen 25:7–11

"This is the length of Abraham's life…died in good old age…and was gathered to his people." The best death is one of old age, then buried by sons to figuratively return to the ancestors. Although the phrase "gathered to his people" may harken back to the dead ancestor cult, it is believed to be used metaphorically at this time.

Psalm 88:10–12

"Do you work wonders for the dead? Do the shades rise up to praise you? Is your steadfast love declared in the grave…Are your wonders known in the darkness?" The implication is no to these questions.

Deut 30:15–20

"See, I have set before you today life and prosperity, death and adversity…and observing his commandments,…you shall live and become numerous." The reward for obeying God is a long life in this world (not an afterlife).

The internal reforms were not the only influences on the ancient Israelites. They were also besieged by the ideas of their neighbors.

Death and the Afterlife in ancient Persia

Key to understanding the religion of Persia is recognizing the necessity of the dualistic cosmology of its founder, Zoroaster.

In the beginning, before time was created, there existed two finite, but uncreated, gods. One was the eternal, totally good Ohrmazd (Ahura-Mazda) and the other was the totally evil Ahriman (Angra Mainyu).[124] They both exist in infinite space separated by the Void. Ahriman attacks the good god and, in response, the good god creates the entire spiritual and material universe in order to get help in fighting the evil god.

---

124. R. C. Zaehner, *The Teachings of the Magi*, 29f. Ohrmazd and Ahriman were the late Persian names for Zoroaster's original names for the gods.

The souls of all humans were created by Ohrmazd and were asked to volunteer to fight the evil one. Ohrmazd then infused wisdom into their souls and said:

> Which seemeth more profitable to you, whether that I should fashion you forth in material form and that you should strive incarnate with the Lie and destroy it, and that we should resurrect you at the end, whole and immortal, and recreate you in material form, and that you should eternally be immortal, unageing, and without enemies; or that you should eternally be preserved from the Aggressor?[125]

Here we see how the souls agreed to descend to earth to fight the "Aggressor" and how the resurrection was promised in the end.

Dualism provides the answers to two important questions that have confounded thinkers for centuries, and still does: why is there evil in a good god's creation, and why is there a creation at all? Zoroastrian dualism's "great merit is that it absolves God from any breath of evil and explains how it could be that creation was actually necessary."[126]

Zoroastrian eschatology follows from its cosmology. At the end-time several things will happen: Ahriman and all his creation will be destroyed, giving Ohrmazd infinity in both time and space; a savior will raise all people's bodies "from the elements into which they had been dissolved and to reunite them with their souls."[127]

Then the resurrected (both saved and damned) will endure a three-day ordeal of molten metal in which all will be purged of all evil, receive bodily immortality, and live forever in an earthly paradise.[128]

125.Zaehner, *The Teachings of the Magi*, 41

126.Zaehner, *The Teachings of the Magi*, 58. Interestingly, it took the genius of St. Augustine a thousand years later to devise an answer to these same questions, without using the idea of dualism.

127.Zaehner, *The Teachings of the Magi*, 142. This solution to the double judgment (of soul immortality and body resurrection) in Christianity was not to be solved for another thousand years. It is still not solved satisfactorily.

128.Zaehner, *Teachings of the Magi*, 147.

Persian (Zoroastrian) influence on Israel

Zoroaster's cosmology and eschatology. In the later biblical period, after the exile, the Israelites were under the domination of the Persian Empire. This was a benevolent rule in that the Persians honored the Jewish religion and had freed them from the Babylonian exile in 538/9 BCE.

When the Jews were exiled to Babylon, they had an opportunity to be re-exposed to Mesopotamian religion and cosmology. With their liberation by Cyrus of Persia, they also had the opportunity to be exposed to Persian religion and cosmology. That they were so exposed can be shown by citing at least these two issues: their mutual relationship was very good for a long period of time[129]; and after the exile, Persian ideas do, in fact show up in the Hebrew Bible.

Just what are these Persian ideas? Edwin Yamauchi says: "the doctrinal areas where Persian inspirations are claimed include teachings on Satan, demonology, angelology, and especially eschatological beliefs, such as judgment, resurrection, apocalypticism, a fiery trial, heaven and hell."[130]

The cosmology of Zoroaster demands the eschatology of the resurrection, since the volunteer martyrs deserve restoration for fighting the evil one and gaining the entire cosmos for the good god. Notice that this same logic would also apply at a later time to the Jews martyred for God in Maccabees.

Although the pre-exilic biblical conception of Sheol, as a lifeless realm of the dead would continue into the first century CE with the teachings of the Sadducees, around the third to second century BCE, the concept of the resurrection had already appeared in the Hebrew texts. This resurrection concept may have been solely intra-Judaic and just coincidental, however, allowing that all of the Persian concepts mentioned above are coincidental would strain credulity.

Leonard Greenspoon claims that: "The Jews would naturally have become acquainted with Persian ideas at the end of the Exile and throughout the early post-Exilic period. And it is in Biblical passages dated from precisely this period

---

129. Bruce M. Metzger and Roland E. Murphy, eds. *The New Oxford Annotated Bible: NRSV* (New York: Oxford University Press, 1994), 581.

130. Edwin M. Yamauchi, *Persia and the Bible* (Grand Rapids: Baker Book House, 1990), 459.

that many commentators have found the beginnings of a clear expression of Hebrew belief in resurrection."[131]

Greenspoon also says: "Scholars have reached a consensus that the belief in resurrection can be detected only in the very late portion of the Hebrew Bible…in Daniel 12, which dates from the second century BCE, and a few are willing to"[132] see it in texts a century or two older. For example, concerning Ezekiel 37:1–15, he says that one scholar "maintains that Ezekiel must have come in contact with Zoroastrian concepts for his vision of the dry bones."[133] These texts from the immediate post-exile to the second century BCE indicate the new beliefs:

> Isaiah 25:7
>
> "And he will destroy on this mountain the shroud that is cast over all peoples…he will swallow up death forever." God will restore Israel and even the dead will be restored.
>
> Isaiah 26:19
>
> "Your dead shall live, their corpses shall rise…awake…the earth will give birth to those long dead."
>
> Daniel 12:1–4
>
> "At that time Michael…shall arise…Many of those who sleep in the dust of the earth shall awake, some to everlasting life, and some to shame and everlasting contempt."

The "Isaianic apocalypse distinguishes between Israel and its foreign oppressor…Part of this restoration will include the resurrection of the dead Israelites."[134] But the oppressors do not also rise to be judged. "Resurrection is

---

131. Leonard J. Greenspoon, "The Origin of the Idea of Resurrection," in *Traditions in Transformation: Turning Points in Biblical Faith*, eds. Baruch Halpren and Jon Levenson (Winona Lake: Eisenbrauns, 1981), 260.

132. Greenspoon, "The Origin of the Idea of Resurrection," 247.

133. Yamauchi, *Persia and the Bible*, 461.

134. George W. E. Nichelsburg, Jr., *Resurrection, Immortality, and Eternal Life In Intertestamental Judaism* (Cambridge: Harvard University Press, 1972), 18.

not a means by which all parties involved are brought to judgment, but an appropriate vindication of the righteous."[135]

If there is a doubt that Isaiah was speaking of the individual resurrection, rather than that of the entire nation or even in a metaphorical sense, Daniel is, without doubt, unequivocal on the issue of the actual resurrection of the individual.

Like the dualism of Zoroaster's judgment, Daniel will go beyond Isaiah by saying that the dead will rise, "some to eternal life, and some to eternal contempt (Dan 12:2b)." Dan 12:1–2 "combines the destiny of the people [community] (V.1) with the destiny of the [individual] dead (V.2)."[136]

So, the Israelites now had an explanation for suffering in this life that was not explained by the Deuteronomist—cosmic justice is available only after death and not in this life.

Death and the Afterlife in Hellenistic Greece

Long before Plato developed his theory of the soul, and long before Ptolemy's conception of cosmology became Church orthodoxy, their predecessors were working on the cosmological framework that would support it.

Two lines of thought culminated in Plato's conception of the afterlife. One was a reaction to the skepticism of the pre-Socratic philosophers who claimed that we are incapable of knowledge of the world. The other was the Pythagorean[137] and Orphic thinkers who claimed that there was an immortal part of humans. Plato, in his quest for an epistemological solution against the skeptics, used the Pythagorean/Orphic theory of the soul to account for being able to have knowledge of the "real" world; that of the Ideal Forms at a cosmological level. The soul of humans was thought to be trapped in the flesh and could know the world imperfectly now, but when freed by death would know completely. In Greek thought, there would be no resurrection of the body, but only the immortal soul would survive death.

---

135. Nichelsburg, *Resurrection, Immortality, and Eternal Life In Intertestamental Judaism* 18.

136. Nico van Uchelen, "Death and the Afterlife in the Hebrew Bible of Ancient Israel," 89.

137. Pythagoras also initiated the development of what was to become the Ptolemaic cosmology—the new mythology was that there was a dualism of the pure celestial and corrupt sub-lunar worlds; the earth was immobile in the center and all the heavenly bodies moved around it.

These concepts were further developed and by Hellenistic times, the ideas spread by the followers of Alexander were to influence many other nations including that of the Jews.

Hellenistic influence on Israel

Interestingly, not too long after the Jews returned from the Babylonian Exile, the Greek Plato was developing his theory of the immortality of the soul that would later have such a profound effect on the Israelites and the subsequent religions based on the Hebrew Bible. Now, the dead were no longer relegated to being under the earth. With Plato's cosmology, the soul would ascend to the stars and later Platonism, in the Hellenistic world, would incorporate the heavenly spheres as locations for the immortal dead.

The (non-canonical Hebrew) Biblical texts, from first century BCE to first century CE, that reflect this thinking include:

> 2 Macc 7:9,11,14
>
> "You dismiss us from this present life, but the King of the universe will raise us up...I hope to get them [tongue and hands] back again...But for you [Antiochus IV] there will be no resurrection to life."
>
> 4 Macc 18:23
>
> "But the sons of Abraham with their victorious mother are gathered together into the chorus of the fathers, and have received pure and immortal souls from God." These and other examples of immortal life are related in this text.[138]
>
> Wisdom of Solomon 1:13; 2:23–24
>
> "Because God did not make death...he created all things so that they might exist...for incorruption, and made us in the image of his own eternity."

---

138. In 4 Maccabees the Hellenistic idea, formulated by Plato, of an individual immortal soul is introduced: "Therefore the soul, Cebes, he said, is most certainly deathless [immortal] and indestructible and our souls will really dwell in the underworld...they will have sentence passed on them..." (*Phaedo* 107).

4 Ezra 7:15–16, 129

> "Now therefore why are you disturbed...consider in your mind what is to come...choose life." Why be concerned with the present mortal state, choose immortal life.

It is in 4 Ezra 7:75 that the concept of the immortal soul is fully developed where Solathiel asks:

> "whether after death, as soon as everyone of us yields up his soul, we shall be kept in rest until [the renewal]...or whether we shall be tormented at once?"

Here we have the statement of immortality that will be inherited by the Christian Fathers. It includes the Platonic immortal soul, the final restoration and judgment, and the concept of the intermediate waiting state.

A summary of foreign influences on Israel

The evolution of an idea

The cosmology of the ancient Israelites was derived from that of their neighbors. Even the later Priestly writer of Genesis 1 still shows the ancient Near East emphasis on ordering the chaos of the primordial waters. As much as the three-tiered cosmology (under-the-earth, earth, heaven) of the Mesopotamians and the Canaanites influenced their concepts of the afterlife (with the cult of the dead under the earth), so the essentially same cosmology did for the early Israelites.

With Josiah's reforms, the cult of the dead was eliminated or driven underground, so that the official Yahweh-only religion had no belief in the afterlife.

With the trauma of the Exile, even though the Jews were subsequently freed by the hand of Cyrus of Persia, the Deuteronomic promise of long life and reward in this life was severely questioned. The resurrection ideas of Persian Zoroastrianism may have offered a model for a post-exilic afterlife scenario that would offer life and reward in a restored paradise[139] on earth for faithful service

---

139. Yamauchi, *Persia and the Bible*, 332-3. The Greek word *paradeisos* (from the Meadian *paridaiza*, Avestan *paridaeza*) was used to describe the paradise of the Garden of Eden (Gen. 3: 8–10). It was borrowed as *pardes* in Hebrew. This would seem to be an instance of a definite influence.

to Yahweh, obviously denied in this life, in a later and better life at the end of time.

As the empire of Alexander the Great spread throughout the world, and the Jews of the Diaspora became more Hellenized, some of them attempted to integrate the ideas of the Platonic concept of the soul into the Jewish religion. The two eschatological concepts were mutually incompatible, so the tendency of the Hellenized Jews was to adhere to Platonic immortality, while the sect of the Pharisees (and their rabbinical successors) held to the resurrection of the body.

Ideas of the afterlife in tension

These two ideas, coming from two separate origins, are obviously incompatible and were therefore held in tension by the larger body of the Jews and later by the Christians.[140]

So, another question for our inquiry becomes: when did the Platonic idea of the body/soul dualism actually enter into the thinking of the Christian Fathers—and why?

In Hellenistic Judaism, close upon the Common Era, the ideas of the Last Days, the Resurrection of the Dead and their Judgment had entered into the consciousness of the Jewish people before the founding of Christianity.

The Theodicy Problem in Israel

As long as Israel was polytheistic, there was no Theodicy problem. However, when Yahweh became the only God, it then became an obvious problem.

In Isaiah 45:7, God is said to create both good and evil since He was believed to be the only power capable of creation. Still, the Deuteronomist had promised the people rewards in the form of earthly benefits for being righteous and, conversely,

140. This dichotomy of afterlife beliefs was only gradually and imperfectly resolved hundreds of years later by the Christian Fathers in the early centuries of Christianity.

promised penalties for sinfulness.[141] Over the centuries, it would become apparent that the promises of Deuteronomy were not ringing true. So, now, how is the justice of God explained? There were at least three successive attempts, illustrated by the following:

1—Job was a righteous man who failed to get the reward promised by Deuteronomy. He is accused by his friends of sinfulness, since that was, after all, the accepted reason for a person's misfortune. Job knows better and wants God to justify His actions against him. This cannot rightly be called a Theodicy since God makes no attempt to justify Himself. He simply asks Job: "Where were you when I laid the foundation of the earth?" In other words, who are you to question me? Job can only accept the mysteries of God's bigger picture and "repent in dust and ashes."

2—The Prophets had a good explanation for the justice of God. They claimed that the people suffered because they failed to live up to their part of the covenant between God and Israel. This was a reasonable Theodicy since the entire Hebrew Bible is filled with the failures of the people to follow God's commandments. Notwithstanding its reasonableness, there would come a time when the people were enduring great suffering and even giving their lives to follow the Laws of God. The older explanations no longer worked and something had to take their place.

3—During the Syrian Persecutions of Antiochus (ca. 165 BCE), the martyrs for the cause of Law and Temple were seen to receive no reward as promised by Deuteronomy in this life so, if there is no reward now, it must come later!

One only has to read 2 Maccabees to see that the resurrection doctrine had come to the fore in the thinking of the martyrs due to their steadfastness against the

---

141. Dt 5:9–10 I, the Lord your God, am a jealous God, punishing the children for the sin of the fathers to the third and fourth generation of those who hate me, [10] but showing love to a thousand generations of those who love me and keep my commandments. Dt 30: 15–18. See, I set before you today life and prosperity, death and destruction. [16] For I command you today to love the Lord your God, to walk in his ways, and to keep his commands, decrees and laws; then you will live and increase, and the Lord your God will bless you in the land you are entering to possess. But if your heart turns away and you are not obedient, and if you are drawn away to bow down to other gods and worship them, [18] I declare to you this day that you will certainly be destroyed. You will not live long in the land you are crossing the Jordan to enter and possess.

Syrian enemy. The writer or editor of chapter six offers his commentary on the reasons for suffering of the Jews:

2 Maccabees 6:12–17

> Now I urge those who read this book not to be depressed by such calamities, but to recognize that these punishments were designed not to destroy but to discipline our people. [13]In fact, it is a sign of great kindness not to let the impious alone for long, but to punish them immediately. [14]For in the case of the other nations the Lord waits patiently to punish them until they have reached the full measure of their sins; but he does not deal in this way with us, [15]in order that he may not take vengeance on us afterward when our sins have reached their height. [16]Therefore he never withdraws his mercy from us. Although he disciplines us with calamities, he does not forsake his own people. [17]Let what we have said serve as a reminder; we must go on briefly with the story.

The horrors of the details of the torture and death of the martyred are so intense that the writer has to offer an explanation as to why God is allowing these things to happen. He falls back on the idea of God's corrective discipline, which is a perfectly good rational for a Theodicy. However, the story of chapter seven seems to offer something else as these excerpts show:

2 Maccabees 7:1–42

> It happened also that seven brothers and their mother were arrested and were being compelled by the king, under torture with whips and thongs, to partake of unlawful swine's flesh. [2]One of them, acting as their spokesman, said, "What do you intend to ask and learn from us? For we are ready to die rather than transgress the laws of our ancestors."
> The king fell into a rage, and gave orders to have pans and caldrons heated. [4]These were heated immediately, and he commanded that the tongue of their spokesman be cut out and that they scalp him and cut off his hands and feet, while the rest of the brothers and the mother looked on. [5]When he was utterly helpless, the king ordered them to take him to the fire, still breathing, and to fry him in a pan. The smoke from the pan spread widely, but the brothers and their mother encouraged one another to die nobly, saying, [6]"The Lord God is watching over us and in truth has compassion on us, as Moses declared in his song that bore witness against

> the people to their faces, when he said, "And he will have compassion on his servants.""C
>
> After the first brother had died in this way...

The rest of the brothers and the mother all died with these words on their lips—

> You accursed wretch, you dismiss us from this present life, but the King of the universe will raise us up to an everlasting renewal of life, because we have died for his laws.
>
> I got these from Heaven, and because of his laws I disdain them, and from him I hope to get them back again."..."One cannot but choose to die at the hands of mortals and to cherish the hope God gives of being raised again by him. But for you there will be no resurrection to life!
>
> I do not know how you came into being in my womb. It was not I who gave you life and breath, nor I who set in order the elements within each of you. [23]Therefore the Creator of the world, who shaped the beginning of humankind and devised the origin of all things, will in his mercy give life and breath back to you again, since you now forget yourselves for the sake of his laws.
>
> My son, have pity on me. I carried you nine months in my womb, and nursed you for three years, and have reared you and brought you up to this point in your life, and have taken care of you. [28]I beg you, my child, to look at the heaven and the earth and see everything that is in them, and recognize that God did not make them out of things that existed. And in the same way the human race came into being. [29]Do not fear this butcher, but prove worthy of your brothers. Accept death, so that in God's mercy I may get you back again along with your brothers.

Clearly, the statement of Theodicy of 2 Macc 6:12–16 is countered by the events of the rest of the verses of chapter seven. Suffering is not due to sin; rather, it is due to the evils of men. However, now there is a reward for suffering—a resurrection to eternal life.

While discussing Maccabees, it should be noted that the belief in the resurrection is amplified by the belief in the efficacy of offering prayers for the dead.

2 Maccabees 12:38–45

Then Judas assembled his army and went to the city of Adullam. As the seventh day was coming on, they purified themselves according to the custom, and kept the Sabbath there.

On the next day, as had now become necessary, Judas and his men went to take up the bodies of the fallen and to bring them back to lie with their kindred in the sepulchers of their ancestors. Then under the tunic of each one of the dead they found sacred tokens of the idols of Jamnia, which the law forbids the Jews to wear. And it became clear to all that this was the reason these men had fallen. So they all blessed the ways of the Lord, the righteous judge, who reveals the things that are hidden; and they turned to supplication, praying that the sin that had been committed might be wholly blotted out. The noble Judas exhorted the people to keep themselves free from sin, for they had seen with their own eyes what had happened as the result of the sin of those who had fallen.
He also took up a collection, man by man, to the amount of two thousand drachmas of silver, and sent it to Jerusalem to provide for a sin offering. In doing this he acted very well and honorably, taking account of the resurrection.

For if he were not expecting that those who had fallen would rise again, it would have been superfluous and foolish to pray for the dead. But if he was looking to the splendid reward that is laid up for those who fall asleep in godliness, it was a holy and pious thought. Therefore he made atonement for the dead, so that they might be delivered from their sin.

Why pray for them if they were to have no future? This passage will be of immense interest to much later Christian theologians when the problem of the intermediate state after death will arise.

We are now at the threshold of the Christian era as shown by **Fig. 28** and **Fig. 29.** To the east of Galilee, across the Jordan River, is the Decapolis (Greek for the *ten cities*). This fact shows the influence of Hellenistic culture on the region in which the Jesus Movement will develop. This will also be the area into which the Jewish-Christians will flee shortly after the martyrdom of James, the brother of Jesus, and the destruction of Jerusalem.

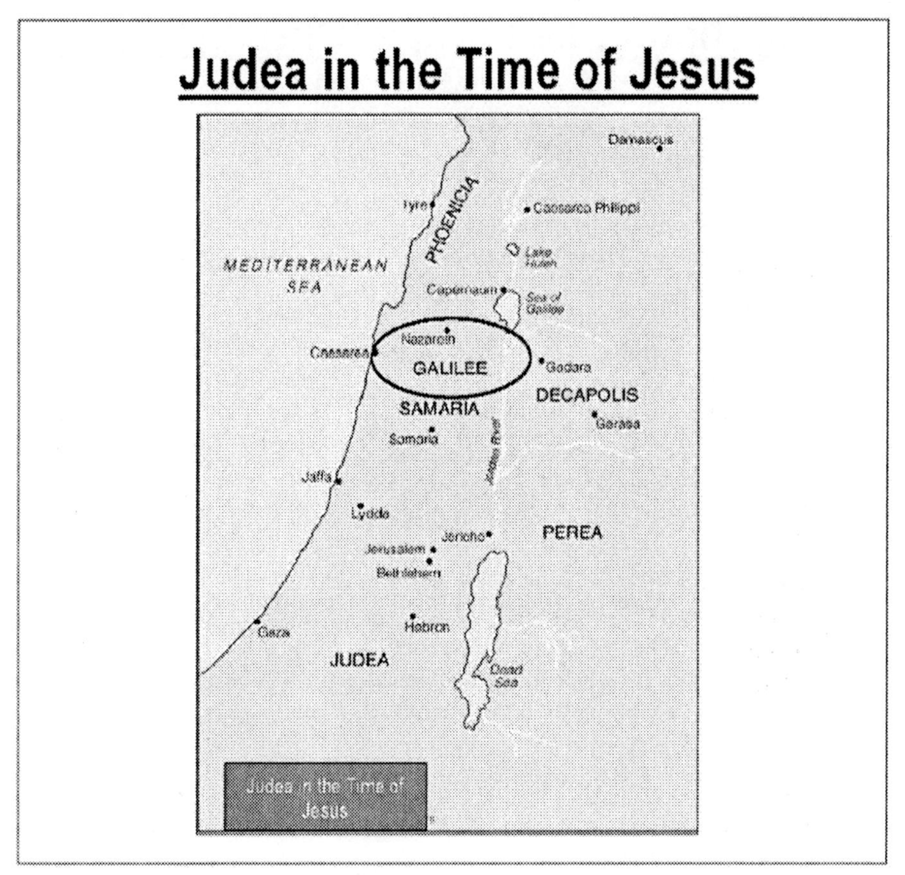

Fig. 28 Judea in the Time of Jesus

We have now traveled over 3000 years of history. It took 2000 of those years to arrive at the establishment of the united monarchy under King David. Over the next 500 years, we see the splitting of the monarchy, the fall of the Northern Kingdom, the Yahweh-only reforms of Josiah, the Exile of the Southern Kingdom, and the return from Babylon to build the second Temple.

For the next 350 years, Judah will be subjugated first to Persia and then to Greece, where it will absorb the customs of their masters. There will come a short period of independence, and then Rome will descend upon the world and ensnare what they will call Judea. All of these powers will have left their mark on the world into which Jesus of Nazareth will descend.

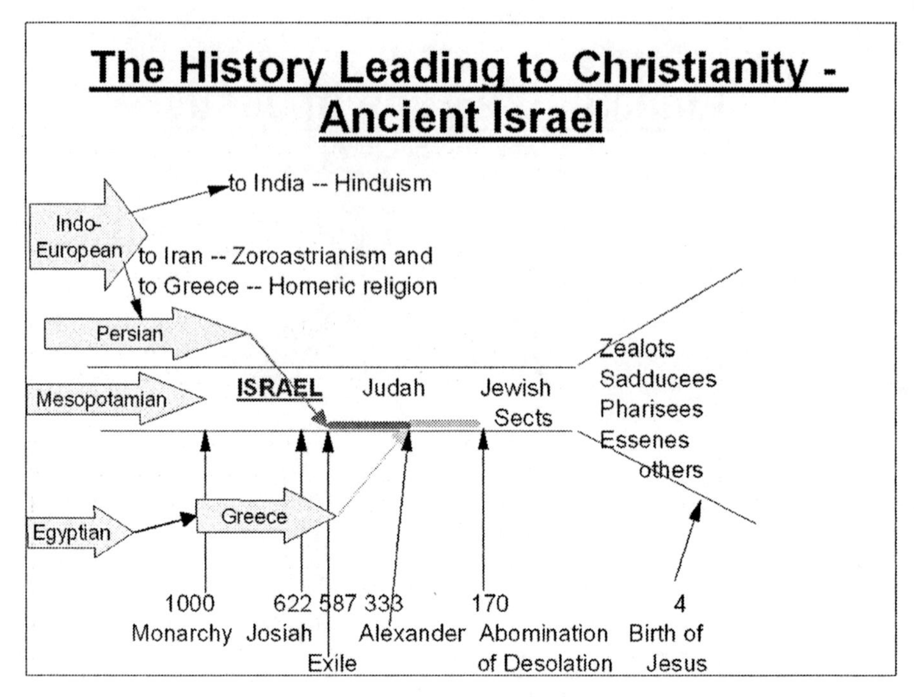

Fig. 29 History Leading to Christianity—the Jews

The World of Early Christianity

"The Kingdom of God is not coming with signs to be observed...for behold, the Kingdom of God is in the midst of you." Luke 17:20–21[142]

All of the empires of the past had fallen. The Jews had been under the rule of so many for so long that a well developed apocalyptic was in place to be transferred onto the new conqueror—Rome.

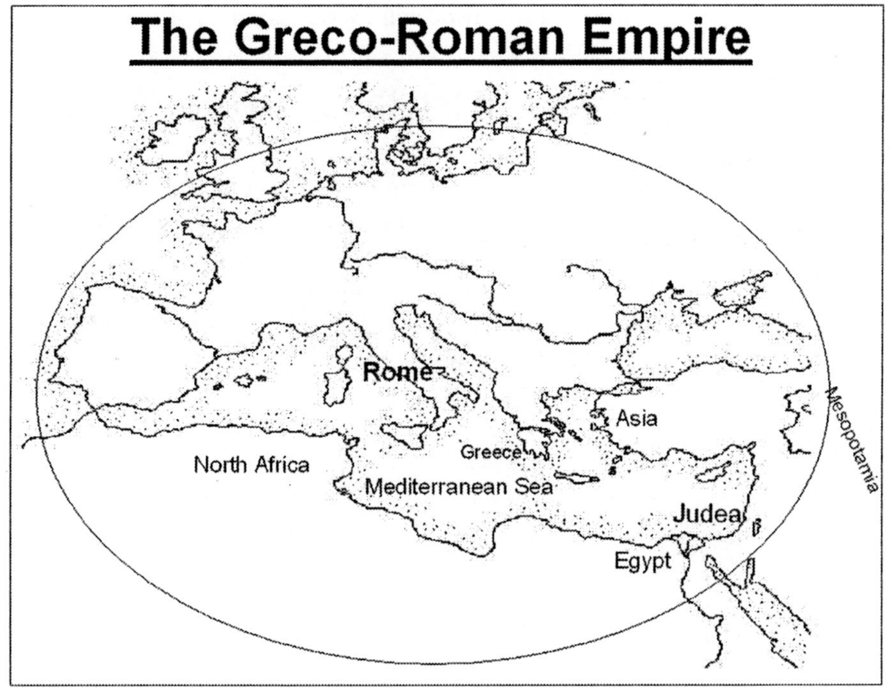

Fig. 30 The World of Early Christianity

142. The Kingdom is already here. This, of course, is counter to the expectations of most of the Jews. In fact, there has never been a clear and unambiguous universal belief on this idea.

The World of Jesus

Jesus was born into a provincial area of Israel, as well as into the larger world of the Greco-Roman empire, **Fig. 30** above.

There is no indication in the Gospels that he was influenced by the Hellenistic religious culture, but that negative evidence does not prove he wasn't. Indeed, if he was familiar with the immortal-soul eschatology of the Greeks, that teaching was soon over-shadowed by the Pharisaic (and Pauline) belief in the bodily resurrection.

Of course, the early Pauline eschatology of the resurrection, was soon overlaid by the Platonic soul of the Hellenistic culture into which Christianity would disperse. A significant part of that Hellenistic culture was the cults of the Mysteries.

The Mystery Religions of the Greco-Roman World

The etymology of the term "mystery" is of importance to understanding the religions themselves. The Greek *myelin* means "to close one's eyes or mouth", therefore, figuratively, to "keep secret". A derivative, *mists* means an initiated person (Myers, 4). I believe that "esoteric" would be a more appropriate term, as it has a more immediate English meaning of "intended for only a chosen few as an inner group of disciples or initiates". However, the term is "mystery" and that is what we'll stay with.

Based on the above comments, my own definition of the term Mystery Religion is: a way of salvation for the individual, where salvation involves the saving of the person from the gloom or oblivion of death by initiation into secret knowledge available to only a select few.

The Eleusinian mysteries

During a famine in the Rome of 496 BCE, the Sibylline Books were consulted and they said that a temple should be built to Ceres, Liber, and Libera who are actually the Roman names for the Greek deities of the Eleusinian Mysteries: Demeter, Bacchus, and Persephone (Dowden, 32). So, this is the oldest of the Greco-Roman Mystery Religions.

It is based on the Greek myth of Demeter and her daughter, Persephone, where Persephone is abducted to the underworld and her mother neglects the prosperity of the world while involved in her quest for her daughter's return. Persephone is eventually returned, but there is a catch—she must stay part of the year in the netherworld with her abductor husband, Hades, and the remaining nine months in the upper world with her mother.

This story was most likely an ancient vegetation myth, where the vegetation shrivels and the seeds are buried in silos under the earth during the dry Greek summer months, and the seeds sprout when the rains come. It came to symbolize the possibility of a resurrection from the dead for those who understood the mystery, as indicated in the Homeric Hymn to Demeter:

> Happy is he among men upon earth who has seen these mysteries; but he who is uninitiate and who has no part in them, never has lot of like good things once he is dead, down in the darkness and gloom.

By the time the Romans came to know these mysteries at Eleusis around 500 BCE, the Eleusinian rites had been performed in Greece for over 300 years.

The cult of Isis and Serapis

The cult of Isis goes back to the ancient Egypt of around 2700 BCE. Serapis is a fourth century BCE construction by the Greco-Egyptian king Ptolemy I from the conflation of Apis, the bull, and the god Osiris. Serapis was the deity who came to be worshiped in the Greco-Roman world.

In the original Egyptian resurrection story, Osiris' brother, Seth, had twice killed Isis' husband, Osiris—once by being thrown into the Nile and again by dismemberment. Isis had twice resurrected Osiris from the dead and thus provided the template on which Egyptian pharaohs; then, later, all people could expect to be "Osirified" or resurrected from the dead.

As it was to be with Plotinus' union with the One (centuries later), the initiate could not wish for and get initiation, but must wait upon the goddess. As Apuleius discovered: "The initiation date for each aspirant was given by direct sign from the Goddess...which without her consent would be an invocation of destruction" (*Golden Ass*, 11.21). Compare this idea with the Christian doctrine of Grace where man can do nothing toward acquiring salvation, but is dependent upon being chosen by God.

The Isis/Serapis cult made its way to Rome around the early first century BCE, where it met with resistance for a time; then was accepted by Emperor Caligula. It was flourishing in the first century CE, and lasted until the Christian destruction of paganism in the late fifth century.

The cult of Cybele and Attis

Another cult that made its way to Rome was that of Cybele (the Great Mother) and Attis. Cybele was in love with Attis, but he had sex with another. Out of remorse, he castrated himself and died; then was forgiven and resurrected by Cybele. His worship allowed his disciples to participate in a similar resurrection. Briefly, his myth is: Attis was born from a virgin. The worship of Attis involved an effigy of him that was hung on a tree; then be buried in a cave. When the tomb was reopened, the god Attis would rise from the dead and proclaim the good news of salvation. In the Roman worship of Attis, an animal's blood, a symbol of Attis' sacrifice, would be poured on worshipers who believed that his blood would wash away their sins.

The cult of *magna mater* (Cybele) was only one of two foreign religions to be deliberately invited into Rome. During the war with Hannibal in 204 BCE, the Sibylline books were once again consulted; as they had been before the introduction of the Eleusinian mysteries in 496 BCE. "A prophecy was found that if ever a foreign enemy should invade Italy, he could be defeated and driven out if Cybele...were brought from Pessinus (in Phrygia) to Rome" (Livy, History of Rome, 29.10). The Great Mother had been worshipped in Phrygia since, at least, 1500 BCE.

The Romans did as recommended, and later were confronted with a religion that threatened to destroy the *mos majorum* of their society. The priests (the *galli*) of Cybele would emulate the frenzied, destructive behavior of her consort, Attis, by castrating themselves for her. As a result, Roman citizens were not allowed to serve as priest until the time of Emperor Claudius, then later Domitian again forbade them this practice.

The cult of Mithras

Mithraism made its way into the Roman world in 67 BCE when the Roman general Pompey defeated the Cilician pirates, who had been practicing the religion (Plutarch, *Life of Pompey*, 24.1–8). With the dispersal of the defeated Cilicians throughout the Empire, the religion had spread and was taken up by the military, whose movements spread it even more.

The cult had an elaborate series of initiations where the initiates would advance through seven grades corresponding to the seven planets. It is believed that the purpose of this seven-step initiation was to reenact the descent and re-ascent of the soul from the celestial realm through the heavenly spheres and back again. This ascent to the realm of the stars recalls Plato's ascent to the ultimate Good and his emphasis on astral immortality.

Cult similarities and differences

Why choose one of these from among the many available? Mithraism offers two major differences from the other three mystery religions discussed above. It was exclusively for males and it offered a more spiritual immortality, on the model of Plato, rather than a resurrection based on the vegetation model of the older mysteries.

In the big picture, the Mysteries are very similar to each other and very different from the Roman religion of *mos majorum*. Whereas, the civic religion emphasized the community and one's place in it but did not offer the individual hope of escaping death, the mystery religions did just the opposite. They stressed the salvation of the individual and insured him or her some form of afterlife; achievable by being initiated into some secret knowledge.

Why would a person choose one over the other? In the first place, some—like the Emperor Julian (ca. 361 CE)—did not choose. He rejected Christianity in favor of the theurgy of the Neo-Platonic Iamblicus; and, also, was initiated into the Eleusinian, Mithric, and Great Mother Mysteries.

Secondly, where a choice is made, the family or community religion into which one is born or grows up, or one's gender, may dictate the preference. For example, men may prefer Mithraism and women may prefer Cybele, but all the Mysteries performed the same sotereological function. Besides, their gods were not jealous, so one could (as did Julian) choose to belong to several mysteries.

In light of the fact that there were so many religions that could meet some definition of mystery, is the category of "mystery religion" useful? On the one hand, yes, in that all of the mystery religions had secret initiations, purifications, an exclusive community and salvation. The category is a useful device to be able to speak of them using a single inclusive term.

On the other hand, the real problem is that the category usually excludes other religions that should also be included. For example, Christianity has initiation rites, and certain rituals could only be attended by the initiated. Clement of Alexandria recognized this in the late second century CE, where he attacked the Mysteries and claimed that Christianity is the true mystery religion that offers "truly sacred mysteries" (*Exhortation*, 12.120). One becomes holy by initiation; God marks the worshipper and gives the guiding light, and the individual is given over to the care of the Father. Clement could have been describing any of the Mysteries, but for a perfect fit, it's Mithraism.

Not only "orthodox" Christianity, but also Gnosticism would fit the category of mystery religion. It appears even more esoteric in that it includes only the sons of Seth. But, if we allowed all of these religions to be included under the same term, that term would lose its ability to describe a particular set of entities.

The term is imbedded in the language of religious study, and it excludes the religions of Christianity and Gnosticism; therefore, as long as we recognize its limitations, it remains useful in describing a unique set of religions of antiquity.

Common themes of the Mystery Religions

Religions like Great Mother and Attis, Orphic, Dionysian, Eleusinian, Mithric, etc., were the opposite of the Olympian and the Roman civil religion; but they held these concepts in common:

A suspension of fate or determinism[143]
A ritual baptism as part of the initiation of new believers
A ritual meal
A god or son of a god who died and was resurrected
A goddess involved in the birth or safety of the child god
An unusual circumstance of birth
A return to the realm of the gods by the savior god

143. The Olympic religionists of Homer and the later Stoic philosophers believed that we are at the mercy of a predetermined fate. But, the Mysteries' gods ruled over the stars themselves, so one's fate was no longer "in the stars."

Mithraism, which was a major competitor of Christianity in the first centuries, had some marked similarities with it. Sunday (day of the Sun) was held to be a sacred day, and the birthday of Mithras was celebrated on December 25. These days were sacred in honor of the *sol invictus* (the invincible sun), which has its deepest roots in the triumph of the winter solstice—when the sun ceased its descent and once again began to rise.

John the Baptist and the proto-Christian Jesus Movement

John's message

God will very soon, at any moment, descend to eradicate the evil of this world in a sort of apocalyptic consummation. This is, of course, the message of an apocalyptic eschatologist.

Jesus, who was baptized by John, called him the greatest person ever, but said that the least in the Kingdom of God would exceed him.

John unequivocally said that the Kingdom was coming in cataclysm. It was to be a true end of the physical world as we know it. This was in the tradition of the Essenes and their more ancient forerunners, the Zoroastrians.

Jesus, on the other hand, claimed that the Kingdom of God was coming in the converted hearts of people, or perhaps by a miracle from the Father that would bless the poor and bring down the rich and powerful.[144]

Most of Jesus' later followers would choose John.

Start of the Movement

The proto-Christian movement starts with Jesus of Nazareth (ca. 4 BCE–30 CE), whose ministry only lasted one (Synoptic Gospels) or three (John's Gospel) years before he was killed by a collusion of Jewish leaders and Roman officials.

---

144. This is contestable, since the New Testament is ambiguous on the nature of the Kingdom, and one could make an argument for Jesus also being an **apocalyptic eschatologist**, depending on what parts of the Bible you read.

The movement's message was: "Repent for the Kingdom is at hand" (Mark 1:15).

This was a development of the Messianic kingdom expected in the late Jewish apocalyptic of Daniel and 2nd Isaiah. As we've seen, such apocalyptic has ancient roots and background influences:

Jewish via Persian/Greek eschatology
Jewish Apocalyptic due to Greek (Hellenistic) rule
Greek Mystery religions

At first, the followers of the movement would have been a new sect of Judaism. If it had remained Jewish, it probably would not have survived the destruction of Jerusalem in 70 CE. Of course, we will never know that for a fact since a counterfactual cannot be proven.

The new sect did not remain Jewish for long and Paul, a Jew, would open it up to the Gentiles of the Hellenistic world.

The new sect, and the established Jewish religion, soon separated and Christianity, as it evolved into the institution we see today, would be established by the Greek Fathers between 100 and 500 CE, further separating Jewish and Gentile Christianity.

The first Christians

The Jesus Movement was not called Christian until the 40's when it got that name at Greek speaking Antioch. Jesus was called Messiah in the language of Israel, which was translated almost immediately into Greek, the language of the new church.

Earlier, the Movement was called the Way or the Nazarenes, perhaps after Jesus' hometown in Galilee. The original focus of the Movement was in the Jewish homeland: first in Galilee, then in Jerusalem.

Peter was the original head of the Jerusalem church and was later replaced by James, the brother of Jesus.

Scholars designate the original followers of Jesus in Jerusalem as Jewish-Christians. These would later be called, among other designations, Ebionites; and they would be branded as heretics by the developing church.

The quest for the historical Jesus

Some of the few things we know for sure about the man, Jesus, are that he rejected the hypocrisy of many of the leaders of the established organized religion, and he preached the coming Kingdom of God.

But, what factual sources do we have to determine who was the Historical Jesus versus the later Christ of Faith? This question will be more fully addressed after learning more about the first few Christian centuries…

Fig. 31 shows the history of Christianity up to the time of John the Baptist and the Jesus Movement.

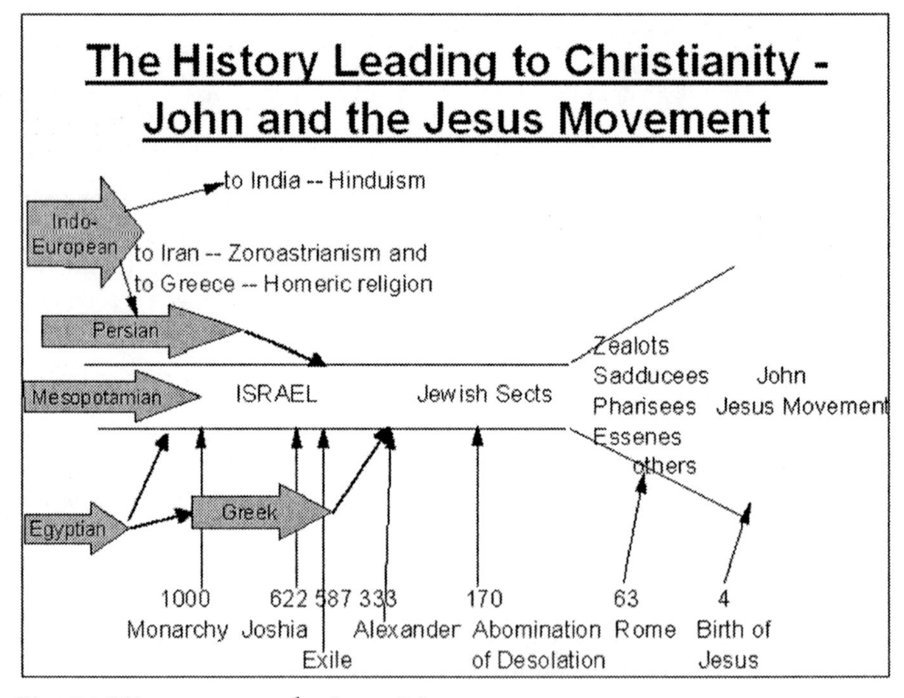

Fig. 31 History up to the Jesus Movement

PART III

The Development of Christianity

TIMELINES: THE BIG PICTURE (1–525 CE)

These timelines **Fig. 32** and **Fig. 33** show key people/events in chronological relationship on a linear timescale.

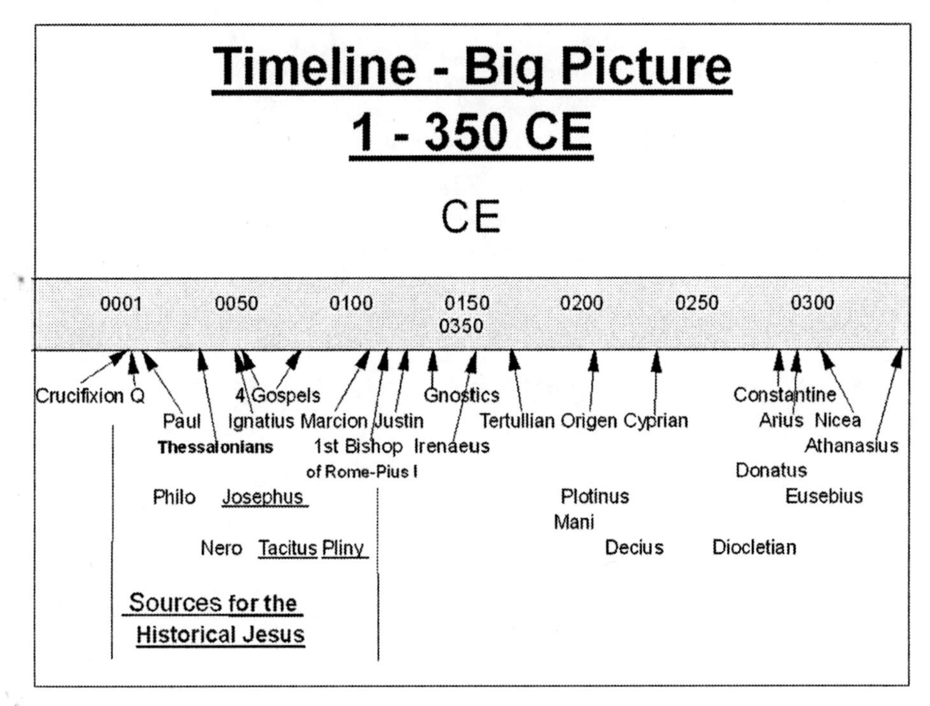

Fig. 32 Timeline 1–350 CE

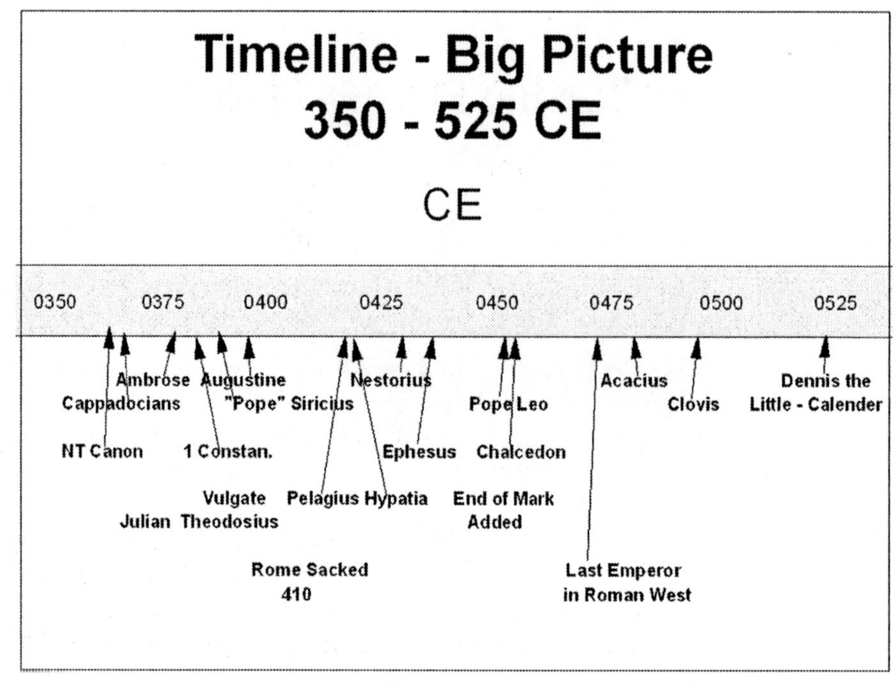

Fig. 33 Timeline 350–525 CE[145]

145. For detailed history of the first 600 years of Christianity, see: W. H. C. Frend, *The Rise of Christianity*, (Philadelphia: Fortress Press, 1984). For a 2000 year history, see: Paul Johnson, *A History of Christianity*, (New York: Atheneum, 1987).

The Evolution of the Afterlife (Encapsulation)

By the time of Pope St. Gregory the Great (ca. 540–604), all of the elements of the Christian church's concepts of the afterlife had been put in place. Heaven and Hell were places that the immortal soul inhabited immediately after death, depending on whether or not that soul had been saved. A third place, purgatory, had also been established, although, it would not be declared a doctrine until 1439 at the council of Florence.

The interesting thing about this state of affairs that make it worthy of devoting several sections, is that these concepts are diametrically opposed to the afterlife model held by almost all Jews in Israel, at the time of Jesus. How could this change come about so quickly? What happened to the older plan for the afterlife in the intervening years?

In order to sufficiently examine this radical change, we are required to look to the distant past and in places foreign to Israel. For instance, we know that people had some inkling of an afterlife, as far back as 50,000 years ago, where we find grave goods buried with the dead which could only be for their support in an afterlife.

However, the first written evidence for an afterlife is found in Egypt in the Pyramid Texts of ca. 2400 BCE. These are painted in the burial pyramids of the Kings of Egypt, declaring the king's continued existence after physical death. Later, in Persia ca. 1200 BCE, we find the texts of the monotheistic religion of Zoroaster, that lays claim to a resurrection of the dead at the end of time.

The most immediate progenitors of Christianity are ancient Israel and ancient Greece but, interestingly, neither of these cultures had a developed concept of an afterlife until quite late in their histories. Around the eighth century BCE, both the books of Homer in Greece and the oldest books of the Hebrew Bible (the Christian Old Testament) have only the most rudimentary idea of a post-mortem existence.

In Israel, the dead are all consigned to the pit, a place called Sheol, where there is no real consciousness of existence and even God cannot make contact with the ghosts of the dead. This idea of a disembodied wraith was a continuation of the still more ancient Mesopotamian "cult of the dead." Strangely, at the very same time that neighboring Egypt had a highly evolved afterlife concept, the Mesopotamians have no hope of post-mortem reward or punishment. Similarly, in Greece, the dead were relegated to an equally bleak place like Sheol, called Hades, where they also had no real existence.

This situation was not to change until the fifth century BCE in Greece (and the second century BCE in Israel) when the concepts of the immortal soul and the resurrection were to develop respectively. Both cultures acquired the new beliefs by importing them from another culture—most probably, Egypt for Greece and Persia for Israel. Even after the introduction of the new beliefs, most of the Greeks and Israelites refused to accept them, since the teachings of the Homeric epics and the Scriptural Torah were too ingrained in the thoughts of each populace to allow room for the new concepts. Many Greek philosophers and the Jewish Sadducees were still unconvinced at the time of Jesus, and soundly denied and even abhorred the idea of an afterlife. Nevertheless, we do find some serious, but limited, acceptance of an in Greece at the time of Plato (ca. 427–347 BCE) and in Israel at the time of the Syrian Greek rule (ca. 200 BCE).

Jesus was a practicing Jew who would have been most influenced by sects other than the Sadducees, and would have believed in the resurrection of the dead. His forerunner, John the Baptist, was proclaiming the apocalyptic vision of the end of the present age and the subsequent resurrection, as developed in the Old Testament Book of Daniel (ca. 165 BCE). The New Testament, which was written between 25 and 100 years of the Baptist's death, is full of these same apocalyptic images. It should, therefore, be safe to say that the earliest Christian afterlife paradigm was one that consisted of the resurrection of the body at the end of the present age, which Paul, the Apostle to the Gentiles, expected "the appointed time" to come very soon.

So, what happened five hundred years later, to that paradigm from the time of Paul to the time of Gregory the Great? As we shall see, Paul's expected end did not come; many new Greek converts to the faith brought along the body/soul dualism of Plato, and the Fathers of the Church accommodated their teachings to the realities of later times.

THREE EARLY CHRISTIANITIES

There are three main branches of early Christianity, which we will consider first in this section.

1—the earliest branch, which stood alone for a brief time, was the Jewish-Christian sect created by the immediate disciples of Jesus.

2—although there may have been others, the next branch that we have knowledge of was the Pauline missionary churches that were to develop into mainline Christianity, by the end of the Third Century.

3—Later, but still alluded to in the New Testament, were the various Gnostic Christian sects who stressed the wisdom of Jesus, as against the redeeming resurrection doctrine of Paul.

In chronological order, first the Jewish-Christians...

Jewish-Christianity (Encapsulation)

By the turn of the First century, the original apostolic church at Jerusalem was gone. Its remnants were scattered, some of which went to Pella across the Jordan River, where we will meet them again later. The immediate cause of this dissolution was the Roman destruction, in 70 AD, of the Temple and the dispersion of many of the people of Jerusalem.

A deeper, more ultimate cause could be traced back 2000 years earlier with the migration of Abraham from Mesopotamia to Palestine. However, for our purposes here, we will only go back to the charge of Jesus to take his message to all of the Jews.

Immediately after the Crucifixion, Peter was the leader of the band of disciples that had abandoned Jesus in his hour of need. The appearance of Jesus to many of them—subsequent to his death—caused a regrouping in Galilee and then in Jerusalem where they did, indeed, spread the teachings of the crucified Messiah.

Peter was now in control of the church in Jerusalem and was bringing many into the Jesus Movement (not yet called Christians). All of the new faithful were Jews, either from the area around Israel, or from the broader Diaspora of Hellenized (Greek-speaking) Jews. As such, the Jesus movement was considered a new sect within greater Judaism. The laws of Moses and the sign of obedience to God, the circumcision, were still the norm of this group, as it was for all Jews. A new belief was that the Messiah had come, and that he had instituted a new way of life that would usher in the imminent Kingdom of God.

The first (and mostly affable) division within the new group was between the Greek and Aramaic speaking Jews. The Greeks set up a separate leadership for their subgroup; although, they still held Peter as the leader of the Jerusalem church. Success was to bring about greater change.

As the new movement spread throughout the Diaspora, non-Jews heard of the teachings of Jesus and wanted to join the movement. They were welcomed into Judaism, as "God-fearing" Gentiles had always been welcomed in the past. But, full conversion to Judaism meant adhering to the laws of Moses and accepting all of the rites attendant with Judaism.

Then came one who had been persecuting the Jews of the new movement. He murdered a Greek-speaking member who had spoken against things important to the Temple officials. The Greek speakers were beginning to stray from the official core of Judaism. Something happened to dramatically change the persecutor, and he began to believe that the resurrection of Jesus had become the turning point in the history of God's dealings with man. So after he had murdered Stephen, Saul of Tarsus became Paul, the greatest advocate of the new movement.

The Jerusalem church eventually saw his conversion as real and agreed that he should be the leader of the mission to the Gentiles while they continued with their mission to the House of Israel. This friendly agreement was to plant the seeds of the death of the original apostolic movement.

By the 40's AD, Paul had founded many new churches throughout the Greek-speaking world. The new converts were eager to join his movement for two primary reasons: it provided an egalitarian ethical system unknown in their world; it fit into the Greek mythical system already in place. They were, however, not as eager to adhere to the rites of Judaism and refused to become Jews.

This caused a problem for Jerusalem, which came to a head in Antioch, where the Jews and non-Jews of the Jesus movement were sharing table fellowship. Even Peter, who had come to Antioch to convert the Hellenized Jews, was participating with the Pauline groups in such unlawful fellowship. The major break came when representatives from James, the brother of Jesus, who was now head of the Jerusalem church, came to Antioch. Peter, in deference to Jerusalem, stopped attending the fellowship and Paul called him a hypocrite to his face (Gal. 2:11 ff).

Things were patched up and at the Council in Jerusalem (ca. 50 AD), James agreed to let the non-Jews stay in the movement without being circumcised, and agreed to a limited amount of the Jewish Law (the Noachide law). The compromise was not to last, and Paul was constantly being harassed by Judaizers in the churches he had founded

The Hellenization of the movement eventually caused the Jews to turn against the Jesus movement and forced them to stop attending the synagogues. On the other hand, the growing numbers of non-Jews in Paul's movement overwhelmed that of the Jewish Jerusalem church. The Jerusalem church found itself to be outsiders to Judaism and to the now independent Pauline movement.

After the Roman destruction of Jerusalem in 66–70 AD, the Jewish Christians found themselves displaced and isolated. The Pauline movement became even more Greek and not only refused to adhere to the Mosaic Law, but it was also beginning to deify Jesus. The isolated Jewish-Christians could not abide either of these developments. Some of them, however, would eventually accept the Pauline theology but kept to the Mosaic Law.

Others could never accept the Pauline theology and so, in due course, the original apostolic Jesus movement was declared heretical by the developing Greek Church and cut off from what was to become orthodox Christianity.

ST. PAUL AND THE ORIGINAL CHURCH

Paul in Brief

Paul (died ca. 65 CE) was born Saul of Tarsus in present-day Eastern Turkey. That would make him a Jew of the Diaspora, therefore, from a Hellenized Culture.

Saul claimed to be a Pharisee who had studied under the famous teacher, Gamaliel. He persecuted the early Jewish Christians at the direction of the High Priest, a Sadducee. Nevertheless, in the famous story of his journey to Damascus, he was converted and started teaching his version of the crucified Jesus to Hellenized Jews and Greeks.

According to his own statement, he went about it without consulting the original Jesus Movement in Jerusalem (Gal 1:8ff). Paul eventually attempted to reconcile his mission with Jerusalem, which led to the first recorded church conflict (Gal 1:18–2:10).

The First Church Conflict

It is impossible to discuss Paul apart from:

The Jewish Diaspora in the Greco-Roman Empire and
The Jewish Christians

Because they are so entangled, we will look at Paul and these subjects together.

Jewish Diaspora in the 1st Century CE

The Jewish people had been living in the Hellenized world since the conquests of Alexander the Great (ca. 332 BCE) and had dispersed throughout that empire.

They had densely populated the entire Eastern coastline of the Mediterranean Sea (from present day Turkey in the north and Egypt in the south), and had established major cultural centers in Antioch, Damascus, and Alexandria.

That part of the world was under the control of the Roman Empire but, as the Romans themselves said, the conquered had conquered the conquerors; so the culture was still Greek. The Jews living outside Israel were very much Hellenized and spoke Greek, but still held to the religion of their fathers, so that synagogues were now scattered throughout the Eastern Roman world, **Fig. 34**.

A Jew seeking to spread a new sect of Judaism would have only to travel from city to city and preach in the local synagogue.

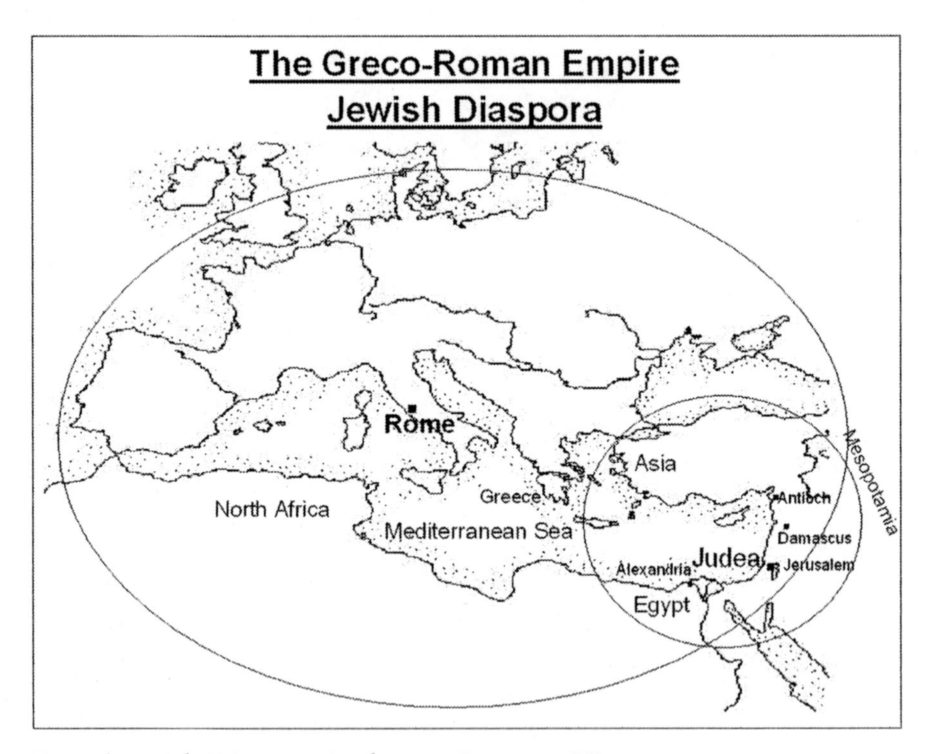

Fig. 34 Jewish Diaspora in the 1st Century CE

Jewish Christians (The Original Church) and Paul

Key events of the original church

The key events of the primitive church are related cryptically below, **Fig. 35.** Assuming 30 CE as the date of the crucifixion, the dates of the interactions between the Jewish-Christians and Paul lie in the approximately 35-year period between 30 and 65 CE. Our sources for these events are found in Paul's epistles and the Pauline Acts of the Apostles.

A careful reading of Paul versus Acts will show the intensity of the conflict. Paul becomes quite angry with the Jerusalem "pillars" and shows it in Galatians (written ca. 55 CE); whereas, the break is minimized in the later Acts (written ca. 85 CE) after the Pauline faction had prevailed.

Approximate Date (possible alternate dates)	**Event**
before 30 CE	Jesus' ministry either 1 year in Galilee (Synoptic Gospels) or 3 years in Judea (John's Gospel).
30	Jesus is crucified and the disciples go to Galilee then to Jerusalem
31	Greek speaking Jews elect their own leadership—the 7 of Acts 6:5 form their own mission
32	Paul persecutes St. Stephen, then converts and begins his ministry
35 (37)	Paul's 1st trip to Jerusalem, sees Peter and James
44 (47–49)	Paul's first mission to the Gentiles wit h Barnabus and Mark
49	Paul's 2nd trip to Jerusalem, sees James now head of Jewish-Christians (Jerusalem Council—1st Christian council held)—Paul is asked to "remember the poor"
49	Paul condemns Peter at Antioch (Gal 2:11ff)
51 (50–53)	Paul's second mission with Silas
51	Paul writes 1st Thessalonians (earliest New Testament work)
54 (53–57)	Paul's third and last mission
57	Paul's last visit to Jerusalem, collection for the poor is refused, final breakup

Approximate Date (possible alternate dates)	Event
62	Death of James, brother of Jesus
63	Flight of Jewish-Christians to Pella in Perinea across the Jordan, ending the mission to Judea
65	Death of Paul in Rome
70	Romans attack Jerusalem, destroy Temple and Judaism forever splits into Christianity and Rabbinic Judaism
after 65	Mark's Gospel written
after 85	Matthew, Luke and Acts written
after 95	John's Gospel written
132	Bar Kochba revolt and defeat—all Jews driven out of Palestine

Fig. 35 Key Events within the First 100 years of Christianity

Incident at Antioch (Galatians 1and 2)[146]

It is uncertain whether this incident took place before or after the Jerusalem Council. It seems likely that it was after, because some resolution of the Jew/Gentile conflict had been accomplished at the Jerusalem Council (ca. 49). Now, it appears that some people in Jerusalem were reneging on the agreement.

The main players in the conflict are James and Paul. James, the brother of Jesus, is the head of the Jewish Christians in Jerusalem, and Paul has been given the OK to be the messenger to the Hellenistic World—first to the Hellenized Jews outside Judea and, later, to just the Gentiles.

Now, some "false brethren" from Jerusalem interfere with Paul's mission at Antioch. Peter had come to Antioch and was participating in the table fellowship with Paul's converts. Since they were all Gentiles, they did not adhere to the practices of the Jews, who were prohibited from associating with non-Jews at such intimate gatherings.

The false brethren disrupt the meeting and chastise Peter and others for participating in an unclean act. Peter and Paul's disciple, Barnabus, are ashamed and retire from the meeting in deference to the Jerusalem representatives.

146.Also see—2 Corinthians 10–13, Acts 15 and 21.

This infuriates Paul and he condemns Peter and Barnabus to their face, and we do not hear of them again. The remainder of Acts is focused entirely on the mission of Paul.

This probably means that the spilt had become irreconcilable (as indicated by the epistle of James, especially, 2:14–26)[147]. Paul and the Jewish Christians would go their own ways. The vagaries of history would decide the ultimate winner of this first Christian conflict.

Paul's Letters

Some of Paul's letters have references to the other two branches of First century Christianity. The most important ones are given below:

Galatians

2: 1–21—Paul initially ignored the original Apostles; then he later opposes Christian missionaries from James, who believe that Gentiles need to follow the Law and that there should be no table fellowship with Gentiles. (Judaizers or Jewish-Christians)

1 Corinthians

15: 1–28—Opposes Christian leaders who taught that they had already experienced a spiritual resurrection and there was no physical resurrection. (proto-Gnostics).

12: 1–13: 13—Other divisive factions. People claiming spiritual gifts (charismata) were interrupting the community. Paul responds with the most beautiful passage in the epistles at 13: 1ff.

Romans

Paul has emphasized three doctrines that were most important to him throughout his ministry:

1—the death and resurrection of Jesus

---

147. "So faith by itself, if it has no works, is dead." Compare Abraham being justified by works in James 2:21 vs. faith in Romans 4:2 This passage is so anti-Pauline that Martin Luther in the sixteenth century would reject James as "an epistle of straw."

2—the immediacy of the coming end time and the Kingdom
3—the salvation of the elect by faith

3: 19–31—These verses most succinctly explain Paul's theology. Elsewhere, he has said that he teaches only Christ and him crucified which means that it is the death and Resurrection of Jesus that atoned for the sins of men and women; and that we are justified to God by faith in Jesus.

His first doctrine was of little importance to the Jewish-Christians, and his second doctrine will be rejected by the Gnostics. These two became the most important doctrines for the early proto-orthodox Christians. The third doctrine will cause great consternation during the entire development of the Christian faith (even to the present time).

Fig. 36 recaps the entire history of Christianity from early Mesopotamia though, the centuries of foreign rule, and influence on Israel—to the foundation of the Jesus Movement and the first Church Council.

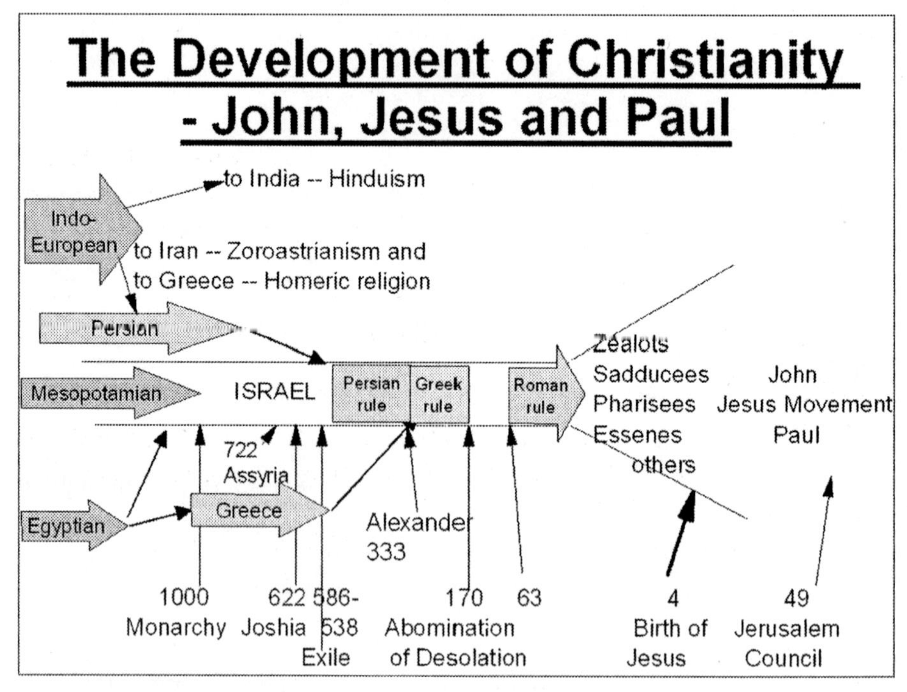

Fig. 36 History and Development of Christianity to Paul and the Jerusalem Council

Paul and the Jewish Christians—a Comparison

We've looked at an early Church conflict, now we'll delve deeper into the problems that arose.

As with any group of strong willed people, opinions had rapidly hardened into factions. The Pauline and Jewish-Christian conflicts are still apparent in the canonical books of Acts and the Pauline epistles, in spite of the years that distanced the writings from the conflicts.

Paul vs. the Jewish-Christians:

> Who exactly was Jesus?
> Who spoke for him?
> What was Jesus' good news?
> How could one join the Movement?

Who exactly was Jesus?

The monotheistic Jewish-Christians would not have more than one God, which relegated Jesus to being a son of man; that is, a human being.

But Paul claimed that Jesus was also somehow divine, that he was the Son of God. He was sent here by God to suffer and die for our salvation. Here, we see the influence of the ancient Mystery Religions with their dying and resurrected god.

This question of the identity of Jesus would foreshadow the great Christological debates of the fourth century.

Jesus was probably not a Pharisee (like Paul claimed to be), nor a Qumran Essene (possibly like the Baptist), but did agree with these sects on some issues. However, he agrees so closely with the teachings of the Pharisee Hillel that it could be argued that he indeed was a Pharisee who wanted to reform the sect.

Who spoke for Jesus?

At first Simon (who was renamed Peter), then James, the brother of Jesus, led the Jewish Christians of the Jerusalem church.

We don't hear of most of the Twelve in Paul's letters or Acts.

Paul laid claim to Apostleship, but the Jerusalem church never recognized him as such.

The Seven of Acts 6 started Hellenist churches throughout the Diaspora.

By the time of the Apostolic Council (ca. 49), there were other "pillars" speaking for the church.

After the Antioch incident, the church split; with Paul working almost exclusively with the Gentiles and the other factions working mostly with the Jews. However, we do see Paul's missions being interfered with by Judaizers and other unknown persons.

The Jerusalem church continued to be a sect of Judaism and had only the intention to reform.

What was Jesus' Good News?

For the Jewish-Christians, the good news was the Kingdom of God. They believed that the Kingdom had arrived (see Gospels of Matthew and Luke). Matthew is the most Jewish-Christian of the Gospels, in that it stresses the keeping of the Law; however, by the time of its writing (ca. 85 CE), Matthew's community had accepted the idea of Jesus being somehow divine.

Paul claimed that the good news was of Jesus' death and resurrection; that works (law) were of no value, and that we are saved by grace and faith alone.

He believed that the Kingdom was still to come very soon (see Gospels of John, Mark, and the Epistles).

How could one join the Movement?

The Jewish-Christians insisted that one follow the Law before being accepted. In order to become a Christian, one had to first be Jewish.

Paul insisted that the Law was not necessary, indeed, was counter to salvation, for Gentiles to join the church

The Jerusalem Council, in the interest of unity, compromised. They allowed that the Gentiles need only follow the Noachide minimal law, which meant refraining from meat sacrificed to idols, fornication, meat of strangled animals, and blood.

This compromise did not last long.

Splinter Jewish-Christian sects would evolve and, eventually, be declared heretical. A main one was the Ebionites.

The Ebionites (A Sect of Jewish-Christians)

A generation after the fall of Jerusalem (ca. 100 CE), the Ebionites were making these claims about Jesus: He—

- was a religious Jew
- adhered to the spirit rather than the letter of the Torah Laws
- taught social justice, judgment for the exploitive rich and the rule of God for the poor
- was chosen as God's son at his baptism but was otherwise not divine
- called for acceptance of the reign of God and living as though it were already here
- was not pre-existent nor born of a virgin

The proto-orthodox Church condemned them as heretics; however, they continued as small enclaves in Galilee and the Trans Jordan (Peraea, Decapolis).

They ceased to exist after 450 CE.

With **Fig. 37**, we will take leave of the history portion of the graphic and concentrate solely on the post-Jesus development of Christianity. By the end of the First century, we have, at least, the two Christianities, as shown below:

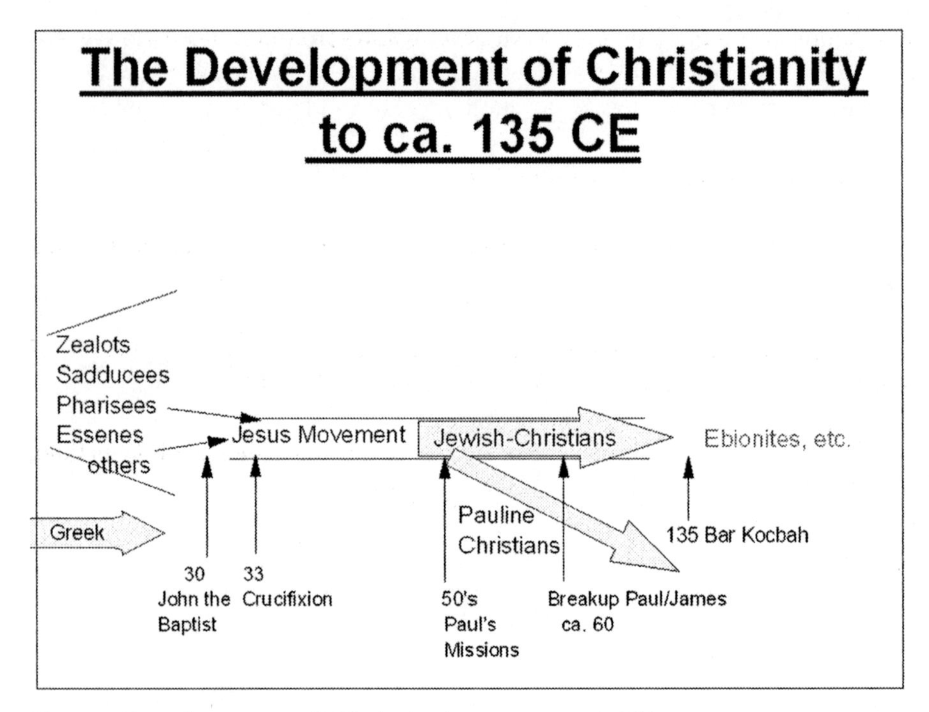

Fig. 37 Development of Christianity to ca. 135 CE

There were several other offshoots of Jewish-Christianity. Some of them, such as the Nazarenes, were closer in doctrine to what became orthodox Christianity than the Ebionites. They all either merged with the mainline Church or were eventually extinguished.[148]

Pauline Christian Theodicy

St. Paul—Five responses to innocent suffering

> "Shall we say that God is unjust?"…
> "By no means!" (Romans 9:14)

1—There is suffering because people are wicked—"since all have sinned and fallen short of the glory of God; they are now justified by his grace as a gift,

148. An important document from ca. 200 CE, the Pseudo-Clementine *Recognitions*, contains a description of a Jewish Christian who finds himself both separated from Judaism and outside of the evolving Greek Christian church.

through the redemption that is Christ Jesus, whom God put forward as a sacrifice of atonement by his blood effective through faith" (Romans 3:23–25).

2—We suffer because of the guilt of our ancestors; the sin of Adam shows the human tendency to evil (Romans 5:12f).

3—Suffering is educational in that it builds character and shows need for God (Romans 5:3–5).

4—The creator himself suffers because of Jesus' death on the cross and because of our evil ways; we must share his suffering (Romans 8:18–26).

5—Suffering is only temporary, since those elected for salvation, a gift from God, will receive an eternal blessed life (Romans 9:14ff).

THE EARLY HERETICS

Marcion the Proto-Gnostic

As with most heretical works, we have nothing of the writings of Marcion, except what quotes we get from his enemies. The primary sources for information concerning him come from the Church Fathers: Justin Martyr (110–165 CE), Irenaeus (120–202), Epiphanius (315–403), Hippolytus (170–236), and especially Tertullian (145–220) who wrote five books (called *Adversus Marcionem*) condemning Marcion.

In these sources we learn that Marcion was born ca. 110 CE in Sinope, Pontus in Asia Minor. His father was the bishop of the church there, and had the unfortunate occasion to see his son expelled from the church at Sinope. This was allegedly for (according to Epiphanius)[149] committing adultery. More likely, he was run off because of his unorthodox beliefs.

Since he was a rich merchant and ship owner, he was able to leave Asia Minor and move to Rome around 135 CE, where he ensured his acceptance by giving the Roman church 200,000 sesterces (a large gift).

While in Rome he met the Gnostic teacher, Cedro, who taught that the God of the Old Testament was not the same as the God and Father of Jesus. This was to be a common assertion among the later Gnostic movements. For now, it propelled Marcion into a radical disassociation from anything to do with Judaism.

Since Paul had been most adamant about ridding Christianity of the Jewish Law, Marcion felt that Paul was the truest representative of the church. Marcion accepted only one gospel as authoritative, that of Luke because he had been a faithful disciple of Paul's. Taking Paul's letter to the Galatians, as a proof text, he explained that "false brethren" had corrupted all of the gospels, except Luke:

---

149. Epiphanius, *Against Heresies* 43.1. Louis Berkhof, *The History of Christian Doctrines.* (London: Banner of Truth, 1978), 52.

> I marvel that ye are so soon removed from him that called you into the grace of Christ unto another gospel; which is not another; but there be some that trouble you, and would pervert the gospel of Christ. (Galatians 1:6–7)

Furthermore, there could be only one gospel:

> But though we, or an angel from heaven, preach any other gospel unto you than that which we have preached unto you, let him be accursed. As we said before, so say I now again, if any man preach any other gospel unto you than that ye have received, let him be accursed. (Galatians 1:8–10)

His radical theology got him summarily excommunicated from the Roman Church in 144 CE.[150] The Church wanted to be rid of him so they returned his gift and bid him to leave. He did leave and used the money to spread his message across the empire.

He built an organization exactly like the Orthodox Church—later Fathers had to warn their people to avoid being duped by a Marcionite church.[151]

Marcion's doctrines

What horrified the Romans so much that they would return his money? It wasn't his rejection of other gospels; it was his rejection of the God of the Hebrew Bible:

> Marcion laid down the position that Christ, who in the days of Tiberius was by a previously unknown god revealed for the salvation of all nations, is a different being from he who was ordained God, the Creator for the restoration of a Jewish state, and who is yet to come. Between these, he interposes a separation of a great and absolute difference as great as lies

150. Marcion was excommunicated by the first sole Bishop of Rome, St Pius I (140–155). This was a major step toward establishing the Papacy. The next steps were: Victor I (189–198), attempting to legislate the date of Easter for the entire Church (Quatrodeciman controversy); St. Stephen I (254–257), using Matthew 16:18 to justify primacy of Rome; St. Siricius (384–399), issuing a decretal claiming that Peter is present in the Bishop of Rome; St. Leo the Great (440–461), claiming universal papal authority. The title of Pope was restricted to the Bishop of Rome in 1073.

151. Cyril of Jerusalem cautioned believers, lest they should be fooled into agreeing with a Marcionite church by error (*Catechetical Lectures* 4:1 4).

> between what is just and what is good, as great as lies between the law and the gospel, as great as is the difference between Christianity and Judaism (Tertullian, *Against Marcion*, IV.6).

His main doctrinal points were a total rejection of the Old Testament and a distinction between the inferior (but just) God of the Jews and the supreme God who sent Jesus as his messenger to save us from the bondage of Yahweh.

Many thinkers, before and after Marcion, would be struck by the crudities and anthropomorphisms of the Hebrew Bible, but the ones who wanted to accept it (like Philo, Ambrose, and Augustine) would see the Biblical myths as allegories of a greater reality. This was not so with Marcion; he could see only the literal meaning of the texts, and rejected them as being beneath the Father of Jesus.

In his *Antitheses* (Contradictions), he laid out all of the offending verses, and used them as proof against the scripture and the God of the scripture. Jesus' God was infinitely better than the barbaric God portrayed in the Old Testament, as stated by Justin:

> And there is Marcion a man of Pontus, who is even at this day alive, and teaching his disciples to believe in some other god greater than the Creator. And he, by the aid of the devils, has caused many of every nation to speak blasphemies, and to deny that God is the maker of this universe, and to assert that some other being, greater than He, has done greater works. All who take their opinions from these men are, as we before said, called Christians.[152]

Tertullian wrote:

> These are Marcion's Antitheses, or contradictory propositions, which aim at committing the gospel to a variance with the law, in order that from the diversity of the two documents, which contain them, they may contend for a diversity of gods also.[153]

For Marcion, a radical Paulinist, Jesus had rejected the Law and the Prophets. He claims the God of the Old Testament is the Creator of this miserable world and

152.Justin Martyr, First Apology, 26, in *Apostolic Fathers* (AF), vol. 1, edited by Cleveland A. Coxe (Grand Rapids: Eerdmans, 1981), 171.

153.Tertullian, AM 1.19, in ANF, vol. 3, 285.

cannot be the God of Jesus. As with most dualists, he considered the flesh so evil that Jesus could not possibly have been born into this world as a human being but only seemed to be human. Therefore, there would be nothing in his theology that would allow anything to do with the flesh: no virgin birth, no crucifixion, and no resurrection. In fact, he thought the body so evil that marriage was forbidden to his followers, which prohibition probably contributed to the eventual demise of the sect.

Even so, the Marcionites gathered enough converts to last into the fifth century. Even though many of them assimilated with the later Manichees, there was still some mention of Marcionites in the tenth century.

Marcion's contributions to the Church

Marcion created the first New Testament canon, which consisted of 10 letters of Paul, an edited Gospel of Luke, and his own Antitheses. This forced the Church to form its own canon, so that there would be no question of what was the truth for the orthodox believers.

One Biblical commentator, F.F. Bruce, suggests that:

> The chief importance of Marcion in the second century lies in the reaction that he provoked among the leaders of the Apostolic Churches. Just as Marcion's canon stimulated the more precise defining of the NT canon by the Catholic Church, not to supersede but to supplement the canon of the OT, so, more generally, Marcion's teaching led the Catholic Church to define its faith more carefully, in terms calculated to exclude a Marcionite interpretation.[154]

Marcion's total rejection of Judaism forced the Church to re-evaluate its relationship with its parent religion. Although the orthodox had abandoned the Law, they, nevertheless, saw that they could not abandon the Jewish scriptures, since Christianity needed their antiquity to retain legitimacy in the Roman world and to claim themselves as the fulfillment of the older revelation.

The Marcionites would reject allegory, accept revelation, and encourage church organization; while their fellow dualists would embrace allegory, reject revelation, and distain organization. Those fellow dualists would be known as the Gnostics.

---

154. F.F. Bruce, *The Spreading Flame* (Exeter: Paternoster Press, 1964), 252.

The Gnostics (Encapsulation)

~ All Gnostics are Dualists but not all Dualists are Gnostics ~

Gnosticism proper occurs in the first century, as various sects of the growing Christian movement. There were several groups of Gnostics with differing views (some of which are discussed later), but one thing they held in common was a belief in the dualism of good and evil, which they concretized by spirit opposed to matter.

Another thing that defined all of the Gnostics was that they valued gnosis (equals knowledge in Greek) above all else. This was not knowledge of the scientific kind, but the intuitive knowing of who you really are—an eternal part of the divine.

Dualism, itself, has a long history that can be traced to the remote past. One of the first systematic dualists was Zarathustra (in Greek, Zoroaster), who is believed to have taught around 1200 BCE. Sometimes dualist religions, such as Zoroastrianism, are confused with Gnosticism; however, Zoroastrianism is itself not Gnostic but its ideas may very well have played a significant role in the later development of Gnostic Christianity.

The most haunting question for those who believe in a good and powerful god is that of the existence of evil in the world. How can such evil be accounted for? As we've seen in Part II, Zoroaster offered an account by positing two forces—one good and one evil—that were in constant battle for supremacy. The presence of the evil force absolved the good god of any culpability for the personal and natural evils in the world, thus, providing the world with the first solution to the Theodicy trilemma.

Although Zoroastrianism was dualistic with the sons of light battling the sons of darkness, it was not Gnostic because it claimed, as did later Judaism, that matter was the good creation of the good god and, therefore, not evil.

The dualism of the Greek Orphics, who flourished around the sixth century BCE, could be considered a forerunner of Christian Gnosticism in that they, indeed, held matter to be evil and that the human body itself, being matter, was a prison for the divine spark that resided within each of us. Their goal was to recognize that they were a soul that had fallen from a lofty place into this fleshly prison and, thereby, recover that place upon leaving the body.

Plato (ca. 385 BCE) was to take up and expand upon this doctrine, and put the force of philosophy behind his concept of the immortal soul. His philosophy was to greatly influence later Jewish and Christian thought concerning the afterlife.

Around the time of Jesus, the Greek ideas (mixed with those of the Persians) had manifested themselves in Jewish literature. The intertestamental Book of Wisdom is clearly Platonic, and the earlier Jewish sect of the Essenes expounded a dualistic religion, much like that of Zoroaster.

In the writings of the Essenes, we find the same battle between the sons of light and the sons of darkness (that Zoroaster had espoused 1000 years earlier). Now the idea of the spiritual, in opposition to the material, intruded on the Jewish idea: that God's creation was very good and matter became held as being lower than spirit.

When Jesus came preaching the Kingdom of God, he was constantly misunderstood by all who heard him. Indeed, the New Testament concept of the Kingdom of God is quite ambiguous, allowing any number of sects to interpret it as they wished. One can read scriptural passages that can clearly be taken as Gnostic and this is what allowed them (and other sects) to flourish.

"The Kingdom of God is within you" is a basic teaching of the Greek Orphics, and evolved into the teachings of various Gnostic groups. All of these claimed that a divine spark resides in a person and what is needed is knowledge of "where you came from, what you are, and where you are going." This is in order to insure that the sparks of divinity ascend to their celestial home, when freed from the prison of the flesh.

Most Gnostics took the Orphic's beliefs to the extreme that claimed that flesh was evil and that the material world had been created by a lesser god. Only those with this knowledge could escape the evil world and return to the world of the highest God.

John the Baptist most likely came out of the dualist Jewish Essene movement which looked forward to the Kingdom, and Jesus' message concerning the Kingdom could easily be a modified version of that movement.

Eventually, the evolving orthodox Church would drive the Gnostic movements underground with its extreme polemic of the second and third centuries.

Nevertheless, the Gnostic beliefs would come back repeatedly throughout history.[155]

The Christian Gnostics

Valentinus (ca. 100–175), Basilides (second century), and others took Plato's dislike of the body to excessive extreme, claiming that it was evil. They also took his Demiurge and translated it into the creator God of Israel and equated it with the flawed Ialtabaoth; thus, making the creation of the world an error that had to be overcome.

Some individuals were thought to posses a spark of the divine substance acquired from Wisdom through her offspring, Ialtabaoth:

> And Ialtabaoth blew some of its spirit, that is, the power of its mother, upon him [Adam].
>
> The Secret Book According to John[156]

In some Gnostic systems, they were the only ones who could hope to return to the divinity after death. This return is modeled on Plato's ladder of ascent to the highest Good, as he spelled out in the *Symposium* (210a–212a). The Gnostics also introduced the non-Platonic concept of a redeemer figure, who was sent by the real God to bring gnosis to those "elect".

The most famous of the Gnostic theologians was Valentinus. He was born in Egypt, and like Marcion, went to Rome about 136 CE where he hoped to be elected as bishop. Rome snubbed him and he left the proto-Orthodox church and went his own way, setting up the largest of Gnostic schools.

His school taught that groups of 30 Aeons made up the spiritual world (the "Pleroma" (fullness) of the Primal Ground of Being who emanates the Aeons). One group of Aeons, the Ogdoad, are called: Depth, Silence, Mind, Truth, Word,

---

155. e.g., Manicheans (third century), Paulicans (seventh), Bogomils (tenth), Cathari/Albigensians (twelfth), and in more recent times: Masons, New Age, Unity, etc.

156. This work is also known as the *Apocryphon of John* and contains the classic Gnostic myth of creation. St. Irenaeus wrote against this work, ca. 180 CE, so it dates from before that time.

Life, Man, and Church. Another group was the Decad (10) and Dodecad (12). The last of the Dodecad was Wisdom, also called Sophia.

Our world was the result of the error of Sophia, who produced a god who did not know of the Pleroma, and thought himself to be the supreme god. This offspring of Sophia was identified with the Creator God of the Hebrew Bible. It was his fault that the material world was created evil. But, he is also credited with providing humanity with the spark of divinity that is able to return to the Pleroma. Christ is the Aeon who is sent by the Pleroma to redeem humanity by bringing the saving knowledge (gnosis) to the spiritual people.

Two hundred years before the great Trinitarian debates of Orthodox Christianity, the:

> Gnostic, Valentinus, the leader of a sect, was the first to devise the notion of the three subsistent entities (hypostases), in a work that he entitled *On the Three Natures*. For, he derived the notion of three subsistent entities and three persons—father, son, and holy spirit.[157]

Philosophical basis of Gnosticism

The philosophical basis of Gnosticism was the problem of good and evil, which is a major topic in this book—Theodicy. Gnosticism starts with the same premise as Marcionism, stated briefly:

> - The world is obviously full of imperfection.
>
> - The perfect Supreme Being could not be the author of such imperfection, since imperfection cannot come from perfection.
>
> - The Hebrew Bible (Christian Old Testament) represents Yahweh as the Creator of the world.
>
> - Hence, since his world is imperfect, its Creator, Yahweh, must also be imperfect.

157. Valentinus Fragment B.

> - Therefore, the religion of the Jews (as found in the Old Testament) is, thus, not the true religion; and Yahweh is not the true God.

This conclusion allows the Gnostic to account for the present world order, without compromising the character of the Supreme Being.

Of course, the next obvious question would be; how did the Creator of this world, Yahweh, come to be? Is he not imperfection brought forth from the perfection of the Supreme Being? So, we must still inquire, "how could Perfection bring forth Imperfection?" Asked another way:

> How did the One—changeless and eternal reality—bring forth the transient world of creation?

This takes us back to the Ionian philosophers of the sixth Century BCE when they looked at the cosmos and wondered, "how did the One (being) turn into the many (becoming)?" The Gnostics will provide an answer.

Characteristics of Gnosticism

That answer is clever, but not entirely new, since they took their solution from a further development of the ideas of Plato. It consists of emanations, where a series of emanations produced Aeons to mediate the perfect Supreme Being to the imperfect world.

Recall that the Egyptian god, Ptah (discussed in Part II), emanated the other gods from his own substance. The Gnostics modeled their cosmology on these Egyptian/Platonic precursors to produce subsequent beings of progressively lesser and lesser perfection, as they receded from the source of Perfection. Finally, a being comes into existence that does not know the Perfection and thinks of himself as all powerful. This lesser being is the Creator God of the Old Testament who creates the material world.

Thus, we have a dualism where matter is evil, but spirit is good. The Gnostics believed that the material world is evil—the goal is to set free the spirit that is entrapped in a physical existence.

They believed this was possible through the reception of secret teachings by which one obtained γνόσις (Gnosis = knowledge).

The Gnostics were extreme dualists, agreeing with the Greek Orphics about the soul being trapped in the body but greatly differing in cosmology.

They adhered to Docetism, where the rejection of the flesh forbade the Messiah to have a real body. His body only "seemed" physical (from the Greek δοκέο to seem).

Just as did Marcion, the Gnostics had great hostility to Judaism and claimed that its God is evil or, at the very least, ignorant and imperfect.

Part of the reason for their short existence was their exclusivity. They held that most humans are ignorant of the divine spark within (dualism of material and spiritual), and were convinced that there were three classes of humans who were predestined to be fleshy (Choics), reasoning (Psychics), or spiritual (Pnuematics).

They, of course, were the spiritual class, but some Gnostics allowed that even the reasoning Psychics could achieve salvation through Christian faith and good works. However, the physical Choics were dammed from the start. They were also fatalistic in that they believed that one cannot help oneself but is dependent on outside help.

Since salvation comes from knowing who you are, where you come from, and where you are going, they thought that Jesus had come from the Supreme Father to provide the help necessary for saving knowledge.

The doctrines of predestination and the need for outside help would continue through subsequent sectarians, including the great St. Augustine and the Protestant Reformers.

There were many sects with various beliefs, however, the two most important were: Basilides (ca. 130) in Alexandria and Valentinus (ca. 140) in Rome. They (and other Gnostic groups) caused much grief for the proto-orthodox church, and forced the development of the orthodox canon and creeds.

Some earliest possible Gnosticisms in the New Testament

Bible Reference	Date of Reference and Issue
Acts 8:9–24	ca. 85, Simon Magus, considered the father of Gnostics
Matthew 4:8–9	ca. 85, Jesus is offered world by its ruler, the Devil (a Gnostic belief)
Revelations 2:2, 6, 15, 20–23	ca. 90, false apostles, Nicolaitans
2 John 7	ca. 95, Docetic deceivers
2 Peter 2: 1–22	ca. 100, escaped the world through knowledge
1 Timothy 6:20	ca. 140, is the first certain reference to Gnostics by name
Jude 4–19	ca. 140, condemned as "certain intruders," possibly Carpocrates, who taught reincarnation
2 Thessalonians 2:7–8	ca. (?), the lawless may be Gnostic
Colossians 2:8	ca. 62(?), possibly a reference to Docetic philosophy

Fig. 38 Some Possible Gnostic References in the New Testament.
Last two are least probable.

The story of Nag Hammadi: the finding of the Gnostic library

The mid-1940's was a marvelous time for the advancement of knowledge of ancient religion.

In 1947, an accidental find of manuscripts written in Hebrew, Aramaic, and Greek (on papyrus, vellum and copper) opened up the world of the ancient Jewish sect, which was known only sketchily heretofore. These became known as the *Dead Sea Scrolls* and have been dated to the first centuries BCE and CE. These scrolls were buried, probably for safekeeping, before 68 CE in caves in the Judean Desert around the site of the Dead Sea enclave—believed to have been inhabited by the Essenes. With this find, we discovered almost all of the books of the Old Testament, as they existed over a thousand years before our previous extant manuscripts.

In 1945, an equally accidental find of manuscripts, written in Coptic (late Egyptian), was made near the town of Nag Hammadi in Upper Egypt. These were in the form of codices, or books, and contained a large store of information (13 leather bound volumes containing 52 texts). It was ca. 350 CE when they were buried. At least 42 of the texts were previously unknown works. Before this find, we knew very little about the Gnostic sect of Christians, except that which was found in the writings of St. Irenaeus and other heresiologists (of the first centuries of Christianity) like Tertullian, Hippolytus, and the much later Epiphanius of Salamis (ca. 315–403).

Obviously, this sect had lost the battle over who would become the Orthodox, and the probable scenario is that the Gnostic Christians buried their books for safekeeping, until such time as they would regain favor. As with the sectarians of the Dead Sea, that time never came.

Some Gnostic literature and their doctrines:

The Nag Hammadi codices discovered in 1945 are only a portion of a larger body of Gnostic literature, which is now fairly large.[158] Here we will look at only a representative sample that illustrates some Gnostic principles:

Letter to Flora from Ptolemy

Ptolemy was a disciple of Valentinus and followed in his tradition with a few modifications. In this Letter to Flora, who was an ordinary Christian, he attempts to persuade her of the truth concerning the Law, as found in the Hebrew Bible.

He tells her that some people say that the Law comes from God and some say the Devil. This is wrong, for in actuality, the Law comes from three sources: God, Moses, and the elders. The Laws created by the latter two are distinct from the legislation of God.

Now the Law of God itself is divided into three parts also:

> Pure but imperfect—his example is the Ten Commandments which Jesus came, not to abolish, but to fulfill.
>
> Interwoven with injustice—his example here is the *lex talionis* (an eye for an eye…), which he claims the Savior did abolish.

---

158. For an excellent book containing the texts of Gnostic scriptures, see: Bently Layton, *The Gnostic Scriptures*, (New York, Doubleday, 1987).

> Symbolic—as an example he gives the law of circumcision, which is to be taken only symbolically. The real circumcision is that of the heart. So, these laws are to be kept, but not physically as before.

If God's Law at its loftiest is pure but still imperfect, what does that say about the God who made them? He is not the highest God! He is only an intermediate God who was the craftsman of this material world and, although just and good, ranks below the true and perfect God who sent Jesus into the world in order to fulfill the pure (but imperfect) Laws, and to give humans the knowledge (gnosis) necessary for their salvation.

This letter to the ordinary Christian, Flora, also indicates that this school of Gnostics believed that both spirituals and psychics could live close to the Pleroma.

The Hymn of the Pearl from the Acts of Thomas

The Acts of Thomas relates the story of one Didymus Judas Thomas,[159] the twin brother of Jesus, as he wanders about preaching and doing miracles. As a small part of the text, there is a beautiful poem that describes the search for a pearl in a far country.

The text of the story is about the son of a King of the East who set out to retrieve a pearl from Egypt. He passes through frightening lands and once there he puts on their style of dress in order to blend in. The Egyptians poisoned him with something that made him forget who he was and what was his purpose. Eventually his plight came to the attention of his parents and they sent a missive declaring:

> Arise, and become sober out of your sleep.
> Listen to the words written in this letter.
> Remember that you are a child of kings.
> You have fallen under a servile yolk.
> Call to mind your garment shot with gold.
> Call to mind the pearl for which you were sent…
> Your name has been called to the book of life,
> …in our kingdom.

159. The name Thomas is Syriac and means "the twin"; he was also called Didymus, which is the Greek equivalent.

Whereupon, he remembers his true nature, accomplishes his mission, puts on his fine garment, and is guided home to the King, carrying the pearl.

On its surface, this is an adventure tale. What of the sub-text? If read allegorically, the story becomes:

> The true God of the spiritual realm
> Sends a soul past the celestial bodies
> To a foreign place in the material realm where it puts on a fleshy garment
> To get educated (gnosis)
> While there, the heavy material garment makes the soul forget who it is
> A missive (Jesus) comes to remind it of its place of origin
> The dirty garment is thrown off
> He is guided past the celestial bodies toward the spiritual realm
> He reunites with the true God, having been educated

This scenario is reminiscent of the "life-death-true life" saying of the Orphics, where one is alive in the spiritual world, falls into death in the material world, then becomes alive again in the spiritual.

The Gospel of Thomas

We have no record of this text from the early Fathers, as we do of the first two texts above. All of our knowledge of this text comes from three fragmentary Greek papyri found at Oxyrhynchus in Egypt in the late 1800's and, more importantly, a full Coptic text found at Nag Hammadi.

It is a "sayings" gospel of the collected sayings of Jesus. The same twin brother, Didymus Judas Thomas, of Jesus is credited with the compilation but this is unlikely. The Coptic manuscript was copied sometime before 350 CE and the original composition likely goes back to the late first century to the mid-second century. This would put it after the other "sayings" gospel we will discuss later (the document known as Q).

Just as we'll see with the earliest part of the Q document, Thomas shows Jesus as a teacher of wisdom. There is no reference to later Christian eschatological doctrines, nor to most later doctrines. The entire work consists of 114 sayings of Jesus. Some representative ones are produced below:

All of the sayings of Jesus cluster about these topics:

The Kingdom of Heaven is within.
Human existence is not true existence.
Salvation is through self-knowledge.

3) Jesus said, "If those who lead you say, "See, the Kingdom is in the sky," then the birds of the sky will precede you. If they say to you, "It is in the sea," then the fish will precede you. Rather, the Kingdom is inside of you, and it is outside of you. When you come to know yourselves, then you will become known, and you will realize that it is you who are the sons of the living Father. But if you will not know yourselves, you dwell in poverty and it is you who are that poverty."

20) The disciples said to Jesus, "Tell us what the Kingdom of Heaven is like." He said to them, "It is like a mustard seed, the smallest of all seeds. But when it falls on tilled soil, it produces a great plant and becomes a shelter for birds of the sky." (cf. Mt 13:31–32, Mk 4:30–32, Lk 13:18–19).

29) Jesus said, "If the flesh came into being because of spirit, it is a wonder. But if spirit came into being because of the body, it is a wonder of wonders. Indeed, I am amazed at how this great wealth has made its home in this poverty."

37) His disciples said, "When will You become revealed to us and when shall we see You?"
Jesus said, "When you disrobe without being ashamed and take up your garments and place them under your feet like little children and tread on them, then [will you see] the Son of the Living One, and you will not be afraid"

46) Jesus said, "Among those born of women, from Adam until John the Baptist, there is no one so superior to John the Baptist that his eyes should not be lowered (before him). Yet I have said whichever one of you comes to be a child will be acquainted with the Kingdom and will become superior to John." (cf. Mt 11:11, Lk 7:28).

50) Jesus said, "If they say to you, "Where did you come from?', say to them, "We came from the light, the place where the light came into being on its own accord and established [itself] and became manifest through their image." If they say to you, "Is it you?', say, "We are its children, we are the elect of the Living Father." If they ask you, "What is the sign of your father in you?", say to them, "It is movement and repose."

51) His disciples said to Him, "When will the repose of the dead come about, and when will the new world come?"
He said to them, "What you look forward to has already come, but you do not recognize it."

53) His disciples said to Him, "Is circumcision beneficial or not?"
He said to them, "If it were beneficial, their father would beget them already circumcised from their mother. Rather, the true circumcision in spirit has become completely profitable."

62) Jesus said, "It is to those [who are worthy of My] mysteries that I tell My mysteries. Do not let your left hand know what your right hand is doing." (cf. Mt 13:11, Mk 4:11, Lk 8:10; Mt 6:3).

70) Jesus said, "If you bring forth what is within you, what you bring forth will save you. If you do not bring forth what is within you, what you do not bring forth will destroy you."

84) Jesus said, "When you see your likeness, you rejoice. But when you see your images which came into being before you, and which neither die nor become manifest, how much you will have to bear!"

113) His disciples said to Him, "When will the Kingdom come?"
<Jesus said,> "It will not come by waiting for it. It will not be a matter of saying "Here it is" or "There it is." Rather, the Kingdom of the Father is spread out upon the earth, and men do not see it."

The Anti-Gnostic Apostle's Creed

The Gnostics:

- denied a divine act of creation;

- believed the redeemer Christ only seemed* to be (Docetism—Jesus was divine, and only seemed to be human);
- believed He did not really suffer;
- believed matter was evil—so resurrection was spiritual.

Hence, the creed…

The Apostle's Creed was formulated to combat Gnosticism:

> I believe in God, the Father almighty, creator of heaven and earth.
> I believe in Jesus Christ, God's only Son, our Lord, who was conceived by the Holy Spirit, born of the Virgin Mary, suffered under Pontius Pilate, was crucified, died, and was buried; he descended into Hell (the dead).
> On the third day he rose again; he ascended into heaven, he is seated at the right hand of the Father, and he will come again to judge the living and the dead.
> I believe in the Holy Spirit, the holy catholic Church, the communion of saints, the forgiveness of sins, the resurrection of the body, and the life everlasting. Amen.

The Apostle's Creed probably dates from the sixth century, but was derived from a late second century form, which was known as the Roman Symbol. This creedal statement was promulgated in order to oppose Gnostic and Marcionite doctrines. There is one God, the Creator of the world, who was the Father of Jesus. Jesus was born into the flesh of a human woman. There will be a judgment of both the living and the dead and a resurrection of the flesh (body). The dualist heretics had denied all of these assertions.

Comparison of true Gnosticism with Marcionism

Marcion held the Gnostic idea that creation was flawed, being the creation of a lesser god. This made him a dualist, who believed in a higher God, and a lower Demiurge, who created this world of matter. But, as said earlier: all Dualists are not Gnostics. Marcion was certainly not a Gnostic, even though some early Christian Fathers, such as Irenaeus of Lyons, Tertullian, and Hippolytus had put him into the same category as the Gnostics.

He may be contrasted with the Gnostics on at least three very important issues:

- Marcion offers no secret doctrines concerning a divine spark imprisoned in a fleshy body.

The term "Gnosis" was not in his vocabulary. Instead, he emphasized belief in Jesus as the redeemer sent by the true God to all people. Salvation was thus available to all men without regard to any kind of spiritual status. It did not involve secret revelations or knowledge of esoteric rituals.

- Marcion has no complex cosmological theories involving a number of heavenly spheres through which the soul has to pass.

Gnostic teachers, such as Valentinus (second century) and Basilides (who taught in Alexandria) taught that salvation was the release of the divine "spark," or pneuma from the "prison" of the fleshly body. After death the pneuma (spirit) has to pass through a number of heavenly spheres; each ruled by a demonic "archon". The number of spheres depended on the particular Gnostic system; Basilides had posited 365 spheres. Possession of Gnosis allowed the spirit to pass through the spheres and be reunited with the "Supreme God".

- Marcion has no complex genealogies designed to insulate the highest being from the material world.

The later Gnostics had multiple layers of gods in order to separate the Supreme God from any responsibility for the creation of this evil world.

Whereas, Marcion would pare his Gospel down to a bare minimum, using only Paul[160] and Luke, the Gnostics produced voluminous texts for their scriptures.

---

160. Marcion used only Paul's epistles. Why? Was Paul a proto-Marcionite, or even an early Gnostic, as some scholars have claimed? Paul was a dualist; his dualism being between flesh and spirit. However, Paul did not believe, as did the Gnostics, that the God of the Old Testament was evil, nor that the world was evil, nor that man's spirit was imprisoned in an evil fleshy body. After all, Christ was born, suffered, died, and was resurrected in the flesh. Thus, Paul still believed in the Jewish concept of a unity of body and spirit; for him there was no Orphic/Platonic/Gnostic immortal soul trapped in the evil body.

The Church Father Tertullian would compare Marcion's reductionism with what he considered Valentinus' expansionism of the scriptures:

> Of the scriptures we have our being before there was any other way, before they were interpolated by [the heretics].... One man perverts the scriptures with his hand, another their meaning by his exposition. For although Valentinus seems to use the entire volume, he has nonetheless laid violent hands on the truth only with a more cunning mind and skill than Marcion. Marcion expressly and openly used the knife, not the pen, since he made such an excision of the scriptures as suited his own subject-matter. Valentinus, however, abstained from such excision, because he did not invent scriptures to square with his own subject-matter...and yet he took away more, and added more, by removing the proper meaning of every particular word (*De Praescriptione Haereticorum*, 38).

Theodicy for the Gnostics

There is evil in the world because it was made flawed by a flawed creator God. Thus, they avoid having the true God be the source of evil.

A major difference in eschatology

The ultimate goal of the Gnostic was to be freed from the bounds of the body (the Kingdom of darkness) and ascend spiritually to the heavens (Kingdom of Light): there to be with God forever.

The early Christian goal was to be resurrected and, with the other saints, rule in the new Kingdom of God that would be established on the earth. Which goal won out?

Both Gnosticism and later Christianity would be modeled on the Platonic concept of the immortal soul ascending non-materially to heaven. Gnosticism would thus intrude on Pauline Christian eschatology—and on other doctrines as well.

Those Greeks Again and Again

By the end of the second century there were three distinct major Christian factions, as shown in **Fig. 39.** The Jewish-Christians were small and isolated by now. The Gnostics were at the height of their influence and the Pauline Christians were the most catholic of them all.

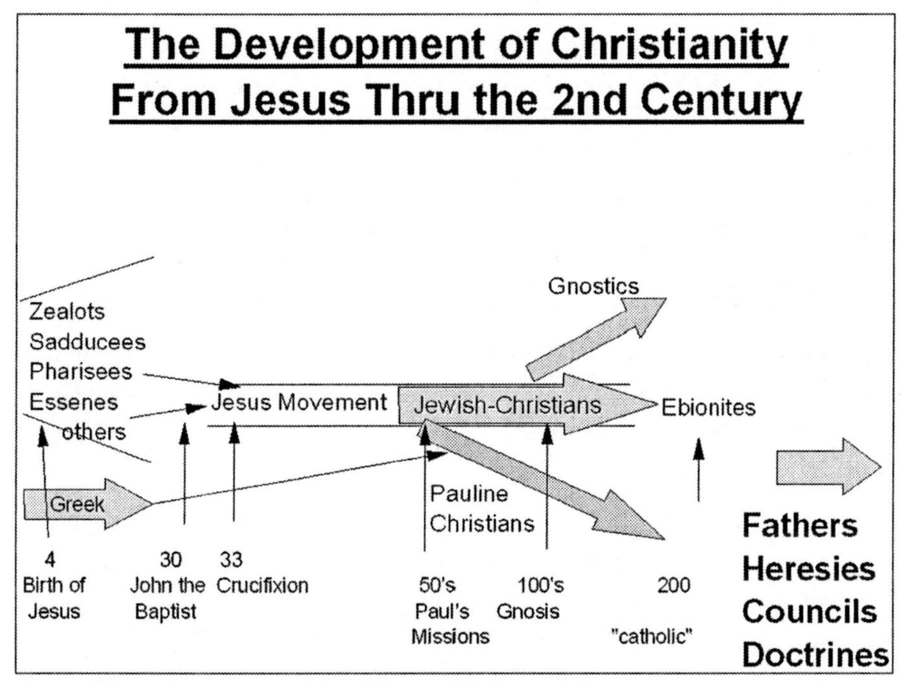

Fig. 39 Development of the Three Christianities

A new philosophy (based on 500-year old Greek thought) was growing that would shake the foundations of two of these Christian groups. The new philosophy favored neither, but was used by both to provide a philosophical basis for their doctrines. The Paulines would use it most effectively and flourish, while the Gnostics would fail.

Plotinus and the New Platonism (Encapsulation)

A revised form of Platonism was founded by Plotinus (ca. 204–270 CE) and promulgated by his disciple, Porphyry. This philosophy became known as Neo-Platonism, since it rests on the original philosophy of Plato. Porphyry[161] describes this link to Platonism:

> So this god-like man above all, who often raised himself in thought, according to the ways Plato teaches in the Banquet, to the First and Transcendent God, that God appeared who has neither shape nor any intelligible form, but is throned above intellect and all the intelligible.[162]

Plotinus was to have an immeasurable effect on subsequent religious thought, especially that of Christianity. Here, we'll briefly look at only two issues: the human soul and the structure of divinity.

Plotinus' Human Soul

As Plato (in the Phaedo 65–84) had done 500 years before, Plotinus was to also posit a duality of soul and body.[163] The Platonic desire was to escape from the world of seeming to the world of the reality of the Forms, the highest being Plato's Good (the One for Plotinus). Indeed, Plato stressed that growth in philosophy is the preparation for death, since it encourages one to progressively separate the soul from the material world. We have seen this philosophy with the Orphics and will see it again in St. Augustine:

> So, when you are such that nothing at all of earthly things delights you, believe me, at the same moment, the same point of time, you will see what you desire.
>
> Soliloquia 1.14.24

---

161. This is the same Porphyry that claimed the Christians of his time had departed from the teachings of Jesus and had made him the god of a new cult. Against the Christians was written by the Roman pagan Porphyry circa 280.

162. Porphyry, *Life of Plotinus*. 23.1-28, trans. A. H. Armstrong. Loeb Classical Library, London: Heineman, 1966.

163. After Plato came Aristotle, the Stoics and the Epicureans who all argued against Plato by claiming that the soul depended on the body (Aristotle) or that the soul was a body [a physical object] (Stoics and Epicureans). Plotinus would have to first disprove their arguments in order to support those of Plato.

Whereas Plato expected the soul to be reunited with the highest Form after death, Plotinus allowed that one could experience a complete union with the ultimate Reality (the One) in this life, and is said (by Porphyry) to have done so on four occasions. This union is possible because the summit[164] of the soul, the human intellect, never completely leaves the realm of the divine, as he says:

> Even our soul does not altogether come down, but there is always something of it in the intelligible (Plotinus 8, 1–3).

As with the earlier dualism of the Orphics, Plotinus' soul falls from the great height into materiality; yet differently from them, only partially. There remains a part of it in the intelligible world through which it may still communicate with the divine. He identifies the soul with the intellect and, since the soul's summit always remains with the divine intellect, he can say that both intellects are one and the same.

This communication is not always a two-way street; it always exists as a union, but we are unaware of it because of our fallen state. Only by being present to our real selves (and rejecting all forms of the material world, including sense perceptions), can we realize this union. It cannot be forced but must await the grace of God.[165] The only action we can take is to be prepared by knowing that we are a duality and by transcending that intrinsic consciousness of self. Plotinus says:

> The man who knows himself is double, one knowing the nature of the reasoning which belongs to the soul, and one up above this man, who knows himself according to Intellect because he has become that Intellect; and by that Intellect he thinks himself again, not any longer as man, but having become altogether the other and snatching himself up into the higher world, drawing up only the better part of the soul (Plotinus 5, 3, 4, 7–12).

---

164. Plotinus departs from Plato who held that the tripartite soul survived death. He agrees with Aristotle that only the summit (Aristotle's mind) survives.

165. Plotinus did not use the term "Grace of God." The later Christian mystics who appropriated Plotinus' philosophy used that term. He simply claimed that we couldn't initiate the experience.

The Structure of Divinity[166]

One of the philosophical problems in ancient Greece was that of the one versus the many. The Ionian philosophers, starting with Thales of Milites, proposed a single substance as the origin and basis of the entire cosmos. Some chose water and some fire as the single original substance, but they then asked how did we get from this basic element to the manifold world we see before us. Plotinus was to address this problem.

Plotinus showed how the "one becomes many" by postulating a hierarchy of divinity in three hypostases:[167]

1. The One Ultimate Being emanates a lower being without any loss of it's own essence;
2. This second divine Being is (Nous), or Mind, which, in turn emanates the third Being in this trinity;
3. The third and lowest divine Being is the animating principle (Psuke), or Soul.

All the many corporeal things, including us, are part of Soul and, as explained above, our only goal should be to return to the One. Plotinus, thus, showed how the material world is an instantiation of God. Although all "souls" were once in communion with the One, estrangement by the fall into materiality has separated them; therefore, there appears to be a multiform world.

This philosophy will be used by the third and fourth centuries Christian Fathers to establish a philosophical basis to underlie the developing complex Christian doctrines. One of the most notable Christian Fathers to use this philosophy will be St. Augustine. It will be noticed in this trinity of Plotinus that the One is equivalent to God—the Supreme Being; Mind is equivalent to the Logos of the One; and Soul is the animating principle that drives the world.

---

166. Plato had posited the single highest Good and subordinate Forms below. Plotinus has his highest entity (the One) emanate a second Hypostasis, the *Nous* or intelligence, which includes the Forms. Then *Nous* emanates a third Hypostasis, the *Psyche* or soul. Matter is then created by *Psyche*, the organizing principle.

167. Hypostasis means "individual being' or "person'. Recall from Part II the Egyptian god, Ptah, who contained within himself all the other gods, being God in multiple persons.

These Platonic issues' (soul and Divinity) impact on later Christianity

Incorporating the Platonic soul into Christian theology caused a problem that has taken a great deal of theological juggling to fix, since it conflicted with the existing Christian doctrine of the resurrection. This problem was mostly overcome by positing a multiple Judgment. The first Judgment is that of the soul, which was judged immediately upon death to go to heaven, hell, or in a later doctrine, purgatory. The resurrection would then take place at the end of the delayed coming of the end of the world, when everyone would undergo a second judgment.

However, this theological problem was so severe that it still lingers today.

The Platonist "view, that God was an immaterial, timeless, and impassible divine being…became a keystone of Christian apologetics, for it served to establish a decisive link to the Greek spiritual and intellectual tradition."[168] However the emphasis on Jesus worship allowed Porphyry to attack this claim to linking Christian thought to Greek philosophy. One reason he did so was that he resented the Christian thinkers having adopted Greek ideas to expound on Christian teaching. Porphyry said Origen "played the Greek, giving a Greek twist to foreign tales" (Eusebius, Eccl. History, 6.19).

The major problem with tying Christianity to Platonism was how to reconcile the transcendent ultimate One with an immanent personal Father figure.

---

168. Robert L. Wilken, *The Christians as the Romans Saw Them*, (Yale University Press, New Haven and London, 1984), 151.

THE CHURCH FATHERS

Here we will briefly look at the most important Church Fathers, primarily their contributions to orthodox doctrine. See essays in later sections ("The Doctrine of *Creatio Ex Nihilo*" on page 185, and "Eschatology in Early Christianity" on page 212), for more details related to the Church Fathers' views on cosmology and eschatology.

After the Apostolic Age, the proto-orthodox Church was led by the "Fathers" of the Patristic Age.

The Apostolic Fathers

Clement of Rome (d. 97)
He wrote 1 Clement in which he says to honor the elders of the church, since they are the appointed leaders. At this time there was generally no monarchical episcopate and most churches were being led by a group of elders. Eschatology: there is an interim existence in heaven for the godly to await resurrection.

Ignatius of Antioch (50–107)
He was the first to use terms "Christianity" and "heretic." At this early time there were some who refused to believe that Jesus was really human and that he only seemed to be; Ignatius fought this error of Docetism. In order to unify the churches, he said that unity requires us to obey the bishops.

Polycarp of Smyrna (69–155)
He was a disciple of the Apostle, John, and mentor of Irenaeus.

Barnabas of Alexandria (late 1st–early 2nd centuries)
He claimed that the Old Testament belongs to the Christians, since the Jews had lost it when Moses broke the tablets at Sinai.

Hermas (second century)
He claimed that we get only one repentance after baptism. Actually, this was a concession since, theretofore, there was no forgiveness after baptism. This is why many delayed baptism until their imminent death.

The Apologetic (Defenders) and Later Fathers

Justin Martyr (100–165)
He was in Rome in 150 CE. His defense of Christianity was that it is old, and this was respected in the Roman Empire. This required that the Old Testament belong to the Christians, since that it is what gave proof to the assertion of antiquity. Both the Jewish and Greek religions contain truth via Divine Reason (*Logos* of the Stoics) which was instilled into the thinkers of an earlier age. The Christian rites looked like the rites of the Greek and Roman Mysteries because of a Satanic conspiracy that allowed the Mysteries to copy the future practices of the true church. He introduced the term "second coming." Eschatology: there is a place to await the general judgment. In his Christology, he held a very undeveloped view that would later give rise to the heresies of Sabellius and, still later, Arius:

> We reasonably worship [Jesus Christ], having learned that He is the Son of the true God Himself, and holding Him in the second place, and the prophetic Spirit in the third *(First Apology*, 65).
> There is...another God and Lord subject to the Maker of all things; who is also called an Angel, because He announces to men whatsoever the Maker of all things-above whom there is no other God-wishes to announce to them....He who is said to have appeared to Abraham, and to Jacob, and to Moses, and who is called God, is distinct from Him who made all things-numerically, I mean, not (distinct) in will *(Second Apology*, 56).

Irenaeus of Lyon in Gaul (150–195)
He wrote *Against the Heretics*, which shows that there were many forms of Christianity in the late second century. One would be in the true church, if one would follow the Apostolic succession. He claimed that the Logos coexisted with the Father. Eschatology: he was the first to claim an intermediate state in Hades to await resurrection, except for martyrs who went directly to their reward.
Both Irenaeus and Justin were millenarians.

Clement of Alexandria (150–215)

He uses Greek philosophy extensively to undergird the doctrines of Christianity, whereas the Gnostics had used it to counter orthodoxy. He said that Greek philosophy and Jewish prophecy was a preparation for Christ. He claims that the sin of Adam was by example, not by generation, as Augustine would later claim.

Tertullian (160–225)

He was from North Africa and the first of the great Latin Fathers. As opposed to the Platonizing Alexandrians, he asked: "What has Athens to do with Jerusalem?" He also believed in the millennium. Eschatology: there is an immediate judgment at death, but all remain in Hades until the resurrection. He mentions the Trinity, but says the Son is created.

His anthropology was among the first of the Fathers, along with Iranaeus, to be taken from the Stoics who believed that humans were a composite of body and soul. He advocated a mixture in which both were corporeal, using the Stoic maxim: *nihil si non corpus* (nothing if not body).

Origen (185–254)

A brilliant Alexandrian, he followed Clement in Platonizing. He merged Greek philosophy with proto-orthodoxy. He said the Bible should be interpreted as required on three levels—body (literal), soul (moral), spirit (allegorical). He was among the first to reject millenarianism in the East; whereas, the West would hold to it for many more years. Eschatology: he rejected eternal punishment and the physical resurrection. He said the Judgment of the soul is at the End, however, the pre-existent soul was kept in an intermediate place of purging until then. Christology: the Son is subordinate to the Father and derived from the Father, although, their relationship was eternal. His doctrines of the pre-existent soul, universal salvation, and subordination would cause him to be condemned by future theologians.

Eusebius of Caesarea (260–340)

He is known for two outstanding things: being a great Church Historian and being the confidant to Emperor Constantine.[169] He wrote the *Praeparatio*

---

169. Constantine's conversion in the early fourth century led first to the acceptance of Christianity; then to its triumph as the religion of the state. He would run the first general church Council that he hoped would help unite his empire. He had a vision that "in this sign (the labarum is from Χρίστος) he would conquer." He was baptized on his deathbed.

Evangelica which claimed that history had proceeded as it did in order to prepare the way toward Christianity. Christology: he defended both Origen and Arius but claimed that the Father's will generated and preceded the Son.

Athanasius (296–373)

Christology: an Alexandrian who fought for Nicean-style orthodoxy against Origen, Eusebius, and the heretic Arius. He is the person most responsible for the concept that Jesus is not derived from, but equal to, the Father. This is a major shift in Christian Platonic hierarchical cosmology. He countered Eusebius' claim of the Father's will generating the Son, by arguing that since the will is changeable, it would be inappropriate to divine nature because the divine would then no longer be eternal.

He sufferred exile on several occasions, since Constantine alternately accepted his theology (Christology); then that of Arius. He would eventually achieve sainthood and Arius would go down in history as the heretic.

St. Augustine (354–430)

He is such a towering figure that we will cover him after the sections on "Heresies" and "Councils" in conjunction with Complex Doctrines.

Church Councils and Heresies

Church Councils (Encapsulation)

Within ten years of the death of The Prophet, in 632 A.D., the Muslims had captured Alexandria and were about to take all of Christian North Africa. In a very short time, the entire area would convert to Islam without a backward look toward their rich heritage of Christianity.

How could such a thing happen in the region that boasted the greatest theologian of the Church, Augustine of Hippo? How was it so easy for these Christians to switch sides? The answers are complex; however, we can simplify by saying that the internal conflicts of the Church contributed greatly to its own demise. Even more simply, we could sum it up in a single word: Christology—the study of defining Christ.

The Christological debates were to consume the attention of Emperor and clergy for many centuries. Indeed, from the very beginning, the followers of Jesus tried to define exactly just who he was and what was his relationship to God. Our earliest written records, the epistles of St. Paul, seem to describe Jesus as the first fruits of the resurrection and, thereby, the adopted Son of God by virtue of that event.

Mark, our earliest Gospel, would appear to move that adoption earlier in Jesus' life, as he becomes the Son of God at his baptism by John. The later Gospels of Matthew and Luke are already claiming that Jesus, at his birth, was the Son of God. By the turn of the first century, John's Gospel, by now completely immersed in the *Logos* of Greek philosophy, identified Jesus as the pre-existing Word of God who was with Him at the beginning of creation.

These documents were selected for inclusion into the canon of the New Testament by the winners of the Christological debates, and the documents that expressed other ideas were consigned to near oblivion by those winners. We, nevertheless, have numerous other sources from Jewish Christians, Gnostics, and many more that we will examine in due course. For now, we will skip forward from the time of John's Gospel (ca. 100 CE) to around 300 CE, the time of Constantine the Great.

Constantine was about to become the sole Emperor of the Empire and was seeking a unifying ideology around which to solidify his far flung lands. The recent persecutions of the Christians had failed to eliminate that threat to pagan solidarity, and the pagan religion was losing its general appeal at the same time that here-to-fore persecuted Christianity was strengthening. By the early 300's, Christianity was made a tolerated religion, along with all of the others. Within a short time, Constantine recognized that here was the cement he was seeking, and made Christianity the preferred religion of the State.

Unfortunately for him, the unity that he saw in this new faith was more apparent than real, and conflicts simmered beneath the surface, as Christians fought one another to define what would eventually become orthodoxy. The greatest threat to his desired unity was the current argument over the status of Jesus. Arius, a presbyter from Alexandria, claimed that Jesus was divine, but that he could not be equal to the Father. After all, common sense would dictate that the Son must be subordinate to the Father. The Bishop of Alexandria would have none of this, and claimed that Jesus the Christ was equal to the Father, for if he were not, how could anyone less than God himself redeem man from his sins?

Constantine was irked by this theological trivia, which was causing a great rift in the church, and called a meeting of the Bishops throughout the Empire to peacefully settle the matter. They were to meet at Nicea in 325 CE and decide, once and for all, the status of Jesus. In spite of Constantine being in attendance, the meeting was rancorous, and this first Ecumenical Church Council took much time in arriving at a conclusion. Basically, Constantine forced a consensus and anyone who did not accede was excommunicated and exiled. Thus, the Arians lost the first round and Constantine now had his unifying force, or so he thought. The persecuted Arians grew in strength, just like all the proto-orthodox Christians had during the earlier persecutions, and they became a force that needed to be reckoned with. Constantine changed his mind and switched to the Arian side and now exiled the Bishop of Alexandria.

A dozen more councils and synods were held over a period of 125 years, going back and forth between the two factions, with each side condemning and excommunicating the other. The details are interesting, but will be glossed over here. Finally, one side gained the political power necessary to force a final conclusion at the Council of Chalcedon in 451 CE. The Jesus of orthodoxy would, henceforth, be equal to God, and they were said to be of the same substance but, nevertheless, constituted two persons.

The losers, now relegated to being heretics, did not quit the fight. Rather, they converted millions of Romans, Greeks, and Barbarians to their side, leaving the Empire theologically divided and politically weakened.

Nowhere were this and other fights more serious than in North Africa; and when Islam marched into that territory with its simple monotheism of a single God, the frustrated inhabitants almost gleefully accepted the peace of mind that it brought.
The above synopsis of two of the first Church Councils gives some indication of the cycle of heresy and orthodoxy that mark the history of the church. In the following chapter, we will look more deeply into them and the other Councils that define the Church, as we see it today. Below is a review of the first seven General Councils recognized by both the Western and Orthodox churches:

Nicea	325	Refuted Arianism and adopted the original Nicene Creed. Jesus is equal to the Father.
Constantinople	381	Condemned Apollinarianism and claimed that Jesus had a human will. Affirmed the deity of the Holy Spirit.
Ephesus	431	Condemned Pelagius' claim that man is not totally corrupted by Original Sin. Condemned Nestorianism and claimed that Jesus is one person.
Chalcedon	451	Condemned Monophysite ("one nature") heresy and claimed that Jesus has two natures in one person.
Constantinople	553	Condemned Theodore of Mopseustia's and other writings as Nestorian.
Constantinople II	680	Denied Monothelitism ("one will") and claimed that Christ had both divine and human wills.
Nicea II	787	Legitimized veneration of icons.

Battlegrounds of Heresy

Since there was such diversity of doctrine in the early Church, an attempt was made by the proto-orthodox Fathers to stamp out what they believed to be false teachings.

The other Christian sects, of course, were doing the same thing.

For some reason one group won out over the others and became the mainline Christian Church with primary bishoprics (**Fig. 40**) in:

Alexandria	Center of Hellenistic Christianity
Antioch	Peter was head of this church after split with Paul
Rome	Pius I (142–155) was first Bishop of Rome
Constantinople	Late-comer after Constantine, ca. 381
Jerusalem	Was re-established late, ca. 451

Fig. 40 Primary Sees of the Early Church

These are the battlegrounds of the many Christianities of the first few centuries. The greatest theological battles will be between the proponents of an overly-human Jesus of Antioch and the overly-divine Jesus of Alexandria. The winner would be called orthodox and the losers were deemed heretics. Below is the listing and chart of these heresies and the church councils that fought them.

MAJOR CHRISTIAN HERESIES

Through the centuries, heresies arose in the evolving orthodox church and each one was eventually declared by the winning side to be non-orthodox. Most disappeared completely, but several continued underground or re-emerged later.

The most important ones were:

The earliest three, we have already seen.

- Judaizers
- Marcionites
- Gnostics

Briefly listed below are the major heresies that came after the Gnostics. They are presented here in outline and tabular format and will be explained further in conjunction with Church Councils.

<u>Montanism</u>

Montanus (ca. 156 CE) was a schismatic who asserted a direct relationship with the Holy Spirit, which brought on speaking in tongues and other charismatic behaviors. He had a strong emphasis on the immanence of Christ's second coming and the New Jerusalem descending from heaven to the earth. He sought a return to the original pure, simple Christianity as against the developing legalism and intellectualism of the proto-orthodox Church. His downfall was that he did these things apart from the structure of the Church and, at least implicitly, challenged the Church's right to interpret revelation.

In response, the Church declared that revelation had ended with the Apostolic Age! Now there was no need for further revelation, nor could there be any. Another response (that was slower in coming), was the eventual elimination of literal apocalyptic expectations by St. Augustine. He will interpret the Millennium allegorically, however, Millenarianism will return over and over again.

Surprisingly, Church Father Tertullian would abandon the proto-orthodox church and join the Montanists.

Manichaeism

Mani (216–276), a Babylonian, claimed the divine was trapped in the flesh of men and that he had the secret knowledge to set free the entrapped goodness of the spirit. Furthermore, the God of the Old Testament, YHWH he argued, was an evil spirit who had entrapped that goodness in creation.

This is, of course, a direct descendant of the Greek Orphics and was essentially a later Gnosticism.

It countered the anthropomorphism of Old Testament with intellectual philosophy and, thus, appealed to the intellectuals of the day. St. Augustine would be a Manichee for nine years before converting to mainline Christianity.

Manichaeism itself would die out but its philosophy would last through its successors: Priscillianism, Albigensianism (also known as Catharism). All would be severely persecuted by the mainline church.

Monarchianism

Meaning "rule of one", Monarchians claimed that God is a single person, the one Father. They argued that Jesus was an ordinary human upon whom came the power of God, usually understood to be at his baptism or his resurrection. Jesus was not God, but God worked in and through him.

This is a form of Adoptionism in that God granted Jesus powers and then adopted him as a Son. There is strong support for this in Paul and Mark.

Modalism

Also known as Sabellianism (ca. 225), which claimed that God is one person in three different modes. The Godhead is a succession of modes where the Father appears as Son and Holy Spirit. Modalism is the argument that God acts in three different modes, but one at a time. Hence, for a time God is Father, then Son, then Holy Spirit. This is also known as Patripassionism, since the Father incarnated himself and became Jesus. This logically leads to the idea that the Father suffers.

This idea was raised as a counter to the Logos theology of Justin, who had taught that the Logos was another God in number, but not in will. This ditheism hurt the arguments against the Gnostics, and Sabellius put forth the view that the Father and the Son are one in order to insist there was only one first principle, the creator God, a single monarch. His good intentions were to label him a heretic.

Arianism

What is the relationship between Christ and the Father?

Arius (250–336) argued that the Father alone was without beginning. The Son, although pre-existent to the creation of the world, was created or made. That made Jesus a lesser, created being.

This was a subordinationist Christology, where Christ is considered subordinate to the Father. The Church Father Origen had proposed a subordinationist Christology a century earlier.

It was the influence of Plotinus that allowed him to say:

> The Father is alien to the Son in substance, for he has no origin. You must understand that the One was, but the Two was not before it came to be.
>
> Thalia of Arius

Arianism would, for a while, become the main Christianity. However, it would be rejected by the proto-orthodox church in 381, but would survive for centuries more. Arius was condemned at Nicea (325), but rehabilitated at Nicomedia (327), Tyre (335), Jerusalem (335), and Constantinople (336). He died the evening before he was to be reinstated to communion.

Donatism

Donatus (fl. 315), a leader of the first major schism, claimed the validity of sacraments depends on the character of the minister. Those clerics, who had lapsed during the persecutions, could no longer dispense the sacraments with efficacy. Therefore, anyone baptized by a lapsed priest must be re-baptized.

This is one of the heresies (technically a schism) that St. Augustine would fight. The others were Manichaeism and Pelagianism.

Apollinarianism

Apollinarius (ca. 310–390), intent on preserving the two natures of Christ as expressed in the Nicene Creed, argued that Jesus was fully human in body, but his mind was the divine Logos (Word). In essence, Jesus was God clothed in human flesh since Jesus' divine mind overshadowed and replaced his human soul. Again, as with most of these men who were bishops or other leaders of the Church, their good intentions led them into what later doctrine would call heresy.

Pelagianism

Pelagius (d. 418) argued that there is no point at which a person loses free will, which was contrary to St. Augustine's doctrine of original sin; one can always choose for God. Each person is responsible for his own sin and working out his own salvation. Man is unaffected by the fall of Adam and is able to keep all of God's laws by his own free will; original sin is not inherited by Adam's progeny.

The Pelagians denied doctrines that held to: predestination, original sin, and that babies are born with sin on their soul and, therefore, subject to the fires of Hell.

Nestorianism

Nestorius (Bishop of Constantinople 428–431, d. 440) in trying to preserve the idea that Jesus Christ existed from the beginning, argued that Mary could not be called the "mother of God." He preferred the term "mother of Christ." He said that Jesus the Christ was two separate persons, the human Jesus and the divine Christ.

Monophysitism

Christ had only one nature.

This was also known as Eutychianism from its primary proponent, Eutyches (ca. 378–454). Monophysitism was a reaction to Nestorius' claim that Jesus was two persons. Instead, they claimed that Jesus had only one nature and that it was divine. This position argued that when the divine and human natures were joined, the divine absorbed the human. Thus, where Nestorius over-emphasized the human nature, Eutyches over-emphasized the divinity of Christ.

Monotheletism

As a possible compromise between the Nestorians and the Monophysites, they claimed that although Jesus did have two natures, he had only one will and that will was divine.

Catharism

This was a heresy of the eleventh Century, which held that the world was created by an evil deity. The most well known sect of the Cathars was the Albigensians. They believed in the doctrines of reincarnation and two gods, one good and other evil.

This was an obvious extension of much older Gnostic and Manichean ideas.

This heresy was responsible for the development of the Papal Inquisition of ca. 1233, which was the forerunner of the more infamous Spanish Inquisition begun in 1478.

Some other heretical ideas

Docetism is a doctrine that cuts across many of these heresies. It insists that Jesus was fully divine, and only seemed to be human. Marcion and the Gnostics were some who held this view.

Kenosis is a doctrine that comes from St. Paul, where he says that Jesus emptied himself and became like us. Some picked up on this statement and twisted it to mean that the god-man Jesus gave up some divine attributes while on earth.

Socinianism—Socinus (1539–1604) denied the Trinity and claimed that Jesus is a deified man. He was among the first to spread Unitarian ideas to Protestants.

Tritheism—the Trinity is really three separate gods.

The Table, **Fig. 41**, below gives an overview of major heresies, their time frame and a brief synopsis.

Century	Heresy	Cryptic Summary
1st	Judaizers	Must be circumcised and follow the Law
1st & 2nd	Gnosticism	Matter is evil, Jesus only appeared to be a man
2nd (late)	Montanism	Charismatic, his teachings are above the church
3rd	Sabellianism	God is one, Jesus and Holy Spirit are modes
3rd	Manichaeism	Two cosmic Kingdoms of Light and Darkness
3rd to 5th	Donatists	Baptism is invalid if priest is not good
4th	Arianism	Jesus is created & subordinate to Father
4th	Macedonius	Holy Spirit is not Divine, is a creation like angel
4th	Apollinarius	Christ is not fully Human, Logos replaces mind
5th	Pelagianism	No original sin, can achieve salvation on our own
5th	Nestorianism	Mary is mother of Jesus—not of God
5th	Monophysitism	Christ had only one nature, a fusion of human and divine elements
7th	Iconoclasm	Pictures of Jesus and saints are sinful
11th	Catharism	Spirit is of God, body is created by evil God

Fig. 41 The Major Heresies

Church Councils

Councils of Bishops were called to define doctrine, usually to oppose some heresy.

The first seven great councils (**bold print** in **Fig. 42**) are called Ecumenical, because they were accepted by the universal (catholic) Church. Also included in the table are some regional councils of interest that occurred during this time interval. There have been a total of 21 Ecumenical Councils that are accepted as such by the Roman Catholic Church.

All seven (plus an eighth, which is not universally accepted) were held in the Eastern Roman Empire and were called by the Emperor. The last thirteen were held in what is present day Italy, France, or Switzerland (see **Fig. 42** and **Fig. 43**).

Council	Date	Heresy/Subject	Issue or Resolution
Nicea I # 1	**325**	**Arianism**	**Jesus is (homoousios) with Father and fully Divine**
Rimini-Seleucia	359	Arianism	Accepted Arianism (homoiousios)
Laodicea	364	Judaize	Sunday vs. Saturday
Constantinople I # 2	**381**	**Macedonius/ Apollinarius**	**Holy Spirit is Divine/Christ is fully Human, elevated Constantinople 2nd after Rome**
Carthage	394	proto-purgatory	Prayers for the dead doctrine
Ephesus # 3	**432**	**Nestorius/ Pelagius**	**Mary is (Theotokos) God Bearer/All have original sin**
Ephesus	449	Eutyches	"Robber Synod", approved Monophysite
Chalcedon # 4	**451**	**Eutyches/ Monophysite**	**Jesus has two natures in one person. Tome of Leo approved. A canon addresses women deacons**
Orange II	529	Augustine/Double predestination	Rejected Double Predestination

Council	Date	Heresy/Subject	Issue or Resolution
Constantinople II # 5	**553**	**Three Chapters**	**Condemned Theodore of Mopseustia's and other writings as Nestorian.** Origen condemned, reaffirmed Trinity and Jesus' Divinity
Toledo	589	Added to Creed	"Filioque"
Constantinople III # 6	**680**	**Monothelitism**	**Denied Monothelitism ("one will") and claimed that Christ had both divine and human wills.**
Nicea II # 7	**787**	**Iconoclasts**	**Legitimized veneration of icons.**

Fig. 42 The First Seven Ecumenical Councils
(plus some other important non-ecumenical Councils).

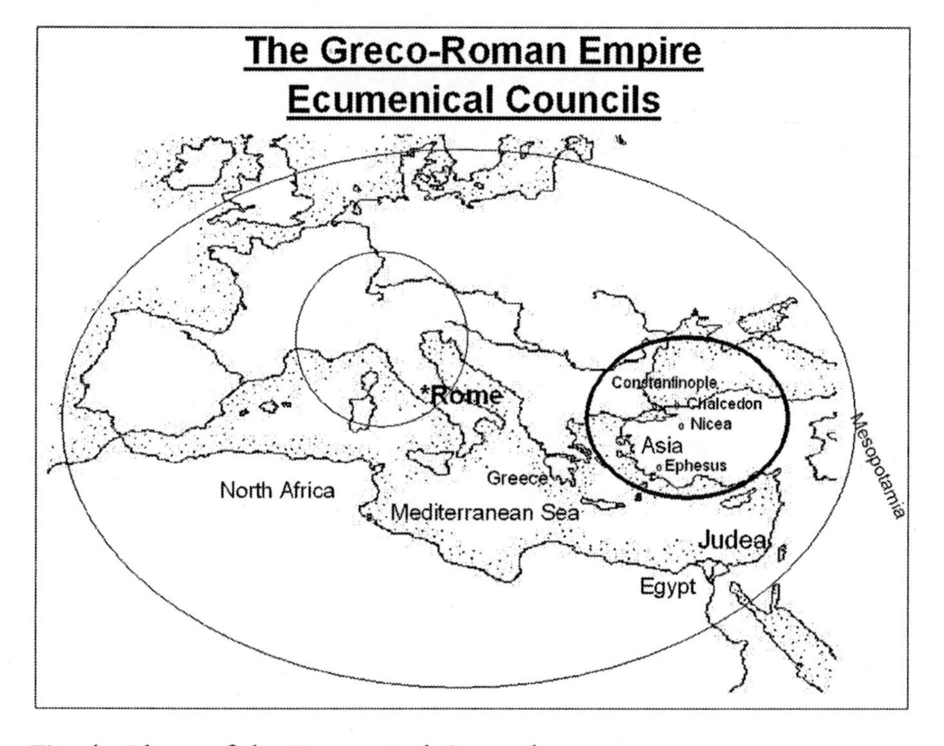

Fig. 43 Places of the Ecumenical Councils
First eight in bold circle, last thirteen in light circle

The following table, **Fig. 44**, completes the list of all Ecumenical Church Councils. These latter fourteen are accepted only by the Roman Catholic Church.

Council	Date	Heresy	Issue or Resolution
4 Constantinople	869	Photius-Patriarch of Constantinople	Condemned him and his council of 867 over the *Filioque*, later Photius was declared a saint by the Orthodox Church
1 Lateran	1123	Lay Investiture	Stopped Lay Investiture, celibacy declared
2 Lateran	1139	Arnold Brescia, Peter Bruys	Ended their errors—some of which led to Albigensian heresy
3 Lateran	1179	Albigenses	Condemned Albigenses and Waldenses heresies
4 Lateran	1215	Abbot Joachim, Albigensianism and Waldensianism	Condemned his Trinitarian errors, Transubstantiation, defined *ex cathedra:* "There is but one universal Church, outside of which there is no salvation."
1 Lyons	1245	Emp. Frederick II	Crusade of St. Louis
2 Lyons	1274	Schism	Temporary reunion with the East—failed over the *Filioque*, Papal elections clarified
Vienne	1311	Templars	Condemned them, new Crusade
Constance	1418	Wyclif, Huss	Ended Great Western Schism, proposed Conciliarism, Huss was burned at the stake
Florence	1443	Council vs. Pope as highest authority	Greek Orthodox reunion failed again, Papal Bull *Cantate Domino* declares *ex cathedra* that everyone outside the Catholic Church is damned
5 Lateran	1517		Discipline, condemnation of Conciliarism, new Crusade promoted

Council	Date	Heresy	Issue or Resolution
Trent	1563	Reformation	Countered Luther, enacted reforms, reaffirmed Catholic doctrines
1 Vatican	1870		Papal infallibility
2 Vatican	1965		Modern adaptations, ecumenism

Fig. 44 The Last Fourteen Ecumenical Councils

The Great Christological and Trinitarian Debates

Development of complex doctrine

Finally, the fourth century Christian Fathers, following the long chain of development from Plato through Philo through Plotinus, accepted the three Hypostases concept of the Neo-Platonists and transformed it into the Trinity of the Christian God.

The Athanasian Creed, written by a Latin writer of the fifth century, is a summation of centuries of work on an incredibly complex doctrine. We shall let it speak for itself:

> **Whoever wills to be in a state of salvation**, before all things it is necessary that he hold the catholic faith, which except everyone shall have kept whole and undefiled without doubt he will perish eternally.
>
> <u>Now the catholic faith is</u> that we worship One God in Trinity and Trinity in Unity, neither confounding the Persons nor dividing the substance. For there is one Person of the Father, another of the Son, another of the Holy Spirit. But the Godhead of the Father, of the Son, and of the Holy Spirit, is One, the Glory equal, the Majesty coeternal.
>
> The **<u>Father</u>** is made of none, neither created nor begotten. The **<u>Son</u>** is of the Father alone, not made nor created but begotten.
>
> The **<u>Holy Spirit</u>** is of the Father and the Son, not made nor created nor begotten but proceeding. So there is one Father not three Fathers, one Son not three Sons, and Holy Spirit not three Holy Spirits. And in this Trinity

> there is nothing before or after, nothing greater or less, but the whole three Persons are coeternal together and coequal.
>
> But it is necessary to eternal salvation that he also believe faithfully the Incarnation of our Lord Jesus Christ. The **right faith** therefore is that we believe and confess that our Lord Jesus Christ, the Son of God, is God and Man.
>
> He is God of the substance of the Father begotten before the worlds, and He is man of the substance of His mother born in the world; perfect God, perfect man subsisting of a reasoning soul and human flesh; equal to the Father as touching His Godhead, inferior to the Father as touching His Manhood. **This is the catholic faith, which except a man shall have believed faithfully and firmly he cannot be in a state of salvation.**

The most serious questions to come before the Councils were those that dealt with the relationship of Jesus to God and man. The first Council defined the relationship between Jesus and the Father in the original Nicene Creed, and the second Council further defined the relationship, by adding to that creed, between all three persons of what became the Trinity.[170]

---

170. The New Testament makes no reference to the doctrine of the Trinity. When St. Jerome (ca. 342–420) translated the Greek 1st Epistle of John into Latin, he (or more probably, a later pious scribe) inserted a reference now called the Comma Johannem (Addition of John) at 1 John 5:7, which reads as translated from the Latin Vulgate to the King James Version: "For there are three that bear record in Heaven, the Father, the Word, and the Holy Ghost: and these three are one."

When Erasmus (1467–1536) was translating the best available Greek texts, he observed that none of his copies contained the Latin Vulgate rendering of 1 John 5:7. The Greek text read completely differently, and he used the Greek manuscripts in his first two editions of his translation of the New Testament (1515). The Church, however, had determined that the Vulgate was The Word of God and forced him to put the insertion back in. To Erasmus' credit, he agreed to do so only if a Greek text could be found with the Vulgate reading in it. Unfortunately, an inauthentic Greek text was produced and he dutifully put it in. The King James Version then used Erasmus' translation with the inserted text. Since then, it has been proven that the Comma Johannem is indeed a later insertion, because there is no valid early Greek text that has it. Nevertheless, the New King James Version still retains the false text.

Jesus' relationship to God

The Original Nicene Creed of 325 CE:

> We believe in one God, the Father almighty, maker of all things, both visible and invisible.
> And in one Lord, Jesus Christ, the son of God, begotten from the Father, only-begotten, that is from the essence (***ousia***) of the Father, God from God, light from light, True God from True God, begotten not made, being of one substance (***homoousion***) with the Father, through whom all things came to be, both those in heaven and those on the earth, who because of us human beings and because of our salvation came down and was incarnate and was made man; he suffered, and rose on the third day, ascending to the heavens, coming to judge the living and dead.
> And in the Holy Spirit.

The cryptic allusion to the Holy Ghost marked the End of 1st Nicene Creed. The Creed adequately explained how Jesus related to the Father. The difficulty was to avoid both:

> - denying his humanity (the Sabellian, Modalism heresies)
> - questioning his divinity (the Arian heresy)

The Creed had condemned those who denied (the Arians) the Father and Son were one in **essence** (ousia) and **substance** (hypostasis) in the anathemas:

> But those who say: "There was a time when he was not;" and "He was not before he was made;" and "He was made out of nothing," or "He is of another "substance" or "essence," or "The Son of God is created," or "changeable," or "alterable"—they are condemned by the holy catholic and apostolic Church.

This Nicene Creed left confusion. How could God be One thing and, yet, consist of two or maybe even three things? The Nicene anathemas had caused even more trouble, since they used *hypostasis* and *ousia* as synonyms. These problems were not to be solved definitively until the Council of Constantinople in 381—even then not everyone would agree.

A problem of Greek vs. Latin

The problem was exacerbated since the West spoke Latin and the East spoke Greek. The Greek words confused the Latins and they mistranslated the key words "ousia" and "hypostasis". The word **Hypostasis** meaning that which underlies (or an underlying reality), was used by the Stoics. It was translated into Latin as **persona,** but they should have used **subtantia**. Unfortunately, **subtantia** was already used to translate **ousia** where they should have used **essentia** so that to the Latins the words **person, substance and essence** were confused.

This caused misunderstandings between West and East! Greek theologians called the Trinity—one essence (*ousia)* in three substances (*hypostases).* Latins did not like three hypostases since that sounded like three gods (or the Tritheism heresy)! Latins theologians called the Trinity—one substance in three essences. Greeks did not like three essences since that sounded like the Sabellian heresy.

The three Cappadocian Fathers resolved the dilemma by redefining some key words.

The Cappadocians said that those words are NOT interchangeable, therefore they claimed: The Father, Son and Holy Ghost are three individuals (hypostases) sharing one essence (ousia)!

St. Athanasius, at a council in Alexandria (362), convinced each side that they believed the same thing, but used different terminology. Both sides kept their own terminology but agreed to the Cappadocian definitions.

The Latins preferred: three **Persons** sharing one **Substance** and ever since, that is the way it has come down to Western Christianity as "God in three persons."

Including the Holy Ghost

After the Council in Constantinople, the Nicene-Constantinopolitan creed now included the Holy Ghost and continued thusly:

> We believe in the **Holy Spirit**,
> the Lord, the giver of life,
> who proceeds from the Father **and the Son**[171],

171. The phrase "and the Son', which in Latin is *Filioque, was* added to the Nicene Creed much later, and this double procession of the Spirit was to be a major cause the 1054 CE split in West/East Church.

> who with the Father and the Son together is worshiped
> and glorified, who has spoken through the prophets.
>
> We believe in **one holy catholic and apostolic** Church.
> We acknowledge one baptism for the forgiveness
> of sins. We look for the resurrection of the
> dead, and the life of the world to come. Amen.

Jesus' relationship to man

Nicea and Constantinople I had solved the problem of how Jesus relates to God (Father and Holy Ghost), at least, for the orthodox. But, now, how does he relate to man?

How does he relate to Man?

Is he a man adopted by God?
Is he just a spirit?
Is he two people, God and Man?

The solutions to these questions (all of which were condemned as heretical) came at the Councils of Ephesus (432) and finally of Chalcedon (451 CE). In a brief summary:

> Mary was the mother of one person who contains both a divine and a physical human **nature**. This melding of the two natures is known as the **hypostatic union**. Jesus Christ is truly man and truly God.

At the time of the Council of Chalcedon, some factions split[172] from the main body of Christianity over these doctrines. The vast majority accepted these complex doctrines on the nature of the Father, Son, and Holy Spirit, as expounded in the Athanasian Creed above. And to this day, they have remained the orthodox beliefs of hundreds of millions of Roman Catholics, Eastern Orthodox and mainline Protestants.

---

172. The Coptics of Egypt are one such non-Chalcedonian group that still exists today.

St. Augustine (354–430), Doctor of the Church (Encapsulation)

Although Mani of Babylon had been dead for 80 years when St. Augustine was born (in what is now modern Algeria), their paths were to cross repeatedly throughout his life. Augustine was the product of the union of a Christian mother and a pagan father and he contended against his mother's faith for many years, before finally succumbing to his mother, St. Monica.

As a young man, he was torn between hedonism and asceticism. For 15 years, until 385, he kept a mistress by whom he had a son, Adeodatus (given by God) and immersed himself in religion and pagan philosophy. At an early age he studied rhetoric and pursued a career as a rhetoritician. He also pursued religion with a passion and became a Manichean for nine years before abandoning that faith around the age of 30.

Manichaeanism was the product of the syncretistic thinking of Mani of Babylon, who combined Christian, Persian, and Gnostic ideas to develop his religion. As with prior Gnosticism, his religion emphasized the dualism between matter and spirit, with the body being the creation of an evil god that, nevertheless, had trapped particles of light from the good creation within itself. It produced a severe asceticism that denied the flesh and sought only to free the trapped light by rigorous practices.

As Augustine grew in wisdom, he recognized the limitations of Mani's religion and sought comfort in the ancient philosophers. He became enamored with Plato and the Neo-Platonists and studied them passionately. All the while, Monica was praying that her son would see the light of the Christian faith and join her in it.

Augustine's career eventually took him from North Africa to Italy where he would meet the future St. Ambrose of Milan. Augustine loved the sermons of the older man, but was restrained from believing his faith because of the crude anthropomorphisms and bad Latin form of the Scriptures, especially of the Old Testament. Compared to the glorious Greek of Plato and his intellectual theories, the Christian Scriptures were unacceptable to educated people like Augustine.

The saintly Ambrose had already recognized the shortcomings of the scriptures (if taken at face value) and taught Augustine that the way to the scriptures was via figurative and allegorical interpretation. This would allow for an Augustinian synthesis of Neo-Platonism and Christianity.

Now that he understood the texts allegorically, instead of literally, Augustine was able to embrace the Testaments; however, he had temporarily traded one problem for another. In his later *Confessions* he cried to God, "I have faith in your Books, but their message is hard indeed to fathom."

Thus, between the pleas of his mother and the intellectualizing of Ambrose, Augustine was able to accept the Catholic faith, and at the age of 33, was baptized in 387. He would then spend the rest of his life fathoming the message.

Even though he would turn on the Manicheans and write voluminously against them, we can see their influence throughout his teachings. He was never to fully eliminate their hatred of the body and its act of procreation. Indeed, his greatest theological innovation, that of original sin, placed that spiritual defect squarely on the organs of reproduction. The original sin of Adam and Eve visited itself on all of their descendants, simply by being born. There was no escape from this sin except by baptism into the Christian faith, and anyone who failed to be baptized was destined for Hell. There were no exceptions, but only the mitigation that unbaptized babies and children would be placed in the level of least torment, due to having added no sins of their own commission.

Augustine struggled against many heresies (such as Donatism, Pelagianism, and Manichaeanism) and fought for many theological issues (such as the Trinity, Free Will, Purgatory, Amillenarianism, and Predestination), that are too complex to elucidate here (some will be discussed in other sections). Because of this labor, he became the greatest teacher, or Doctor, that the Church has ever known.

The Accomplishments of St. Augustine

Augustine fought **three major heresies** as defined above:

Manichaeanism
Donatism
Pelagianism

And, he defined or influenced **several major doctrines:**

Trinity (neo-Platonic: One—Mind—Soul)[173]
Original Sin (all are guilty of damning sin)
Predestination (all are fore-ordained to Heaven or Hell)
Purgatory (influenced the concept of a third place for souls upon death)
Amillenarianism (there would be no thousand year rule after the second coming; Christ's reign had already started)[174]

Theodicy of St. Augustine

Evil exists because **God created the world from nothing** (*creatio ex nihilo*), so creations, not being of the substance of God, are necessarily less than good and capable of evil.

Evil comes from created things simply because they are less than God.

Humans are doomed because of Original Sin. The "Fall" of Adam and Eve in the Garden of Eden condemned all future humanity. Without the saving sacrament of baptism, everyone is condemned to Hell.

Augustinian theodicy depends on the cosmological idea of creation *ex nihilo;* therefore, using this doctrine we will investigate him more fully.

---

173. Augustine used several analogies to show the rationality of the Trinity doctrine. One was the Neo-Platonic cosmology. When combined with another Greek idea, that of the Logos, the Trinity was given a superb philosophical basis. Key to this was the first century Jewish philosopher Philo who had shown that the Greek Logos could be associated with the Word of God. John was to use this in his Gospel to describe the Son. The "Mind" of Plotinus was also equivalent to the *Logos*, giving the relationship of Mind = Logos = Son. This mirrored Augustine's Trinity of: Father (One), Son (Mind), Holy Spirit (Soul).

174. During the second and third centuries, many Church Fathers spoke of the 1000-year reign that would follow Christ's second coming (premillenialism). Origen in the East and Augustine in the West dispensed with this idea. It was not a systematic Christian doctrine until revived around 1830 by John Darby. Today, the doctrine is widely accepted by many denominations and is the subject of best-selling novels.

The Doctrine of *Creatio Ex Nihilo* (Essay)

> In the beginning when God created the heavens and the earth, the earth was a formless void and darkness covered the face of the deep, while a wind from God swept over the face of the waters. Then God said, "Let there be light" (Gen. 1:1–3).

In the above quote from Genesis there is no explicit indication that God created the heavens and the earth out of "nothing." In fact, at the time that the Priestly redactor penned these lines ("perhaps during the Babylonian exile"),[175] the common concept of creation was one of ordering a primal chaos, including the primeval darkness. "God created out of chaos (not *ex nihilo*), as shown by the prefatory verse that portrays the earth as once being a chaotic waste: stygian darkness, turbulent waters, utter disorder."[176]

The question for the modern reader, then, is this: did the Priestly writer intend to imply a creation out of nothing (*creatio ex nihilo*) and, if he did not, then when did this concept arise? Of even more importance is: why would one interpretation of creation, or another, matter to later generations?

The ex nihilo interpretation appears to have mattered a great deal to Augustine, almost a thousand years later, in the fifth century CE.[177] That being the case, it is the intent here to address the foregoing questions, specifically as they apply to Augustine. That is: how did he come to the doctrine that God created the world ex nihilo and why was it so important to his theology?

The ancient background

The late Jewish background

The first apparent indication in the biblical record, that the world was created out of nothing, is in the non-canonical Hebrew book of 2 Maccabees, written in the

175. Bruce M. Metzger and Roland E. Murphy, eds. *The New Oxford Annotated Bible: NRSV* (New York: Oxford University Press, 1994), xxxvi.

176. Bernhard W. Anderson, "Introduction: Mythopoetic and Theological Dimensions of Biblical Creation Faith," in *Creation in the Old Testament*, ed. Bernhard W. Anderson (London: Fortress Press, 1984), 15.

177. Augustine, *Confessions* 11.5 ff, trans. R. S. Pine-Coffin (London: Penguin Books, 1961), 257 ff.

first century BCE, about 400 years after the assumed writing of Genesis 1,[178] where it says:

> I beg you my child, to look at the heaven and the earth and see everything that is in them, and recognize that God did not make them out of things that existed. (2 Macc. 7:28).

Could it be that this citation was the biblical foundation for the ex nihilo doctrine? We shall see that Augustine does use it, but we will maintain that it was not, by its author's intent, a real predecessor to the doctrine.

The possibly contemporary, or slightly later, Wisdom of Solomon (first century BCE) explicitly states the opposite view: God's power is described by "your all-powerful hand, who created the world from formless matter." (Wisdom 11:17).

So, there is either a disagreement between them, or as some scholars claim,[179] neither of these passages speaks of creation ex nihilo.

The Platonic debt

In order to fully determine where Augustine got his ideas on creation, we must consider that the Christianity of the fifth century CE was deeply indebted to an even older tradition—that of the fourth century BCE Plato.

Plato himself came at the end of a fairly long line of thinkers who had attempted to make sense of the cosmos. He was the inheritor of several key ideas from his predecessors[180] which he synthesized into his cosmological construction that appears in several of his works and culminates in his *Timaeus*. There Plato asks:

---

178. Origen, *On First Principles* 2.1.5, trans. G.W. Butterworth (New York: Harper Tourchbooks, 1966), 80.

179. Gerhard May, *Creation Ex Nihilo: The Doctrine of "Creation out of Nothing' in Early Christian Thought*, trans. A.S. Worrall (Edinburgh: T&T Clark, 1994), 6–8.

180. Briefly, these predecessors were Heraclitus ('nothing can be known'), Parmenides ('there is nothing to know'), and Anaxagoras (Mind orders matter). Each of these thinkers handed down an extremely important (but incomplete) principle that was addressed, in turn, by the others and, in the hands of Plato, was solved to the satisfaction of many succeeding generations. R.D. Archer-Hind, Introduction and annotations to *The Timaeus of Plato*, by Plato. (New York: Arno Press, 1973), 3–19.

> As for the...cosmos...we must ask...whether it has always existed and had no beginning, or whether it has come into existence and started from some beginning. The answer is that it has come into being.[181]

So, we see that Plato does break with much of Greek philosophy in that he claims the world is not eternal, thus agreeing with the story in Genesis. It certainly has been due, in part, to this belief that later Christians were to accept him as "the" worthy philosopher.

Plato also anticipates the Augustinian concept of time where he states: "So time came into being with the heavens."[182] The reason Plato gives for this is that time cannot exist without the motion of bodies, which is in partial agreement with Augustine. Augustine will refine the motion to be of any material bodies; whereas, Plato had specifically noted only the heavenly bodies.[183]

Plato's concept of evil also anticipates that of Augustine's.[184] Plato believes that evil is not a substance; rather, it is a defective presentation of the Idea.[185] This concept, as we shall see, will play a most significant role in Augustine's refutation of the Manichaean's doctrine of evil.

Augustine will say that space, as did time, also came into being with the creation of the world. Can the same be said of the thinking of Plato in the *Timaeus*?

Plato had initially posited two forms of reality: first the unchanging, uncreated Forms; second, the sensible, created material copy of the Forms. Later, he needed a third type of reality, which he calls the "receptacle of becoming," or simply space.[186] Space, like form, is also eternal and indestructible. But, when empty of

181. Plato, *Timaeus* 28C, trans. Desmond Lee, *Plato: Timaeus and Critias* (London: Penguin Books, 1977), 41.

182. Plato, *Timaeus* 38B (52); Augustine, *City of God* 11.6, trans. Henry Bettenson (London: Penguin Books, 1972), 435-6.

183. Augustine, *City of God* 11.6 (435); 12.16 (491); Confessions 11.23 (271).

184. Augustine, *Concerning the Nature of Good, Against the Manichaeans 4, in A Select Library of the Christian Church. Nicene and Post-Nicene Fathers.* First Series, Vol. 4: *The Writings Against the Manichaeans and Against the Donatists, ed Philip Schaff* (Edinburgh: T&T Clark, 1887; repr. Grand Rapids: Eerdmans Publishing Co., 1996), 352; also see *Confessions* 7.16 (150); *City of God* 12.8 (480).

185. Archer-Hind, *The Timaeus of Plato.*, 33.

186. Plato, *Timaeus* 52A (71).

any material, is it nothing? Plato says it is in that we "say that everything that exists must be somewhere and occupy some space, and that what is nowhere in heaven or earth is nothing at all."[187] So, do material objects also define space as well as time? It would seem so, but space is as pre-existent as matter, and did not come into being with the creation of the world, as does time. Indeed, he says that the space already "was characterized by the qualities of water and fire, of earth and air."[188] On the one hand, this would seem to be more like the pre-existent primeval chaos of Genesis.

On the other hand, a case might possibly be made for the assertion of creatio ex nihilo in Plato,[189] but the old Greek philosophical concept of "nothing comes from nothing" appears to have ruled in his day. As we shall see, a great deal of time would elapse before this Greek concept was to be displaced. Many primary sources indicate an adherence to the idea of the pre-existence of matter; some important ones being: the first century BCE Wisdom of Solomon, Philo, Justin, Athenagoras, Hermogenes, and even the late second century Clement of Alexandria.

We will look at some of these and at the later Christian precedents of Augustine's creatio ex nihilo.

Philo and the early Christian Fathers background

Philo of Alexandria (first century CE)

By the time of Middle Platonism "the cosmogony of the Timaeus is systematized into the characteristic "Three principles" doctrine: the three first ontological principles, thought to be equal in rank; God, Ideas and Matter, constitute the world."[190] Philo speaks of creation of the non-existent, but this simply means

187. Plato, *Timaeus* 52D (71-2).

188. Plato, Timaeus 52D (72).

189. We learn in *Timaeus* 34C that the "soul is prior to matter, which can only mean that matter is evolved out of soul", hence, matter was not pre-existent. This exegesis was not accepted by the Middle Platonist, nor most of the Fathers after Tatian. Nor, indeed, is it by most scholars today. Archer-Hind, Introduction to The Timaeus of Plato, 91n12, 92n1, 105 n13.

190. May, *Creatio Ex Nihilo: The Doctrine of "Creation out of Nothing' in Early Christian Thought*, 4.

that the creator brought "something not being into being."[191] Middle Platonism apparently did not envision the possibility of a creation ex nihilo.

Justin Martyr (c. 95–165 CE)

Justin took what was accepted as this Middle Platonic view of creation for granted. He believed that God created the world from pre-existing matter, as shown by the following excerpts from his *First Apology*: "And we have been taught that in the beginning He of his goodness, for people's sake, formed all things out of unformed matter."[192]

Justin compares "the biblical creation story and the creation myth in the *Timaeus*," and claims that Plato took the doctrine from Genesis,[193] where he says:

> And that you may learn that it was from our teachers…that Plato took his statements that God made the Universe by changing formless matter…So that both Plato and his followers and we ourselves have learned, and you may learn, that the whole Universe came into being by the word of God out of the substratum spoken of before by Moses.[194]

Justin also held that darkness, as well as matter, was pre-existent, as he says:

> "But we all hold this common gathering on Sunday, since it is the first day, on which God transforming darkness and matter made the Universe."[195]

Tatian (d. after c. 172 CE)

Although he was a disciple of Justin, Tatian disavows the pre-existence of matter that had been accepted by his predecessors.

---

191. May, *Creatio Ex Nihilo: The Doctrine of "Creation out of Nothing' in Early Christian Thought*, 16.

192. Justin Martyr, *First Apology* 10.2 in *The First and Second Apologies* I.10.2, trans. Leslie William Barnard, Ancient Christian Writers 56 (New York and Mahwah: Paulist Press, 1997), 28.

193. May, *Creatio Ex Nihilo: The Doctrine of "Creation out of Nothing' in Early Christian Thought*, 122.

194. Justin Martyr, *First Apology* 59.1 (ACW 56.64-5).

195. Justin Martyr, *First Apology* 67.7 (ACW 56.71).

Tatian attacks the philosophers of Greece, including Plato, specifically for the doctrine of the soul.[196] Then he goes on to condemn what was considered to be Platonic creation, stating the doctrine plainly:

> For matter is not without beginning like God, nor because of having beginnings is it also of equal power with God; it was originated and brought into being by none other, projected by the sole creator of all that is.[197]

And, also:

> It is possible to see that the whole construction and creation of the world has derived from matter, and that matter has itself been produced by God...raw and formless before its separation...orderly after its division.[198]

Theophilus of Antioch (bishop ca. 169 CE)

Theophilus, along with Tatian, seems to be one of the earliest Christian Fathers to disagree with the Platonic concept of pre-existent matter, saying that having matter and God both uncreated makes them equal: "if matter is uncreated it must also be immutable, and equal to God."[199] This would argue against God's sovereignty as the sole first principle.

Theophilus "praised Plato for acknowledging that God is uncreated. But then he criticized Plato for averring that matter is coeval with God [and therefore] equal to God."[200] Thus:

---

196. Tatian, *Oratio Ad Graecos* 3.2-3, trans. Molly Whittaker, Oxford Early Christian Texts. (Oxford: Clarendon Press, 1970), 9.

197. Tatian, *Oratio Ad Graecos* 5.3 (OECT 11).

198. Tatian, *Oratio Ad Graecos* 12.1 (OECT 23).

199. Theophilus of Antioch, *Ad Autolycum* 2.4, trans. Robert M. Grant, Oxford Early Christian Texts. (Oxford: Clarendon Press, 1970), 27.

200. Ted Peters, "On Creating the Cosmos," in *Physics, Philosophy, and Theology: A common quest for understanding*, eds. Robert J. Russell, William R. Stroeger, S.J. and George V. Coyne, S.J. (Vatican City: Vatican Observatory, 1988), 278.

> "then according to the Platonists God is not the Maker of the universe, and as far as they are concerned the unique sovereignty of God is not demonstrated."[201]

Theophilus anticipated many of Augustine's ideas on both the creation and the creator where he claims that, concerning the creation:

> the holy scripture spoke not about this firmament [the vaulted ceiling] but about another heaven which is invisible to us.[202]

Explicitly, Theophilus tells us what God did and why:

> God made everything out of what did not exist [2 Macc. 7:28], bringing it into existence so that his greatness might be known and apprehended through his works.[203]

On the reason for creation, Augustine would have to disagree with Theophilus, but he would agree with Plato in that: "the reason for the creation of the universe was God's good purposes to create good."[204]

Irenaeus (c. 120–202 CE)

Irenaeus provides us with a great deal of knowledge concerning the Gnostics, and he condemns them for believing that matter was produced by a lesser deity where he says:

> He Himself called into being the substance of His creation, when previously it had no existence. But the assertion that matter was produced [by the Aeons...Sophia's passion]...became matter—is incredible, infatuated, impossible, and untenable.[205]

---

201. Theophilus, *Ad Autolycum* 2.4 (OECT 27).

202. Theophilus, *Ad Autolycum* 2.13 (OECT 49); Augustine *Confessions* 12.13 (289).

203. Theophilus, Ad Autolycum 1.4 (OECT 7).

204. Augustine, *City of God* 11.22 (454); also see Plato *Timaeus* 30A (42).

205. Irenaeus of Lyon, *Against the Heresies*, 2.10.4, in *The Ante-Nicene Fathers. Vol. 1: The Apostolic Fathers.—Justin Martyr.—Irenaeus, eds Alexander Roberts and James Donaldson* (Buffalo: Christian Literature Co., 1886), 370.

Interestingly, at this time, at least some Christian Fathers still thought of God as having made the world from his own substance, as Irenaeus says:

> He made all things, to whom also He speaks, saying, "Let Us make man after Our image and likeness;" He taking from Himself the substance of the creatures [formed], and the pattern of things made, and the type of all the adornments of the world.[206]

Later Fathers, including Augustine, would dismiss this assertion. Indeed, Augustine would have to deny this, because it would be necessary for created things to not be of God's own substance in order for him to refute the Manichaeans. He would later say: "The Maker is one thing, the thing made is another."[207] Also, that God: "gave existence to creatures he made out of nothing; but it was not his own supreme existence."[208] "And when man was made, God gave to his body a soul which was created out of nothing."[209] Augustine's meaning here is that the Maker is not corruptible, but the thing made, by not being equal, is corruptible. This will be the key argument against the Manichaean concept of evil.

Tertullian (d. ca. 220 CE)

Tertullian provides a more developed idea of *creatio ex nihilo* than Irenaeus. He says that God did not create from pre-existing matter or from his own substance. The remaining alternative was from "nothing".

Thus, Tertullian disagrees with the earlier conclusion of Hermogenes whose

> "fundamental thesis is that the Lord made all things either out of Himself, or out of nothing, or out of something, in order that, upon demonstrating that He could neither have made them out of Himself nor out of nothing, he may consequently affirm the remaining possibility…out of something…that something was matter."[210]

206. Irenaeus, *Against Heresies* 4.20.1 (ANF 1.488).

207. Augustine, *Acts or Disputations Against Fortunatus the Manichaean 12, in A Select Library of the Christian Church. Nicene and Post-Nicene Fathers.* First Series, Vol. 4: *The Writings Against the Manichaeans and Against the Donatists, ed Philip Schaff* (Edinburgh: T&T Clark, 1887; repr. Grand Rapids: Eerdmans Publishing Co., 1996), 116.

208. Augustine *City of God* 12 (473).

209. Augustine *City of God* 14 (568).

210. Tertullian, *The Treatise Against Hermogenes*, 2.1 (ACW 24.27).

Hermogenes certainly had good intentions here in that he attempted to avoid having God be the creator of evil, since it would follow that if God created everything, He, therefore, must necessarily create that which is evil. Hermogenes' excellent logic might have solved the problem of evil, but by this time, it was obvious to the Christian Fathers that such reasoning would make matter the equal of God (*deo aequalis*), subverting the primacy of God alone. Hermogenes had to be refuted, and he was by the logic of Tertullian:

> But even if matter had existed, we would believe that it also had been made by God, for by laying down the rule that nothing is unborn except God, we would win our case...The main point is clear now: I find that nothing was made except from nothing, because I know that what I find was made, once did not exist. Also if something is made out of something, it draws its origin from something made...[matter]...on the understanding that these, too, were made by God.[211]

Clement of Alexandria (c. 150–215 CE)

Surprisingly, even at this late date, we find that Clement still held to the Middle Platonic doctrine of matter, since he accepted the teachings of Philo.[212] Philo starts with the *Timaeus'* assumption of the pre-existence of matter, which Clement follows, and also "that the universe was generated and had a beginning...that its origin did not take place in time."[213] Thus, we have a link from Plato, through Philo, through Clement to Augustine, which shows the antiquity of the belief that the world's creation did not take place in time.

Clement agrees with Augustine on the creation being "not in time", but much as Tatian had done to Justin, Origen was to do to Clement; that is, to disavow his mentor's assertion of the Platonic doctrine of the pre-existence of matter.

211. Tertullian, *The Treatise Against Hermogenes* 33.1 (ACW 24.71).

212. Salvatore R. C. Lilla, *Clement of Alexandria: a study in Christian Platonism and Gnosticism*, (Oxford: Oxford University Press, 1971), 191-2.

213. Lilla, *Clement of Alexandria*, 198-9.

Origen (c. 185–254 CE)

Origen was one of the first of the Christian Fathers that took the above mentioned statement from 2 Maccabees 7:28 "as the first unequivocal statement in scripture of the doctrine of creatio ex nihilo."[214] Augustine would also later use this passage from 2 Maccabees.[215] In the cited article, Goldstein argues that Origen was mistaken and that the verse does not assert creatio ex nihilo at all.[216]

Origen had also used Hermas, Mand. I.1 to support his claim:

> First of all believe that God is one, who created and set in order all things and caused the universe to exist out of nothing.[217]

Gerhard May claims that neither of the writers in Maccabees (written between 104–63 BCE) nor in Hermas (late first century CE) originally intended to claim creation *ex nihilo* and that the Christian Fathers even in the mid-second century CE had not yet formulated the doctrine. However, by the late second century they had seen in the Platonic notion of creation from pre-existing matter a source of the heresies. By then, as we've seen with Tatian, Theophilus and Irenaeus, the Christian Fathers had come to understand that the only solid grounding for the belief that there was only one God and that he was the sole creator lay in the doctrine of creation ex nihilo.[218]

Origen says that:

> I cannot understand how so many distinguished men have supposed it [matter] to be uncreated, that is, not made by God himself...but in its nature and power the result of chance...[then they charge with impiety those who deny God, yet]...they themselves are guilty of a like impiety in saying that matter is uncreated and co-eternal with the uncreated God.[219]

214.Jonathon A. Goldstein, "The Origins of the Doctrine of Creation Ex Nihilo," *Journal of Jewish Studies* 35 (Aug 1984): 127.

215.Augustine, *Nature of Good* 26 (NPNF 1st ser. 4.356-7).

216.Goldstein, "The Origin of the Doctrine of Creation Ex Nihilo," 127.

217.Origen *On First Principles* 2.1.5 (80).

218.May, *Creatio Ex Nihilo: The Doctrine of "Creation out of Nothing' in Early Christian Thought*, 6 ff.

219.Origen *On First Principles* 2.1.4 (79).

Augustine agreed with Origen here, but elsewhere would have to accuse Origen of error[220] because Origen also thought that "the reason for the world's creation was to restrain evil, not to establish good."[221] This, of course, was the very claim of the Manichaeans, so Origen's opinion, left unrefuted, would have lent support to them.

Ambrose (c. 337–397 CE)

By the time of Ambrose, the ex nihilo doctrine was fully accepted by the Christian Fathers, as we see by his writings concerning the Son: "How, then, can He, Who out of nothing fashioned all things, be Himself created out of nothing?"[222] And, "for how did the Son, who created all things out of nothing..."[223] In his *Hexameron*, he is explicit about the creator:

> The Creator...is He who in a moment of His power made this great beauty of the world out of nothing, which did not itself have existence and gave substance to things or causes that did not themselves exist.[224]

And,

> All things, which spring from nothing, reach their perfection and again diminish in perfection, being subject to decline...for He Who has created all things from nothing has the power...[225]

---

220. Augustine seems to mimic Origen's own words here by saying: "I cannot express my astonishment that so learned and experienced a theologian should have..."; Augustine *City of God* 11.23 (455)

221. Augustine *City of God* 11.23 (455).

222. Ambrose, *Of the Christian Faith, 1.19.126, in A Select Library of the Christian Church. Nicene and Post-Nicene Fathers.* Second Series, Vol. 10: *Select Works and Letters. ed Philip Schaff and Henry Wace* (New York: Christian Literature Co., 1896), 221.

223. Ambrose, *Of the Christian Faith* 5.6.68 (NPNF 2nd ser. 10.293).

224. Ambrose, *Hexameron* 1.4.16, in *Saint Ambrose: Hexameron, Paradise, and Cain and Able*, trans. John J. Savage, The Fathers of the Church 42 (New York: Fathers of the Church, Inc., 1961), 16.

225. Ambrose, *Hexameron* 4.8.31 (FOC 42.154).

Ambrose hints at the imperfection of that which springs from nothing, and Augustine would learn that doctrine most intimately from Ambrose and would later use it to greater effect.

The Gnostics background

Against Heresies

We have reviewed the evolution of the idea of *creatio ex nihilo* as Augustine received it and have seen its importance to the Christian Fathers in establishing the sovereignty of God. In order to establish why the doctrine is so important to Augustine, we will have to step back and look at a serious contender to what was to become the orthodox view of Christianity—Gnosticism.

> Inasmuch as certain men have set the truth aside, bringing in lying words and vain genealogies, which, as the apostle [Paul in 1 Tim. 1:4] says, minister questions rather than the godly edifying which is in faith.[226]

Thus begins the preface to Irenaeus' polemic against the heresies of Gnosticism. Irenaeus goes on to give a detailed description of Valentinian Gnosticism, as expounded by Ptolemaeus, a brief rehearsal of which follows.

Valentinian Gnosticism

The Valentinians claim that "in the invisible and ineffable heights above there exists a certain perfect, pre-existent Aeon,…a being invisible and incomprehensible. Eternal and unbegotten."[227] Coexisting with this ungenerate "Profundity" was Thought (also known as Grace and Silence). At some time, Profundity decided to emit from Himself the beginning of all things by depositing a seed in the womb of Silence. Silence gave birth to Mind who is equal to Profundity and is called the Only-Begotten, Father and Beginning of all things. Truth was also emitted, forming the original Tetrad of Profundity, Silence, Mind and Truth. Mind then emitted Word and Life who themselves united to emit Man and Church. With these last four, we have the original Ogdoad which is the root and substance of all things.

---

226. Irenaeus, *Against Heresies* Preface (ANF 1.315).

227. Irenaeus, *Against Heresies* 1.1.1 (ANF 1.316).

Then the emitted Aeons, Word and Life, emitted ten more Aeons, and Man and Church emitted twelve more Aeons. Now we have thirty Aeons in the Valentinian system, which are "wrapped up,...in silence and are known to none."[228] They are the Ogdoad (8), the Decad (10) and the Dodecad (12) all dwelling in the Pleroma or fullness.

The youngest of the Dodecad, Wisdom (Sophia), passionately sought to know the Profundity and the result of this inappropriate passion was a formless substance, which "had its beginning from ignorance and grief, and fear and bewilderment."[229] This substance was the Intention of Wisdom, called Achamoth.

Irenaeus goes on to explain how Achamoth originated the material, ensouled and spiritual substances and from these the elements that participate in the creation of the world, primarily matter, and the creator-God or Demiurge.

The universe of the Demiurge and his creatures exists outside of the Pleroma and do not know the Pleroma. The function of Gnosticism, then, is to achieve salvation by coming to "know" the Profundity of the Pleroma; hence, the Gnostic's admonition (found in Clement of Alexandria's *Excerpta ex Theodoto* 78.2) to question: who we were, what we have become, where we were, whither we were cast; wither we hasten, whence we are redeemed, what birth is, what rebirth is.

In summary, the Valentinian Gnostic doctrine of the fall and the salvation of the divine element in humans is:

> - Sophia (Wisdom) was the origin of sin and she degraded and thrust the divine element into the non-Pleroma world through the materialism of her mistake.
> - Recovery of the fallen Pleroma or spiritual element in the world is brought about by the intervention of a "savior', the activity of the Demiurge, and the distinction of humans into three kinds: pneumatic, psychic and hylic or "spiritual, material, and animal"[230]
> - Reintegration is accomplished by separating the divine element from matter and returning it to the Pleroma.

---

228. Irenaeus, *Against Heresies* 1.1.3 (ANF 1.317).

229. Irenaeus, *Against Heresies* 1.2.3 (ANF 1.318).

230. Irenaeus, *Against Heresies* 1.7.5 (ANF 1.326).

This scheme continues the dualism between spirit and matter, as was found in Plato, and would be in the later Manichaeans. So, as we've seen:

> The idea of *creatio ex nihilo*...was elaborated to exclude the Gnostic teaching that matter is evil, the work of a lesser being, not the work of the God who redeems.[231]

Thus, the Valentinian and other early forms of Gnosticism were effectively dealt with by the early Christian Fathers, using the doctrine of *creatio ex nihilo*. Later, Augustine would need this doctrine against a more extreme foe.

The Manichaeans background

Manichaeus (c. 216–277)

Now an even more extremely dualistic form of Gnosticism had reared its head in the form of Manichaeanism. It promised such certainty that even the young Augustine was taken with its doctrine. It was much like its predecessor, Valentinian Gnosticism, in that its goal was the recovery of all spiritual elements back to the realm of the divine. Mani's myth could be considered extreme by comparison to Valentinus in that there was never a single realm of the divine (the Valentinian Pleroma) having only one high god. Instead, as we've seen in earlier religions, there were two divine realms: one of Light and one of Darkness, ruled by two separate (good and bad) uncreated high gods. This cosmology had the effect of solving the problem of evil in the world, which most certainly accounted for its appeal to the young Augustine.

Mani came from Persia and echoes of the Persian religion can readily be seen in his myth. Zoroaster, many centuries before, had posited two such dualistic realms: one ruled by the good Ahura-Mazda; the other by the evil Ahriman; both in a constant struggle. However, there the essential similarity ends.

With Valentinus' theology, the world was created in order to recover from the error of Sophia. But, with Mani's, the world was necessarily created because the Good God wanted to protect himself from the Evil God.[232] After the invasion of

---

231.Ian G. Barbour, "Creation and Cosmology," in *Cosmos as creation* ed. Ted Peters (Nashville: Abringdon Press, 1989), 125.

232.Augustine *City of God* 11.22 (454).

the realm of Light by the realm of Darkness, particles of Light had become imbedded into the Darkness of evil gross matter that was to make up the human body.

Augustine will refute this dualism many times; here he does so in *Two Souls*, saying that the Manichaeans:

> say that there are two kinds of souls, the one good…said…to have proceed as a certain part from the very substance itself of God; the other evil, which…pertains to God in no way whatever…one time distinct…now commingled.[233]

As with the theology of earlier Gnostics, human bodies contained the divine element (as did all matter to a greater or lesser degree). For the Manichaean it was the duty of humans to liberate the Light from matter, which they did by eating those foods containing the greatest portion of Light, digesting it and freeing the Light.[234]

Augustine (354–430 CE)

Once Augustine had become convinced of the truth of the Catholic faith, he vehemently refuted his previous beliefs, and the main weapon of this refutation was the Christian Fathers' doctrine of *creatio ex nihilo*, now brought to its finest statement in the arguments of Augustine.

Many scholars have defined what God's creation of everything *ex nihilo* meant for Augustine. Two such scholars are Gerhart Niemeyer and Keith Ward. Gerhart Niemeyer claims that "*Deus creator omnium*" is the phrase that captures Augustine's entire ontology and the fact that God created all things out of nothing means that mutable things therefore both are and are not. "They are needy [their]…being is threatened by nothingness and must adhere to God to save

233.Augustine, *On Two Souls, Against the Manichaeans 12.16, in A Select Library of the Christian Church. Nicene and Post-Nicene Fathers.* First Series, Vol. 4: *The Writings Against the Manichaeans and Against the Donatists, ed Philip Schaff* (Edinburgh: T&T Clark, 1887; repr. Grand Rapids: Eerdmans Publishing Co., 1996), 104.

234.Augustine, *Reply to Faustus the Manichaean 6.4, in A Select Library of the Christian Church. Nicene and Post-Nicene Fathers.* First Series, Vol. 4: *The Writings Against the Manichaeans and Against the Donatists, ed Philip Schaff* (Edinburgh: T&T Clark, 1887, repr. Grand Rapids: Eerdmans Publishing Co., 1996), 169.

it."[235] Keith Ward says: for Augustine "the doctrine of creation ex nihilo simply maintains that there is nothing other than God from which the universe is made, and that the universe is other than God and wholly dependent upon God for its existence."[236]

In both of these statements, I believe they are correct, but that there is also more to it. Augustine does use *creation ex nihilo* to deny that the world is something which emanated from God.[237] Even more so, *creatio ex nihilo* was Augustine's way of denying Manichaean view that the soul is of the same substance as God. It also allowed him to refute the Manichaean necessity of the Good God's having to create the world in order to salvage His parts. Augustine says:

> the most high God, that made heaven and earth, not of a foreign substance, but of nothing—not from the pressure of necessity, but from the plenitude of goodness—not by the suffering of his members, by the power of His word.[238]

Thus, in this one sentence, Augustine lays claim to the concepts of "world created from nothing", "world is not begotten of God's substance" and also that "the world is not even necessary" to God, as it was for the Manichaean restoration of the Kingdom of Light.

The difference between the words "begotten" and "created" holds the key to whether the soul is of God, or only from God. The Manichaeans said the soul is begotten of God and is thus of God's own nature, whereas Augustine says the soul is created from nothing.

This theme of being "created" allows for the soul's having, like the Platonic copies, a less perfect resemblance to the reality of the Forms. Augustine will conclude:

---

235. Gerhart Niemeyer, "History and Civilization," *Anglican Theological Review: Supplementary Series* 7 (Nov 1976): 83.

236. Keith Ward, *Religion and Creation* (Oxford: Clarendon Press, 1996), 290.

237. As we've seen in Neo-Platonism and even earlier Egyptian.

238. Augustine, *Reply to Faustus the Manichaean 22.69 (NPNF 1st ser. 298); see also, On the Literal Interpretation of Genesis: An Unfinished Book* 1.2, trans. Roland J. Teske, The Fathers of the Church 84 (Washington: Catholic University of America Press, 1991), 146; *Nature of Good* 27 (NPNF 1st ser. 357).

And when I asked myself what wickedness was, I saw that it was not a substance but perversion of the will when it turns aside from you...the supreme substance.[239]

And,

man's nature created good...it was made changeable...since created from nothing...the will in that nature can turn away from good to do evil.[240]

And,

Therefore, there can be "only one unchanging Good...[mutable] things [are]...not supreme goods"[241]

So, the created soul is neither of the same substance, nor of the same supreme existence; evil is not a substance, and created things are mutable. Evil comes from created things simply because they are less than the immutable substance of God.

Summary and conclusion

As to where he got the notion of *creatio ex nihilo*, we can say that Augustine inherited it from the earlier Christian Fathers after Justin Martyr. Before Tatian and Theophilus, the concept did not appear to be in the Christian consciousness, until it was needed to combat the Gnostics in the second century. Then, with the need to refute the Manichaeans, Augustine once again brought it to the fore.

The reason why the answer to the "why *ex nihilo*" was so important to Augustine was this; it allowed his great conclusions, thusly:

- one God created everything, therefore, the body and all of creation is good.
- God created not of his own substance, therefore the created things are not the highest good but are imperfect and capable of evil.

It allows Augustine to finally say:

Whence is corruption? It is hence, because these natures that are capable of corruption were not begotten by God, but made by Him out of

---

239. Augustine *Confessions* 7.16 (150).

240. Augustine *City of God* 15.21 (635).

241. Augustine *City of God* 12.1 (472).

> nothing…So we see that it is unreasonable to require that things made out of nothing should be as perfectly good as He who was begotten.[242]

This is the great achievement of Augustine; by using *creatio ex nihilo*, he can explain the problem of evil in the world without having to resort to dualism.

Augustine may be seen to mark the complete dominance of Orthodoxy. To be sure, many conflicts continued but the factions disagreeing with Augustine would eventually be overwhelmed. **Fig. 45** shows the state of Christian development around the fifth century.

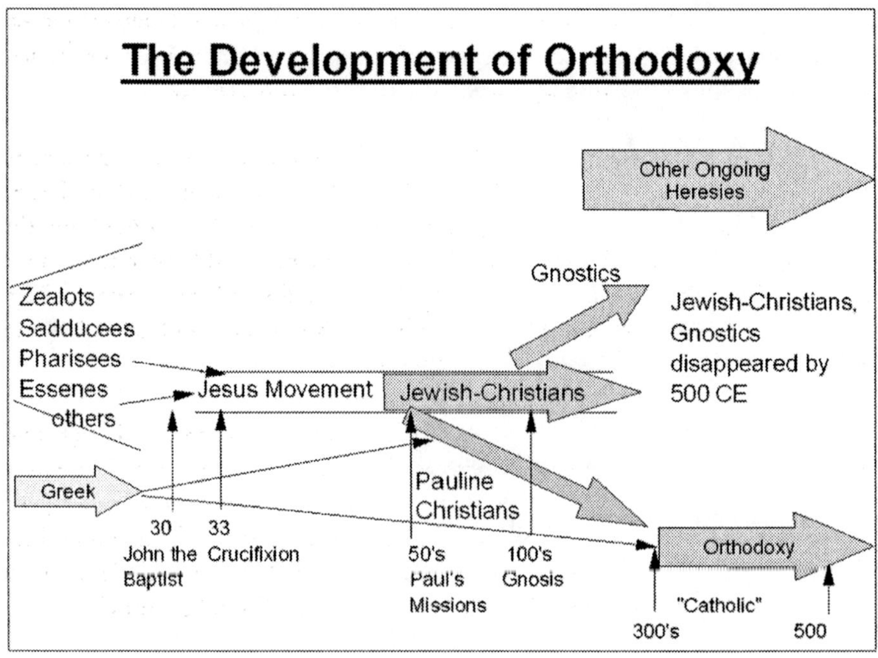

Fig. 45 The Development of Orthodoxy ca. 400 CE

242. Augustine, *Against the Epistle of Manichaeaus called Fundamental 36.41, in A Select Library of the Christian Church. Nicene and Post-Nicene Fathers*. First Series, Vol. 4: *The Writings Against the Manichaeans and Against the Donatists, ed Philip Schaff* (Edinburgh: T&T Clark, 1887; repr. Grand Rapids: Eerdmans Publishing Co., 1996), 148.

The Making of the New Testament (Encapsulation)

Continuing with "The Making of the Hebrew Bible" from Part II…

In 1611, King James of England requested that a group of scholars compile an English version of the Bible based on the best available ancient language manuscripts. This effort resulted in the much beloved text containing the now archaic English we have come to associate with the language of religion….

All of the New Testament was written in Greek by, and for, the Greek speakers of the emerging Church. The earliest books of the New Testament are those letters composed by Paul for the benefit of his missionary churches throughout the Greek world. The first book of the New Testament would, therefore, be 1 Thessalonians written around the year 50 CE. The four Gospels were written between 65 CE for Mark to 100 CE for John; with Matthew and Luke, both of which depend on Mark, written around 85 CE.

During the first two centuries of the church, there were scores of Gospels and innumerable other letters written by diverse adherents to the new faith. These were written by various competing sects within the church, and were quite incompatible with one another. The books that eventually won acceptance for inclusion into the New Testament were those written by the winner of the competition, which was the group that became the Greek-language-oriented Catholic Church.

The earliest extant list of books that were considered acceptable to be included in the New Testament dates from ca. 200 CE. It contains all of the current books, except Philemon, Hebrews, James, 1 & 2 Peter, and 3 John but also includes the Wisdom of Solomon and the Apocalypse of Peter, both of which were later rejected.

The Church was to eventually modify this list to those books that conformed to the dominant theology. Even then, the Western and Eastern bishops quibbled over them, and would have rejected Hebrews and Revelations, respectively, but for a political compromise. Bishop St. Athanasius of Alexandria's festal letter of 367 CE contains the list of books that were eventually adopted as canonical by the Church. It was this canon that was translated, at the request of the Pope, into the definitive Latin version by St. Jerome in 405 CE.

Thus, for over a thousand years, this was the Holy Bible of all orthodox Christians in the West, until the Protestant Reformation.

The Canon of the New Testament

The early years

The Church was expecting the immediate end of the world, so there was no urgency to document for the future. However, oral traditions kept the early stories of Jesus and his followers alive.

The New Testament canon, as we have it today, contains writings from 50 to 150 CE. Paul wrote many letters to his wayward churches, which were collected and became the earliest New Testament books.

Irenaeus of Lyon (ca. 180) argued that Matthew and John were written by disciples of Jesus, and Mark and Luke by disciples of the Apostles; therefore, they were worthy of inclusion.

Marcion's heretical canon encouraged the development of a standard set of writings that would help to avoid non-orthodox beliefs.

The Muratorian canon, a Latin document dating from ca. 200 CE, contains all of the current 27 books except:

Hebrews
James
1 and 2 Peter
3 John

But it adds books that are not in the later New Testament

> Wisdom of Solomon
> Apocalypse of Peter
> Two forged letters from Paul to Laodicea and Alexandria
> The Shepard of Hermas, but is recommended for private reading only

The Canon is closed

St. Athanatius's Festal letter (ca. 367) is the first document to contain all of the current 27 books. His list of acceptable books eventually won the day, but first there was serious political accommodation. The book of Hebrews was contested by Western Latin Christianity, and the book of Revelations was contested by the Greek speaking East. A compromise assured that both books would be included in the final list.

Under Pope Damasas, the canon was determined in 382 CE at Rome, and finally ratified at the Council of Carthage (ca. 419), closing the New Testament forever.

There were criteria for including any book into the canon; it had to be:

Apostolic—believed to have been written by an apostle or a disciple of an apostle.
Ancient—thought to be written during the 1st century.
Ubiquitous—widely read throughout all of Christendom.
Correct—contained the proper acceptable theology/doctrine of the dominant church.

The following tables (**Fig. 46** and **Fig. 47**) give the consensus of Bible scholars on the supposed author and approximate date of each New Testament book:

Canon of the Gospels

Book	**Author**	**(Ca. Date)**
Matthew	Anonymous	85 CE
Mark	Anonymous	70
Luke	Anonymous	85
John[243]	Anonymous	95
Acts	same author as Luke	85

Fig. 46 The Canon of the Gospels

243. Some in Rome said "we ought not to have" the Gospel of John because it compromises Jesus' humanity, and was a main gospel of the Gnostics.

Canon of the Epistles and Revelations

Unfortunately, some authors and dates are not known and others are scholarly guesses.

Book	Author	(Ca. Date)
Romans	Paul	58
1 Corinthians	Paul	55
2 Corinthians	Paul	56
Galatians	Paul	54
Ephesians	?	?
Philippians	Paul	62?
Colossians	Paul?	62?
1 Thessalonians	Paul	52
2 Thessalonians	Pseudonymous	?
1 Timothy	Pseudonymous	?
2 Timothy	Pseudonymous	?
Titus	Pseudonymous	?
Philemon	Paul	?
Hebrews	Anonymous	before 70
James	Pseudonymous	? possibly 110
1 Peter	Pseudonymous	?
2 Peter	Pseudonymous	100?
1 John	Anonymous	140?
2 John	Anonymous	?
3 John	Anonymous	?
Jude	Pseudonymous	140?
Revelation	John of Patmos?	90?

Fig. 47 The Canon of the Epistles and Revelations

The compilation of the New Testament

Just as we discovered multiple authorship and redaction over an extended period of time with the Old Testament, so have we found the general evolution of the

Gospels. Luke and Matthew wrote independently but both used two common sources. We are certain that one was Mark and, fairly certain, that there was a "sayings of Jesus" text that they also used. This hypothetical text was given the name "Source", which in the Biblical scholars' German is Quelle, or Q for short.

Q will figure prominently in the quest for the historical Jesus.

Luke and Matthew also each had another independent source, which has been called "L" for Luke and "M" for Matthew.

This scheme is illustrated graphically in **Fig. 48,** thus:

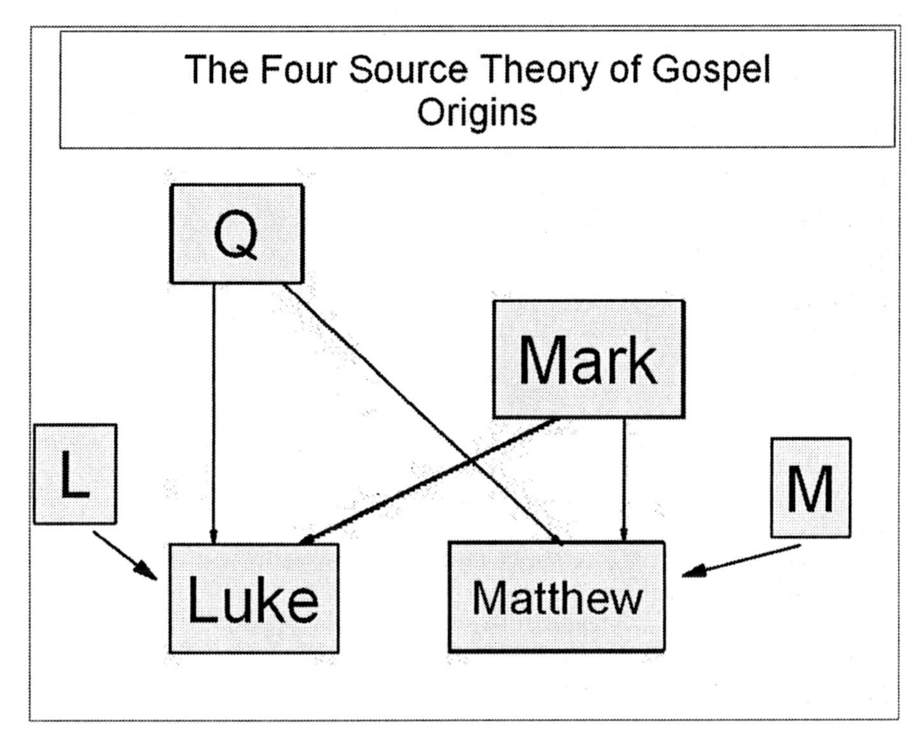

Fig. 48 Origin of the Gospels—Four Source Theory

QUEST FOR THE HISTORICAL JESUS

If we are to have a quest, we need something to look for. In this case, it's the human Jesus. Where shall we look? What are the sources of information about Jesus? There is some contentious archeological evidence, such as the shroud of Turin, and the more recent bone box of James the brother of Jesus. These are questionable and we don't have much else. No, our best places to look for the historical Jesus is in written documents.

These come in two types: Christian and non-Christian sources.

Non-Christian Sources

If we look at non-Christian references to Jesus within 100 years of his death, we find only these three:

> Pliny the Younger (governor of Bithynia in Asia Minor ca. 111–131 CE) writing to Trajan (112 CE), has the line, "Christians were singing hymns to Christ as God."
>
> Tacitus (in 115 CE), *Annuals of Rome*. Mentions Christians as being persecuted for hatred of the human race, who were followers of Christ who was crucified when Tiberius was emperor.
>
> Josephus (ca. 95 CE), *Jewish Antiquities*. Says Jesus was called a messiah, had a brother James, and was a wise man who did spectacular deeds. Text shows later interpolations in **bold print.**[244]

244. Now there was about this time Jesus, a wise man **if it be lawful to call him a man**, for he was a doer of wonders, **a teacher of such men as receive the truth with pleasure.** He drew many after him **both of the Jews and the gentiles. He was the Christ.** When Pilate, at the suggestion of the principal men among us, had condemned him to the cross, those that loved him at the first did not forsake him, **for he appeared to them alive again the third day, as the divine prophets had foretold these and then thousand other wonderful things about him**, and the tribe of Christians, so named from him, are not extinct at this day (*Antiquities* 18:63–64). And so he convened the judges of the Sanhedrin and brought them a man called James, the brother of Jesus who was called the Christ, and certain others *(Antiquities* 20.196–208*)*.

This is a possible reference:

Suetonius (ca. 69–140 CE), *Lifes of the Twelve Caesars.* This claims that the Jews were driven out of Rome for rioting at the instigation of "Crestus" by Claudius, who reigned 41–54 CE. If this were indeed a reference to Christ, it would be the earliest mention of the historical Jesus in non-Christian sources.

This next reference would be too late for our 100-year criteria, but it shows his story was well known by this time.

Lucian of Samosata (ca. 115–200 CE), *The Passing of Peregrinus.* This quote from Lucian's satire mentions the crucified man:

> It was then that he [Peregrinus] learned the wondrous lore of the Christians, by associating with their priests and scribes in Palestine…. and they revered him as a god, made use of him as a lawgiver, and set him down as a protector, next after that other, to be sure, whom they still worship, the man who was crucified in Palestine because he introduced this new cult into the world.

That's the extent of it outside of the New Testament. How about inside?

Christian Sources

Since Paul was concerned with the death and resurrection of the Christ, and not with the person of Jesus, that leaves the Gospels.

But, the Gospels were written very late, contain layers of later theology, and were not designed to be historical; so, how do we get at the historical person of Jesus by using them?

We do it by applying 150 years of scholarship using these scholarly criteria:

- independent attestation (multiple witnesses)
- dissimilarity (against witnesses' vested interest)
- contextual credibility (coincides with other known facts)

The Gospels as non-historical documents

A comparison of the Synoptic and John's Gospels, **Fig. 49**, will illustrate that major issues are not treated the same, and even quite differently. One or the other has to be wrong, if you assume they are literal historical documents. The other option is to assume they are theological documents not intended to be factually historical; that is, they are non-historical.

Issue	**Synoptic Gospels**	**The Latest Gospel**
	Matthew, Mark, Luke	**John**
Virgin birth[245]	Mentioned in Matthew 1:23 (quoting Isaiah 7:14) and Luke	John 1:45 calls Jesus son of Joseph, virgin birth not mentioned
Jesus as Son of God	From the time of birth or baptism	From the time that the universe was created
Description of Jesus	Jesus' humanity emphasized	Jesus' deity emphasized
Jesus equal to God	No	Yes
Jesus' theology	Essentially the Judaism of the time	Largely separate from Judaism
Kingdom of God	Main theme	Background theme
Basis of personal salvation	Good works, helping the poor	Belief in Jesus as the Son of God
Duration of ministry	One year	Three years
Location of ministry	Mainly in Galilee	Mainly in Judea, near Jerusalem
Ceremonial event at the Last Supper	Communal meal only	Foot washing
Who carried the cross?	Simon	Jesus alone
Visitors to the tomb on Sunday with Mary Magdalene?	One or more additional women	Mary Magdalene went alone

Fig. 49 Non-historical Character of the Gospels

245. Matthew 1:23 quotes from the Greek Septuagint, where the Hebrew word המלע (*almah* = young woman) was translated as παρθενος (*parthenos* = virgin). The virgin birth doctrine is thus aquired via the Greeks, not the Hebrew Old Testament.

The Q Source

When did we find the document called Q? Is it like the finds of the Dead Sea Scrolls or the Nag Hammadi texts? Unfortunately, we do not have an actual document called Q! It is a hypothetical document that scholars believe must have existed because Matthew and Luke, which were written independently, contain material from some common source (in German, Quelle). That common source has been named Q.

Protestant and Catholic Bible scholars have isolated the Q sayings by examining those common verses in Matthew and Luke, and have reconstructed what must have been the original document. So, Q is right there in the Gospels.

If you've ever wondered at the contrasting portraits of Jesus in the Gospels, you might have suspected that they were written over a period of time that saw the unfolding of major events in the life of the Jesus Movement community. In some places Jesus is represented as a wise man, healer of the sick, and champion of the underprivileged. At other times we see Jesus in the role of apocalyptic eschatologist; then, as a God in the later Gospel.

We see this development in the entire Gospels and in the much smaller Q source. Scholars have further isolated layers of writings that show a theological development over a short period of time.

These layers are called:

Q1, Q2 and Q3

We can use them to glimpse the historical Jesus within 20 years of his crucifixion, and before the various factions added their flavor to the story.

Q1—Describes Jesus as a Philosopher/Teacher

Prior to the writing of Q1, the Gospel message was passed verbally among individuals and groups. About 50 CE, this oral tradition was written down as Q1. Q1 covers the following topics:

who will belong to the "Kingdom of God"
treating others (the Golden Rule)
loving even enemies

do not judge others
good people produce good things
dedicating oneself to the Kingdom
telling others about the Kingdom
asking for God's help through prayer
proclaim the message confidently
don't worry about tomorrow
don't worry about food, clothing, possessions
behave humbly
the Kingdom is here or will soon arrive
the cost of being a follower
the cost of rejecting the message

Jesus is described as a devout Jewish man from Galilee, but there are no indications as yet that he was considered more than a gifted human being. He was not thought of as a Messiah, but rather as a philosopher and teacher.

If this is indeed the earliest writings of the Jesus Movement, we can see that in Q1 the original Christians appeared to be centered totally on concerns about their relationships with God and other people, and their preparation for the breaking in of the Kingdom of God on earth.

Completely absent from consideration are almost all of the doctrines that we associate with Paul's epistles, or modern day Christianity.

Q2—Describes Jesus as an Apocalyptic Prophet

A short time later, the scenes were added of the coming end of the world with its judgment. Q1, of course, had been accepted by the Movement and was considered the standard teaching text of the community. So the additional sayings were inter-woven within the existing Q1 story in order to integrate the judgmental texts, as part of his original message.

The new sayings were written in response to the serious civil unrest and upheavals in Palestine (associated with the Roman-Jewish war around 60 to 70 CE). Q2 includes statements of judgments against those who refused to listen to Jesus' message and those who had rejected them. Apocalyptic appears in the form of John the Baptist and the coming Judgment. Jesus tells John of his miracles that show he is the awaited Messiah:

> the blind receive their sight, the lame walk, the lepers are cleansed, the deaf hear, the dead are raised, the poor have good news brought to them.

This is the quote we've seen in the Essene Scroll 4Q521 and Isaiah 61:1, which is now reflected in Luke 7:22 and Matthew 11:4.

Instead of the simple hopefulness of God's bounty taking care of his people, we see an "us" versus "them" attitude, and "they" are the ones who had better be afraid of the coming Judgment.

Q3—Describes Jesus as now speaking for God

Even more additional sayings appear to have been added during the mid 70's CE. This was at a time that the Roman-Jewish war had concluded, after the Jews and Jewish-Christians had been driven from Palestine.

These new sayings describe the followers of Jesus as retreating from the violence and civil unrest of society, and looking forward to the time of their deliverance when the Kingdom would finally arrive. Jesus was upgraded beyond his original Q1 status as a teacher (and his later Q2 status as apocalyptic prophet), and is now described as the son of the Father God who interacts with Satan, and reveals the Father to whom he so chooses.

Other Christian writers would be aware of this "sayings Gospel," and Matthew and Luke built their Gospels, in part, around Q and Mark.

This developing theology in Q was all integrated into the Gospels of Luke and Matthew, making them very ambiguous. Because of this ambiguity, one can read almost anything into the Gospels, so that scholars and denominations still debate exactly who and what Jesus was.

Then, confusing the situation even more, we also have the further development of:

> Pauline theology
> First Century and later additions of the Church Fathers

The following **Fig. 50** shows the corresponding locations where Q is found in Matthew and Luke and the proposed breakdown into the Q1, Q2 and Q3 components.

QS[246]	Q1	Q2	Q3	Description	Luke	Matthew
3		x		John the Baptist	3:3	3:5–6
4		x		Baptist preaching	3:7–9	3:7–10.
5		x		The coming one	3:16–17	3:11–12
D[247]				Baptism of Jesus	3:21–22	3:13–17
6			x	Temptations	4:1–13	4:1–11
p				Jesus in Nazareth	4:16a	4:13.
7, 8	x	x		Beatitudes	6:20–23	5:2–12
p				Woes	6:24–26	
9, 10	x			Love enemies, 2nd mile	6:27–35	5:38–48 7.12
10–12	x			Judging	6:37–42	7:1–5 10:24–25 15:14
13	x			Integrity	6:43–45	7:16–20 12:33–35
14	x			Test of good person	6:46	7:21–23
14	x			Hearers and doers	6:47–49	7:24–27
15		x		Centurion	7:1–10	7:28 8:5–13
16		x		John's question to Jesus	7:18–23	11:2–6
17		x		Jesus about John	7:24–28	11:7–11
p				John, tax collectors	7:29–30	21:28–32
18		x		Children in agora	7:31–35	11:16–19
19	x			Would–be follower	9:57–62	8:18–22

246. QS numbers (designating probable sayings of Jesus) are taken from: Burton L. Mack, *The Lost Gospel: The Book of Q & Christian Origins*, (HarperSanFrancisco, 1993), 260-1.

247. John S. Kloppenborg, *Q Parallels*, (Polebridge Press, 1988). Sayings not in Mack. For Kloppenborg, sayings marked by d are doubtful, sayings marked with p are probable.

QS[246]	Q1	Q2	Q3	Description	Luke	Matthew
20 21 22 23	x	 x x x		The mission of The seventy	10:2–11 10:12 10:13–15 10:16	9:37–38 10:7–16 11:20–24 10:40
24			x	Jesus grateful to Father	10:21–22	11:25–27
25		x		Blessedness of disciples	10:23–24	13:16–17
d				Limit mission to Israel	none	10:5–6, 23
d				Great commandment	10:25–27	22:35–39
26	x			Lord's prayer	11:2–4	6:9–13
d				Midnight friend	11:5–8	
27	x			Answer to prayer	11:9–13	7:7–11
28, 32		x		Beelzebub	11:14–20	12:22–28
28, 29		x		Binding strong man, not against me	11:21–23	11:29–30
30		x		Unclean spirit	11:24–26	12:43–45
31			x	True blessedness	11:27–28	
32		x		Sign of Noah	11:29–32	12:38–42
33		x		Light of body	11:33–36	5:15 6:22–23
34		x	x	Against Pharisees	11:39–52	23:24–36
35–37	x	x	x	Fearless confession	12:2–12	10:26–33
38	x			Divider	12:13–14	
38	x			Rich fool	12:16–21	
39 40				Anxious over life Treasures	12:22–34 12:33–34	6:25–33 6:19–21
d				Watchful faithful	12:35–38	
41		x		Watchful faithful	12:39–40	24:43–44
42		x		Faithful servants	12:42–46	24:45–51
43		x		Cause of division	12:49–53	10:34–36

QS[246]	Q1	Q2	Q3	Description	Luke	Matthew
44		x		Signs of times	12:54–56	16:2–3
45		x		One's accuser	12:58–59	5:25–26
46	x			Mustard seed, yeast	13:18–21	13:31–33
47		x		Narrow door	13:24–27	7:13–14 7:22–23 25:11–12
48		x		Many will come	13:28–30	8:11–12 19:30 20:16
49			x	Lament over Jerusalem	13:34–35	23:37–39
d				Sheep falls in pit	14:5	12:11
50	x			Humility	14:11 18:14	
51	x			Great dinner	14:16–24	22:1–10
52	x			Cost of discipleship	14:26–27 17:33	10:37–38 10:39
53	x			Savorless salt	14:34–35	5:13
54		x		Lost sheep	15:4–7	18:12–14
54		x		Lost coins	15:8–10	
55		x		God and mammon	16:13	6:24
56			x	Violence to Kingdom	16:16	11:12
56			x	The Law No divorce	16:17–18	5:18 5:32 19:9
57		x		Causing sin	17:1–2	18:6–7
58		x		Forgiveness	17:3–4	18:15 18:21–22
59		x		Faith like mustard seed	17:6	17:20–21
d				Unprofitable servant	17:7–10	
p				Kingdom and signs	17:20–21	

QS[246]	Q1	Q2	Q3	Description	Luke	Matthew
60		x		Day of Son of Man	17:23–24, 37	24:26–28
60		x		Days of Noah	17:26–27	24:37–39 10:39
60		x		Days of Lot	17:28–30	none
60		x		Two in Field	17:34–35	24:40–41.
61		x		Talents	19:12–27	25:14–30
62			x	Greatness in Kingdom, 12 tribes	22:28–30	19:28

Fig. 50 The Q Document

Eschatology in Early Christianity (Essay)

This essay will discuss the concept and development of the Afterlife and the Judgment of the Dead (in late Judaism and early Christianity) in more detail. The emphasis here is on the Christian development, whereas, in the Part II "Religions of Ancient Israel" section, we concentrated on historical pre-Christian eschatology.

Introduction and Background

A serious situation arose in early Christianity when the promised Last Days did not appear.

According to the Scriptures, God had promised a judgment on all his people. It was assumed by the first generations of Christians that this judgment would take place in the immediate future on the Last Days when Jesus would return at the Second Coming (*Parousia*). In the meanwhile, since the Last Days did not come, where did the faithful go who died until that event would happen? As long as the end seemed imminent, people could prepare for it accordingly. Now, what were they to do? A series of questions arose in reaction to this situation.

If the faithful were not to be judged until the delayed Last Days, where did they mark "time" between their present death and the future Last Days?

If they were, indeed, to be judged at the Last Days; yet, they existed "someplace" until that event, just when were they selected in order to await a reward or punishment? Was it immediately or later, and in what condition were they in the meantime?

If they were to be judged immediately upon death, what was the purpose of the original Judgment at the Last Days?

These questions, brought about by the delay of the Parousia, had to be answered by the early Church in order to provide a coherent theology.

This inquiry will trace the evolution of Christian eschatology, and how the ideas of the general judgment (in the last days) changed to that of an individual and particular judgment, which slowly came to be realized in Christian dogma by the sixth century.

In order to explore that evolution within the first six centuries of Christianity, we must step back and look at some of the theological concepts that were the precursors to the later thinking of the early Church Fathers.

A recapitulation of foreign influences on Israel (from Part II)

The cosmology of the ancient Israelites was derived from that of their neighbors. Even the later Priestly writer of Genesis 1 still shows the ancient Near East emphasis on ordering the chaos of the primordial waters. As much as the three-tiered cosmology (under-the-earth, earth, heaven) of the Mesopotamians and the Canaanites influenced their concepts of the afterlife (with the cult of the dead under the earth), so the essentially same cosmology did for the early Israelites.

With Josiah's reforms, the cult of the dead was eliminated or driven underground, so that the official Yahweh-only religion had no belief in the afterlife.

With the trauma of the Exile, even though subsequently freed by the hand of Cyrus of Persia, the Deuteronomic promise of long life and reward in this life was severely questioned. The resurrection ideas of Persian Zoroastrianism may have offered a model for a post-exilic afterlife scenario that would offer life and reward in a restored paradise[248] on earth for faithful service to Yahweh. This reward, obviously denied in this life, would be forthcoming in a later and better life at the end of time.

As the empire of Alexander the Great spread throughout the world, and the Jews of the Diaspora became more Hellenized, they attempted to integrate the ideas of the Platonic concept of the soul into the Jewish religion. The two concepts were mutually incompatible, so the tendency of the Hellenized Jews was to adhere to Platonic immortality, while the sect of the Pharisees (and their rabbinical successors) held to the resurrection of the body.

---

248. Yamauchi, *Persia and the Bible*, 332-3. The Greek word *paradeisos* (from the Old Persian *paridaiza*) was used to describe the Garden of Eden in the *Septuagint* (Gen. 3: 8–10). It was borrowed as *pardes* in Hebrew. This would seem to be an instance of a definite influence.

These two ideas, coming from two separate origins, are obviously incompatible and were therefore held in tension by the larger body of the Jews and later by the Christians.[249]

So, another question for our inquiry becomes: when did the Platonic idea of the body/soul dualism actually enter into the thinking of the Christian Fathers—and why?

For the time being, close upon the Common Era, the ideas of the Last Days, the Resurrection of the Dead, and their Judgment had entered into the consciousness of the Jewish people before the founding of Christianity.

The Kingdom of Heaven—General Judgment in the Last Days

It would seem that this consciousness was bequeathed to the Jesus movement, for by the time of Jesus (less than 200 years after the Maccabees), the resurrection was a key part of the Jewish religion, accepted by all major sects except the Sadducees. It was certainly considered part of the message of Jesus who is said to have proclaimed that all would arise on the Last Days at his return; the dead would arise and be judged by God.

At the time of the Jesus movement, the Pharisaic resurrection was held to be the method to gain eternal life. The early Christian idea was that those who had already died in Christ—and those still living at the End Time or Last Days—would all arise in the flesh and be judged,[250] some to eternal life and some to eternal darkness.

Did the resurrection of Jesus usher in the Last Days? Many believed that Jesus was the first fruits of the harvest; he was the first to arise in the End Times. So, the question of exactly what the End Times was is left open to interpretation—at least for now. How did the early Church view it? Most probably, at face value as clearly stated in the Bible in Mark, where it says, "Truly I say to you, there are some standing here who will not taste death, before they see the kingdom of God come with power" (Mark 9:1).

---

249. This dichotomy of afterlife beliefs was only gradually resolved hundreds of years later by the Christian Fathers in the early centuries of Christianity.

250. 2 Pet. 2:4,9; 1 Thes. 4:13–5:11; 2 Thes. 2:1–15; 1 Cor. 17:26–31.

Here we have a continuation of the apocalyptic ideas first introduced in the time of Daniel. This is the legacy given to the early Church.

The Parousia of first century Christianity

If the resurrection and the End Times were "at hand." then there would be no theological problem of the Judgment. But, the End Times weren't at hand and there is a problem. This caused the early discussion of what happens to us between death and the Last Days.

In his article, "Thinking about the second Coming", Borg claims that there is nowhere in the New Testament where it speaks about the second coming of Christ in our [today] present time or any [other] future time.[251] Borg says, "In short, the texts tell us that many Christians believed that the second coming of Jesus would occur in or near their time. And, to say the obvious, they were wrong."[252] So, what were the more thoughtful among them to do as the Parousia was delayed? They could either have moved it into a future time, or they could see it as already having already happened. Some books of the New Testament chose to do the latter with a "realized eschatology" in the first century. Others would later ignore that approach and look for the eschaton in their future.

It was only toward the end of the first century, with the delay of the End Times that the Platonic ideas, reinvigorated by the Jewish Philo, arose among the Christians. This most likely happened because it was necessary in order to allow an immediate reward to the martyred—much as had happened with Daniel and the Maccabees two centuries earlier.

We start to see this transition in John 5:24 and 6:39, where the End Time kingdom is already at hand; whereas, some other New Testament books, especially Revelations, claim that the End Time is not yet come. Nevertheless, the promise of the resurrection is assured at <u>some</u> future time.

---

251. Marcus J. Borg, "Thinking About the Second Coming", *Bible Review*, no. 10 (Aug. 1994): 16.

252. Borg, "Thinking About the Second Coming", 16.

Eschatological doctrinal developments in the early Patristic Age

By the time of the second century, the eschaton was being moved firmly into the future by the Apostolic and Patristic Fathers; and with this movement, the aforesaid questions at the beginning of this essay arise. Let us look at some of the solutions proposed by some key theologians: Clement of Rome, Barnabus, Papias, Justin, Irenaeus, Clement of Alexandria, Tertullian, Origen, Cyprian, Lactantius, Basil, Gregory of Nazianzus, Gregory of Nyssa, Augustine, and Gregory the Great.

Note that in discussing the Judgment, it is impossible to avoid reference to closely related topics, which are all generally categorized as "last things" or eschatology: millenarianism (chiliasm), Parousia, judgment, resurrection, paradise, hell, purgatory, and restoration (apocatastasis).

The Apostolic Fathers (late 1st and early 2nd centuries)

God's future kingdom on earth dominated Christian eschatology in the first and second centuries:

In the period of the apostolic church, an apocalyptic eschatological expectation dominated both thought and practice.[253] The Apostolic Fathers generally confine themselves to confirming the eternal and inextinguishable fire that awaits sinners.

In their thinking, the Judgment is universal and final, and it is Christ who will be the judge. He will separate the good from the bad, and death and destruction will be the fate of the wicked.

Second Clement claims that Christ will return to judge the living and the dead (2 Clem 1:1), and Barnabus says that the justice of the Judgment is the beginning and end of our faith (Barn 1,6).[254]

---

253. T. A. Burkill, *The Evolution of Christian Thought,* (Ithaca: Cornell University Press, 1971), 47.

254. G. Filoramo, "Judgment," in *Encyclopedia of the Early Church,* edited by Angelo DiBeradino, trans. Adrian Walford (New York: Oxford University Press, 1992), 457.

The New Testament and Apostolic writing concerns itself mostly with the general judgment, but hints at the particular Judgment immediately after death, so Peter and Paul, according to Clement, went directly to the holy place to join the martyrs and saints (1 Clem 5:4–7).[255]

"Clement's notion of an interim existence in heaven for the godly, before the bodily resurrection, should signify that he was not a chiliast."[256] Thus, he appears to be able to hold both a spiritual and a physical resurrection simultaneously, avoiding millenarianism (chiliasm); and being among the earliest to accept the Platonic immortality of the soul.

Papias, however, was "a firm believer in the millenarianism of (Rev. 20:4–6), maintaining that, after the resurrection of the dead, the Kingdom of Christ would be set up on earth for a period of a thousand years."[257]

So, we see that the earliest Christians had, by no means, settled on a consistent theology.

The Gnostics (2nd century)

The Gnostics rejected the goodness of material creation, and therefore, the resurrection of created bodies. Their doctrine of predestination eliminated the need for a Judgment (a doctrine which Marcion had attributed to the God of the Old Testament).

The Gnostic heresies had to be refuted, and in doing so, the refuters supported the Pharisaic resurrection;, thereby, delaying general acceptance of the Platonic body/soul dualism for quite some time.

Justin Martyr (ca. 100–165).

Both body and soul "become participants in immortality…As Christ promises immortality also to the body, he excels the philosophical representations upon the subject of future life".[258] This is a direct attack on the Platonic idea of the soul

255. Filoramo, "Judgment", 457.

256. Charles E. Hill, *Regnum Caelorum* (Oxford: Clarendon Press, 1992), 72.

257. Burkill, *The Evolution of Christian Thought*, 27.

258. Reinhold Seeberg, *Text-Book of the History of Doctrines*, Trans. Charles E. Hay (Grand Rapids, Michigan: Baker Book House, 1966), 117.

alone being immortal. Many early Fathers claimed that the soul was not essentially immortal; but due to the resurrection, both body and soul would participate.

He accepted millenarianism, but allowed that it was not held by all, even those of good faith in his Dial 80.2,[259] but was against the eschatological spiritualism of the Gnostics.

Justin anticipated Clement and Origen by using the word "apocatastasis" as an idea of redemption, but it was left to Origen to define it as the restoration.

He claims that hell is delayed until the final judgment for demons and the damned whose souls know, in the meantime, a preliminary form of punishment; but he attests the eternity of fire as punishment for both damned and demons

Thus, in the works of Justin, there does seem to be a hint of a particular Judgment at the moment of death. At death the souls of the good and wicked both are given separate dwelling places; the place of good being better than the place of the wicked. There they both await the day of judgment.[260]

Irenaeus (ca. 140–200)

Like Justin, Irenaeus is also against the eschatological spiritualism of the Gnostics, and he accepted millenarianism saying, "the end will come when the devil shall have once more recapitulated the entire apostate throng in the Antichrist."[261] Then Christ will appear after the first six thousand years of the world, the resurrection, and the seventh one-thousand years will be the earthly kingdom of Christ.

He says that all people, save the martyrs, descend into Hades, there to await the resurrection.[262] So, there is now an intermediate state to await the resurrection: Hades for all except the martyrs.

---

259. Hill, *Regnum Caelorum*, 3.

260. Hill, *Regnum Caelorum*, 22f.

261. Seeberg, *Text-Book of the History of Doctrines*, 134.

262. Filoramo, "Hell-Hades", 372.

Clement of Alexandria (ca. 150–215)

Clement is a forerunner of Origen, holding that the punishing fire is not punitive, nor eternal, but rather a healing to allow eventual admission into the final restoration; what he calls apocatastasis. This idea of a restorative fire is an ancestor of the later concept of purgatory. He also rejected millenarianism and would pass that belief on to Origen.

He "was the first to distinguish two categories of sinners and two categories of punishment in this life and the life to come...two fires, a "devouring and consuming" one for the incorrigible, and for the rest, a fire that "sanctified" and "does not consume..."[263] And, he says that "God's absolute goodness implies that punishment can only have a pedagogical, purifying, and healing function, not only in this life, but after death as well."[264]

He claimed that the sin of Adam was by example and not by generation;[265] whereas, Augustine would later claim that sin was transmitted by generation and, thus, develop the doctrine of original sin.

Tertullian (ca. 155–220).

"Tertullian stands in continuity with the apocalyptic of late Judaism and early Christianity."[266] He believed, along with the New Testament and some earlier Christians, that the end was near, therefore "akin to the "consistent eschatology" of the New Testament, or at least the Gospels."[267] Thus, he accepted millenarianism,[268] but prays for the deferment of the end in order to have "more time to convert the heathen and save all men."[269]

---

263. Jacques LeGoff, *The Birth of Purgatory*, trans. Arthur Goldhammer (Chicago: University of Chicago Press, 1984), 54.

264. John R. Sachs, "Apocatastasis in Patristic Theology," *Theological Studies*, no. 54 D (1993): 618.

265. Johannes Quasten, *The Ante-Nicene Literature after Irenaeus*, Vol. 2 of *Patrology* (Westminster, Maryland: Christian Classics, Inc., 1986), 31.

266. Jaroslav Pelikan, "The Eschatology of Tertullian," *Church History* 21 (Je 1952): 110.

267. Pelikan, "The Eschatology of Tertullian" 113.

268. Quasten, *Patrology*, 318.

269. Pelikan, "The Eschatology of Tertullian", 116.

However, the delay of the Parousia caused Tertullian to believe that the "end" in the New Testament passage should be taken as the end of the individual life rather than of all things. So, the end day actually referred to the day of one's death. This immediate judgment was of the earliest explanations of the "particular judgment'. He noted that with the exception of the martyrs, there is for all souls a general place in Hades, until the resurrection, in which there are *supplicia* and *refrigeria* (where it is all right to pray for the dead).[270]

The Parousia, when it did finally come "would be the revelation *substantialiter* of that kingdom which was now already present."[271]

Although Tertullian believed in the soul being still in Adam until it was reborn in Christ, he did not hold the idea that infants who died before baptism were condemned.[272] That remained for Cyprian, Augustine, then Gregory the Great.

General and Particular Judgment through the sixth century CE

Origen (ca. 185–251)

Origen disputed Justin and Irenaeus concerning the earthly Jerusalem and spoke of a heavenly city, and he rejected millenarianism, "the belief that there would be a golden age on earth under the rule of the returned Messiah."[273] Thus, Origen effectively killed chiliasm in the Christian East.

For him, apocatastasis meant the restoration to the original state of souls at the end time, thus even demons may be restored in final order.[274] He therefore interpreted symbolically the details of the Parousia, judgment and hell-fire denying the materiality of infernal fire[275], saying that the fire was rather from the conscience of the guilty soul.[276]

---

270. Quasten, *Patrology*, 288, 338f.

271. Pelikan, "The Eschatology of Tertullian", 118.

272. Jaroslav Pelikan, *Development of Christian Doctrine* (New Haven: Yale University Press, 1969), 89–90.

273. Burkill, *The Evolution of Christian Thought*, 71.

274. Jaroslav Pelikan, *The Emergence of the Catholic Tradition (100–600, vol. 1 of The Christian Tradition: A History of the Development of Doctrine* (Chicago: University of Chicago Press, 1971), 151; Quasten, *Patrology*, 87–92.

275. Sachs, "Apocatastasis in Patristic Theology", 626.

276. Seeberg, *Text-Book of the History of Doctrines*, 159.

He rejected eternal punishment because Christ had come to save those who perished.[277] But he did claim that the souls of the wicked…would continue to burn after Judgment Day for a "century of centuries'.[278]

He wanted to interpret Judgment spiritually so it could be accepted by the educated believer. He believed neither in the resurrection of the flesh nor in the everlastingness of the material world; in true Platonic style."[279]

Origen claimed that the true Judgment is the universal one that will happen at the end of the world, when a final separation between good and evil as judged by works will occur. The works of each will be tested by fire in "the Day" as indicated by 1 Cor 3:11–15,[280] but he has an intermediate place through which souls pass a school of testing[281] and even the fire of hell has no other purpose than to purify. Judgment is not to frighten but to stimulate the will to flee evil. A just distribution of rewards and punishments is not possible on earth, so there must be a Judgment in the world to come. This is reminiscent of the late Jewish thought in Daniel and Maccabees.

Origen was to have many attackers against his teachings. One in particular was Methodius (died 311), who waged a direct attack, claiming that the goal of the Christian life is immortality via the resurrection and that the soul is not what is resurrected but rather the body of "bones and flesh."[282] For Methodius, immortality of the body is to be attained after the destruction of the present world, which will result in a reconstruction of the original creation.[283]

Origen's allegorizing of the resurrection, and his insistence on the pre-existence of the soul, caused many to also oppose the Platonic immortality of the soul and; thus, held back the harmonization of the two concepts (of bodily resurrection and immortality of the soul), for almost 200 more years.

---

277. Sachs, "Apocatastasis in Patristic Theology", 624.

278. LeGoff, *The Birth of Purgatory*, 56.

279. Burkill, *The Evolution of Christian Thought*, 71.

280. Sachs, "Apocatastasis in Patristic Theology", 625.

281. Seeberg, *Text-Book of the History of Doctrines*, 159; Sacks, "Apocatastasis in Patristic Theology", 625.

282. Pelikan, *Emergence of the Catholic Tradition*, 48.

283. Seeberg, *Text-Book of the History of Doctrines*, 191; Quasten, *Patrology*, 129, 134–136.

Cyprian of Carthage (ca. 200–258)

"Cyprian, like Origen, believed in a purifying fire after death."[284] And, both Cyprian and Origen accepted infant baptism as a part of the sacramental practice of the Church, but both were asking: "Whose sins" were being washed away? Origen may have hinted at the concept of original sin because of this question, but it would be Cyprian who would be the first teacher of the Church to connect the original sin of Adam with "the wages of sin being death," therefore making it necessary that infants should be baptized in order to save them from damnation.[285] Thus, Augustine was later able to appeal to authority for his own doctrine of original sin.

Lactantius (ca. 240–320)

He accepted millenarianism and in spite of his philosophical enlightenment, "he is far from interpreting spiritually the statements of John's apocalypse."[286] He even adds apocalyptic items to it, such as: at the end of the seventh millennium, the Anti-Christ will be defeated, the already risen just will be as angels "dazzling as snow', and the unjust will go down to eternal torment.

So, Lactantius, like Irenaeus and Tertullian, believed that:

- until the first Judgment, Hades and deferment are common to both the impious and the just.
- at the first Judgment, all will pass through the fire, but the just will not suffer.
- then will come the millenarian reign, the final struggle and the general resurrection, with the sinners finally condemned at the general Judgment.

Lactantius' eschatology mirrors that of Zoroaster where: All those who are judged have to pass through the fire (both the good and bad). The good will not suffer but the bad will burn.

---

284. Seeberg, Text-Book of the History of Doctrines, 197.

285. Pelikan, *Development of Christian Doctrine*, 80, 87.

286. Hans Von Campenhausen, *Men Who Shaped the Western Church*, trans. Manfred Hoffmann (New York: Harper & Row, Publishers, 1964), 72.

The three Cappadocian Fathers (ca. 329–395)

Basil rejects Origen's apocatastasis because he claims that eternal punishment cannot end or else eternal life would also end.

Gregory of Nazianzus saw the Maccabees as anticipating Christian martyrdom and the Maccabees mother as Mary.

He believed, like Origen that "sinners will be judged and punished for their transgressions both in this world and the next"[287] and that the chief suffering of the condemned is spiritual and consists of alienation from God.

Although sometimes he seems to hold more traditional concepts of eternal punishment, he still allows that this is unworthy of God, "and if punishment is remedial in nature, it hardly seems possible that it could be eternal."[288] The mercy of Jesus who said to forgive sins until seventy times seven, forced him to conclude that "Condemnation that never forgives…is evil."[289]

Gregory of Nyssa, like Origen and Nazianzus before him, also believes that there may be universal salvation.

He believes in a "renewal of all things" in which all will ascend into heaven. Since this is a restoration to the original creation before sin came into the world, it means the total destruction of evil, therefore universal salvation.

The final restoration will take place at the general resurrection as indicated in 1 Cor 15, where Paul says "every creature of God will become what it was from the beginning, before it had absorbed any evil"[290], even if it takes a final purifying fire after the resurrection.

Augustine (354–430)

He claims that all will be submitted to Christ's Judgment upon death. There are no categories, as there were thought to be by earlier Fathers (i.e., Ambrose had

---

287.Sachs, "Apocatastasis in Patristic Theology", 629.

288.Sachs, "Apocatastasis in Patristic Theology", 630.

289.Sachs, "Apocatastasis in Patristic Theology", 631

290.Sachs, "Apocatastasis in Patristic Theology", 635.

said that the Judgment coincides with the Parousia and that there are three categories: 1) the just—not judged; 2) impious already judged; and 3) sinners who must be judged).

He completely rejects the ideas of Origen and the Cappadocians concerning universal salvation and the eternity of punishment, as Gregory the Great would also later do.

For Augustine, Hell is not symbolic; rather, it is real and eternal with no help for the soul once in there, but Hell's fire is not the same intensity for all, so damnation is graded according to the measure of guilt. It will be lightest of all for the children who have "only inherited from their ancestry, [and] have superadded none."[291]

He gave much attention to the intermediate state and is considered the creator of purgatory, where purification takes place immediately after death, although he opposed Origen concerning universal salvation of all men, he "believed that there were "temporary punishments after death" and that it was appropriate to pray that some of the dead be granted remission of sins."[292]

He set the standard for all Christians in the West when he gave up on millenarianism, doing for the West what Origen had done 200 years earlier for Eastern Christianity.[293]

Gregory the Great (ca. 540–604)

Gregory is credited with fixing the central aspects of the doctrine of purgatory. Gregory wrote that "some are judged and perish, others are not judged but perish (also immediately). Some are judged and reign, others are not judged but reign (also immediately."[294]

He followed Augustine in rejecting Origen's symbolism and insisted on eternal punishment where the damned enter Hell immediately on death and where there is no possibility of hope.

291. Seeberg, *Text-Book of the History of Doctrines*, 365.

292. Pelikan, *Emergence of the Catholic Tradition*, 355.

293. Pelikan, *Emergence of the Catholic Tradition*, 129.

294. LeGoff, *The Birth of Purgatory*, 94.

He followed generally in Augustine's footsteps, but to him he "added a crude superstition and mythological speculation touching angels, demons, etc., as found especially in his "Dialogues'."[295]

Also, like Augustine, he claims original sin through Adam and transmitted by the impurity of the "carnal delight" of conception. Thus "the consequence of Adam's sin…is the damnation of unbaptized children dying in infancy."[296]

He believed that some sins can be forgiven even of those that are in the fires of purgatory and the rites of the Church, such as the Mass, is effective for freeing souls from their suffering.[297]

Conclusions

The Christian eschatological ideas of Judgment did not evolve smoothly. As has been shown, some theologians anticipated the particular Judgment, and the intermediate state, well in advance of these ideas finally being codified by the time of Augustine and Gregory the Great. In fact, the intermediate state was not to be called Purgatory until the eleventh century.

Although these doctrines were haltingly arrived at, the questions asked at the beginning of this essay will be answered briefly below, stating eschatological ideas as they had developed by the sixth century. But first, summarizing:

The Last Days and the resurrection are moved out into the future. The Platonic "immortal soul," when finally accepted, resides in an intermediate state between death and the resurrection. A preliminary sorting of the good and bad is done immediately upon death at a particular Judgment. The final sorting, at which the resurrected body is joined to the soul, is done at the general Judgment.

Thus, our original questions can be answered:

1) If the faithful were not to be judged until the delayed Last Days, where did they mark "time" between death and the Last Days?

---

295. Seeberg, *Text-Book of the History of Doctrines*, 2.17.

296. Seeberg, *Text-Book of the History of Doctrines*, 2.22.

297. Pelikan, *Emergence of the Catholic Tradition*, 355–356.

Early theology allowed that martyrs go straight to their reward, but everyone else waited in Hades (later, also in a third place).

2) If they were indeed to be judged at the Last Days, yet exist "someplace" until that event, when were they selected in order to await a reward or punishment?

As the Platonic "soul" was accepted, the particular Judgment was seen as taking place immediately upon death. The souls of the martyrs would go to heaven, the others to an intermediate purifying place. By the time of Gregory the Great, those to be damned would immediately enter Hell.

3) If they were judged immediately upon death, what was the purpose of the Judgment at the Last Days?

The Judgment at the Last Days was the general Judgment, at which the resurrected body would join the soul for final judgment. Some would immediately be in paradise, some condemned eternally to Hell and the majority purified for a time in the "third place," which would eventually be called Purgatory.

Christianity Fragments

The Middle Ages (ca. 476–1453 CE)

The Middle Ages (see **Fig. 56**) are so named by the people of a later age in order to distinguish their age of rebirth from that of a thousand years of intellectual darkness that lay behind them. The darkest years of which were the Dark Ages.

The Dark Ages

The Dark Ages (also called Early Middle Ages) is usually dated from the fall of Rome ca. 476 CE to around 1000 CE. Although it was the decay of Roman infrastructure and Greco-Roman artistic and scholarly activities that are blamed for the long disintegration of European civilization, some credit for the Dark Ages must fall on the institutional Church. Perhaps, Eusebius said it best:

> It is not through ignorance of the things admired by them…It is through contempt of such useless labor that we think so little of these matters; we turn our souls to the exercise of better things.

With this statement, Eusebius turns away from and, for centuries, retards the endeavors of the natural philosophers [scientists] and turns toward the contemplation of God and heaven. While the latter may be desirable, it is the former that will eventually bring humanity out of the darkness of superstition and physical suffering into the enlightenment of reason and physical comfort.

Breakdown of Christianity in the East

Rise of Islam

While all of the **internal bickering** over the nature of Christ and the Trinity was going on within Christianity, a new religion was being born.

That religion was to solve many of their controversies by eliminating gods who became men, multiple god-like persons, and…

By converting half of Christendom.

St. Augustine's North Africa was overwhelmed by Islam around 640 CE, and the Dark Ages settled more deeply upon the Western world. But, fortunately for later generations, the light of learning was kept alive in the Islamic world awaiting the resumption of philosophical inquiry in the West.

East-West Schism

Islam contributed to the eventual breakup of the Catholic Church by taking over two of the three original bishoprics of Alexandria and Antioch, leaving only the ancient See of Rome as the sole survivor. Rome then pursued a path to pre-eminence in the Christian world. However, Constantinople had been elevated to the status of a major bishopric after becoming the capitol of the Roman Empire and resented Rome's claims.

The Eastern and Western Churches split, and their leaders excommunicated each other in 1054. The primary reasons were:

> Rome wanted to be the sole leader and the Eastern Sees rejected that desire.
>
> It was politics that sparked the split, but doctrine had always been an excellent source of division. The final doctrinal straw was the inappropriate insertion of the "Filioque" clause into the supposedly closed Nicean Creed.

And then Islam would take the East too! Constantinople became Muslim in 1453.

Saintliness, Corruption and Arrogance

The Islamic world was in the ascendancy during this time while Europe was in decline.[298]

---

298. One cannot help but note the reversal of fortune of these two powers in the present day. The Islamic fundamentalism of today proves the point that once people have decided that all useful knowledge has been received from a sage of long ago; there is no need to ever think again. Hence, an entry into a dark age.

The Roman Catholic Church now ruled Europe with near absolute power and as we all know: "absolute power corrupts absolutely!" As with the corruption of the Jewish Temple in the times of Jeremiah and again of Jesus, the great Church was destined to be corrupted, too.

There were, as always, many instances of true religious devotion; but there were severe faults that arose in resonance to this corruption:

> Crusades—seven attempts to reclaim the Holy Land from the Moslems by force between 1095 and 1270. In the process, Jews and Orthodox Christians were indiscriminately massacred. The Church's promises of eternal life to the participants is reminiscent of today's promises to fanatical religious suicide bombers;
>
> Inquisitions—the use of torture to obtain confessions of heresy were authorized by the Popes in the13th and 15th centuries;
>
> Persecutions—the Cathars, Wycliffe, and Huss (reformers before the Reformation) were persecuted and burned at the stake;
>
> Financial corruption—greed, simony, and worldly pursuits were rampant for centuries during the Middle Ages and until the Council of Trent;
>
> Bad churchmen—hypocrisy, in regard to religious vows, was also ubiquitous.

But, there was also a positive side in the midst of corruption.

St. Francis of Assisi (ca. 1182–1226 CE) was the son of a rich man. As a youth, he did the usual young person's things; he partied hard, and he wanted to be a knight to fight in the crusades. But, eventually, he realized what he really wanted lay outside the riches of his father and the glamour of the crusades. He chose to take Jesus up on his commandment: that all who would be his disciples must give up wealth and earthly power and take up his cross and follow him.

Francis remained true to the Church, even though there were at least two very good reasons to abandon it. The churchmen were corrupt or, at least, arrogant and prideful; and there was already a reform movement, the Cathars, in progress that rejected the Church's behavior in favor of a return to the simplicity of the early Christian movement. Francis was attempting to do the same kind of reform but he, instead of rebelling against the Church, went directly to Pope Innocent III (Pope, ca. 1198–1216 CE) and asked for his support in creating a lay order of poor friars.

The Pope agreed! Why? There are probably many reasons but one stands out: the Pope needed a counter to the rebel Cathars (Albigensians). The Church was not providing this vehicle for spirituality, so it was being provided from without, by heretics. The Reformers of the day were the Albigensians, and they threatened the power of the papacy.[299] The Pope was able to attack them on two fronts: first, with a bloody crusade against them; and now, with Francis, by providing for their ideals within the confines of the Church.

In an interesting juxtaposition of developments involving the two major mendicant preaching orders founded at this time, Pope Innocent III used St. Francis as a counter by example to the Cathars and St. Dominic was dispatched to argue against the Cathar leadership. When argument failed, the Pope ordered a full-scale crusade against them. This would shortly lead to the Inquisition which the Order of St. Dominic would direct.

Pope Innocent III was not necessarily a corrupt man, as were many other Popes of the Middle Ages; but he was extremely arrogant. He claimed that princes have power over the body, but priests have power over the soul. He reasoned that, since the soul is more important than the body, the priesthood was greater than the secular rulers; and the Pope was, therefore, the most powerful person in the world.

Innocent III called for and ratified the 12th Ecumenical Council held in Rome in 1215 (Lateran IV) where:

- The doctrine of transubstantiation was made official; that is the bread and wine is actually transformed into the body and blood of Jesus.
- The discipline of the clergy was reformed.
- Jews and Muslims were directed to wear distinctive dress.
- The heresies of Albigensianism and Waldensianism were condemned.

---

299. For details on the Papacy, see: Richard P. McBrien, *Lives of the Popes*, (HarperSanFransisco, 1997).

- Secular powers were asked to help suppress these heresies.
- Innocent defined *ex cathedra* (from the chair of Peter) that—

"There is but one Universal Church, outside of which there is no salvation."

This essentially damned the rest of the world and arrogated all power to the Church.

Within one hundred years, Pope Boniface VIII (ca. 1235–1303) would arrogate that power directly to himself:

> "That there is only One, Holy, Catholic and Apostolic Church we are compelled by faith to believe and hold, and we firmly believe in her and sincerely confess her, **outside of whom there is neither salvation nor remission of sins**....Furthermore we declare, state and define that it is **absolutely necessary for the salvation of all human beings that they submit to the Roman Pontiff.**"
>
> Pope Boniface VIII *Unam Sanctam* (November 18, 1302 CE)

Such absolute power begs for corruption and, for over three centuries before the Reformation, the Church was corrupt in:

Pastoral government (simony, manner of rule, immorality)
Piety (exaggerated devotions, superstitions)
Theology (decadent Scholasticism)

Many good churchmen tried to get the Church to reform from within, but some really bad Popes would thwart that possibility. The Church survived the most corrupt Pope ever, Alexander VI (1492–1503), who was most notorious for nepotism, greed, and sexual misconduct.

A few years later, Leo X (1513–1521) was not to be so fortunate, for his pontificate would coincide with a man with a tortured soul who would stand up to him. This would, thereby, mark Leo, for all time, as the person most responsible for the Protestant Reformation.

In **Fig. 51**, we have the development of Christianity from Paul to the end of the Middle Ages.

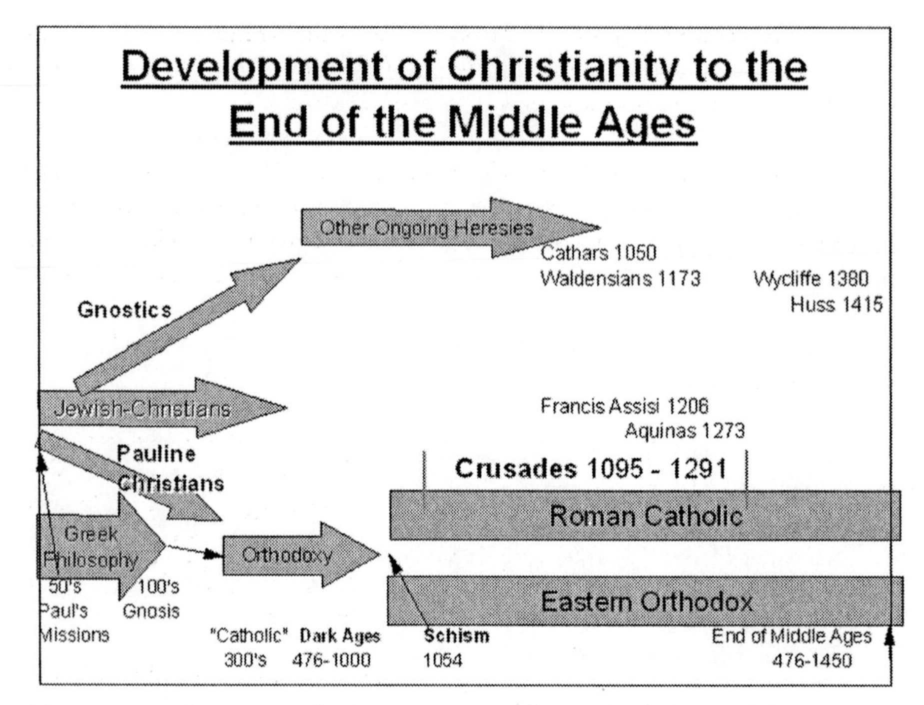

Fig. 51 Development of Christianity to the End of the Middle Ages

Breakdown of Christianity in the West

The Renaissance

The people who had named the Middle Ages were now in ascendancy. The Middle Ages had ended and Europe began the long way back to the glories of the past. St. Francis had helped the rebirth by rejecting the rigidity of the medieval Scholastics, and had inspired people with his love of nature. Now, the natural world inspired artists as piety had done before. Learning became more centered on humanity, and the Humanist era had begun.

In 1453, this rebirth (renaissance) of the human spirit was also aided by the fall of Constantinople to the Muslims. Fleeing Islam, the scholars of the East came to Italy bringing their books and reintroduced the West to Greek learning.

Humanism brought with it a new way of looking at the world. Learning was no longer based on divine (i.e., Church) authority but on the investigations of natural phenomena. The age of the scientific method was fast approaching.

Secular scholarship (without Authority) opened the minds of many to other possibilities than those available heretofore. Without the absolute iron hand of the authority of both Church and state to restrain them, many saw and took new paths of their own choosing. One such path was to lead to the Protestant Reformation.

The Reformation

There had been earlier attempts at the internal reformation of the Church. The Fourth Lateran Council (1215), convened by Pope Innocent III, had enacted significant reforms that sought to control abuses by the clergy and laity. He was somewhat successful in that the Church survived intact for another 300 years, until the abuses again grew to such proportions that something had to change. They did change when the Church started selling salvation.

The Church, and especially the Pope, claimed the power to loose and bind one's penalty for sins based on the Bible text:

> Whatever you bind on earth shall be bound in heaven, and whatever you loose on earth shall be loosed in heaven.
>
> Matthew 16:18–19

This was taken to mean that the Church could offer forgiveness, or withhold forgiveness, of the penalty for sin. Since the penalty for sin was an eternity in Hell, or a very long time in Purgatory, forgiveness was much to be desired. The corruption of this doctrine came in the form of indulgences that were essentially "get out of Purgatory" passes for cash. Martin Luther would be the catalyst for the change.

Martin Luther

Martin Luther (1483–1546) was obsessed and tormented by his belief that he was full of sin, and that God was so separate from Man that he could do nothing to bridge the gap. He became an Augustinian monk and lived a severely disciplined life in order to relieve his feelings of unworthiness. The Church taught that we are worthless sinners due to our fallen nature, but offered a way out by allowing that our good works would gain favor with God.

All his discipline and good works could not convince Luther that he was anything but a sinner and condemned by God, and there was nothing he could do about it. However, he was a teacher and, through his teaching from the epistles of Paul, he began to see a way out of his despair. He reasoned his way to salvation thusly:

- Man could not get close to God by his own actions since he was driven toward evil by the effects of original sin.

- Man could do nothing of his own power, and God alone could intervene to set him free from sin. Man could not coerce God to do so.

- Nevertheless, sinners should live in hope, since God had sent Jesus into the world of sinners, then God must have faith in Man.

- Salvation is thus available through faith alone.

By 1517, Luther was convinced that he had found the solution to his torment and believed that good works were of absolutely no value to one's salvation. Imagine his rage when, at the behest of Pope Leo X, John Tetzel entered Germany selling indulgences. Luther believed this practice would dupe people into believing that they could buy their way out of sin with no consideration of faith whatsoever.

These people were being condemned to Hell by their own Church, since God would not be duped by a pretense of repentance. Selling salvation for money was bad enough, but damning the very souls the Church was supposed to save was the ultimate immorality. The practice must be stopped and salvation, by faith alone, must be taught to these lost souls.

The austere Augustinian monk could no longer abide the financial and spiritual corruption of selling indulgences, so he tried to reform the Church from within. Unfortunately for the unity of the Church, his attempt did not work. After a battle of wills, he was excommunicated in 1520, and was now free to carry on his reforms from the outside.

Renaissance humanism had migrated from Italy into Northern Europe, and there it had settled in well. It provided a compatible environment for the ideals of the German, Luther, which allowed his new brand of Christian thought to flourish.

Thus, Luther had split from Mother Church and developed his major **doctrinal** views: 1) justification by grace through faith, and 2) the priesthood of all believers.

It was the latter doctrine that would encourage the bifurcation of Christianity we see today.

John Calvin (1509–64)

In 1510, Luther was in Rome, as a delegate of his Augustinian order, when John Calvin was celebrating his first birthday. It was while he was in Rome that he tried desperately to rid himself of his feeling of total worthlessness. On bended knees, he ascended the 28 steps of the famous *Scala Santa* in order to receive the indulgence attached to this ascetic performance. He felt no better for the task and went back to Wittenberg, where he developed his idea of "justification by faith alone."

If Luther had tried to reform from within, the next significant reformer did not. He would read the works of Luther and leave the Church to become the founder of the second great branch of Protestantism.[300]

St. Paul had taught a doctrine of predestination in Romans 8 and 9 and in Ephesians 1:

> [8:29] For those God foreknew he also predestined…[30] And those he predestined, he also called; those he called, he also justified; those he justified, he also glorified.
> [9:14] What then shall we say? Is God unjust? Not at all! [15] For he says to Moses, "I will have mercy on whom I have mercy, and I will have compassion on whom I have compassion." [9:16] It does not, therefore, depend on man's desire or effort, but on God's mercy.

300. The first was Lutheran. Calvin's was Reformed from which developed: Presbyterian, Congregationalist, Baptist, United Church of Christ, and others. A third early branch was the Anabaptists: Brethern, Amish, Mennonite, etc. A forth early branch was the Anglican: Methodist, Episcopal, Pentecostal, Quaker, etc.

> 1:4 For he chose us in him before the creation of the world to be holy and blameless in his sight. In love 5 he predestined us to be adopted as his sons through Jesus Christ, in accordance with his pleasure and will.

How is this predestination to be understood? One possibility is that since God is omniscient, he has foreknowledge of how people will behave in the future and, thus, has predestined them to eternal life, or not based on that foreknown behavior. But, this possibility leaves the decision to be saved in the hands of human beings and would seem to take away God's sovereignty. St. Augustine, in his battles with the Pelagian heresy, had come to the conclusion: since humans are corrupt and incapable of gaining salvation on their own, that God alone must have decided whom to save. And, since God is the same for all eternity, he would have made his decision in eternity, before time began. God also had to decide whom to pass by—the mass of perdition—and allow to be damned (see his *Enchiridon*). St. Augustine, following Paul, says:

> "Because whom He did before foreknow, He also predestinated to be conformed to the image of His Son, that He might be the first-born among many brethren. Moreover, whom He did predestinate, them He also called," to wit, according to His purpose; "and whom He called, them He also justified; and whom He justified, them He also glorified." (Rom. 8:29). All those things are already done: He foreknew, He predestinated, He called, He justified; because both all are already foreknown and predestinated, and many are already called and justified; but that which he placed at the end, "them He also glorified",...this is not yet accomplished. Although, also, those two things-that is, He called, and He justified-have not been effected in all of whom they are said,-for still, even until the end of the world, there remain many to be called and justified,-nevertheless, He used verbs of the past tense, even concerning things future, as if God had already arranged from eternity that they should come to pass.
>
> ...
>
> Whosoever, therefore, in God's most providential ordering, are foreknown, predestinated, called, justified, glorified,-I say not, even although not yet born again, but even although not yet born at all, are already children of God, and absolutely cannot perish.... From Him, therefore, is given also perseverance in good even to the end; for it is not given save to those who shall not perish, since they who do not persevere shall perish.
>
> St. Augustine, On Rebuke and Grace, chap 23

During the Reformation, Calvin revived the doctrine that St. Augustine had promulgated over a thousand years earlier. Calvin now also concluded that since God was totally sovereign and his will never changed, it was the logical conclusion that God must have decided one's fate from all eternity; he necessarily predestined who was saved and who was damned. This notion harkens back to that of the Stoics where everything was fated to occur, and the only thing you could do was go along. The added element beyond the Stoic philosophy, which made this a much bleaker outlook, was that now a person was immortal and lack of salvation lasted for eternity.

Predestination

The Church, for reasons of its own effective continuation and in spite of its admiration for Augustine, could not allow that doctrine of "double predestination" to stand, and it was declared invalid at the Council of Orange in 529 CE. Now, with Calvin, it was back and the elect of God would be saved and the rest of the mass of damnation would not.

Election was a gift of God and no one could know if they were among the saved, nor could they do anything about it. The best one could do is believe that if they had been led into the right Christian way of life that this might show evidence of election. An upright life, church membership, worldly success,[301] and experience of being "born again" would provide some indication that you were one gifted with election.

The Reformed church of Calvin codified the doctrine of unconditional predestination, in chapter three of the Westminster Confession of Faith (1647):

> God from all eternity did, by the most wise and holy counsel of His own will, freely and unchangeably ordain whatsoever comes to pass: yet so, as thereby neither is God the author of sin, nor is violence offered to the will of the creatures, nor is the liberty or contingency of second causes taken away, but rather established.
>
> By the decree of God, for the manifestation of His glory, some men and angels are predestinated unto everlasting life, and others foreordained to everlasting death.

301. This indicator has been thought to be a main ingredient in the rise of capitalism. Being a good steward of money was evidence that you were saved.

> These angels and men, thus predestinated and foreordained, are particularly and unchangeably designed; and their number is so certain and definite, that it cannot be either increased or diminished.
>
> Those of mankind that are predestinated unto life, God, before the foundation of the world was laid, according to his eternal and immutable purpose, and the secret counsel and good pleasure of His will, hath chosen in Christ unto everlasting glory, out of his mere free grace and love, without any foresight of faith or good works, or perseverance in either of them, or anything in the creature, as conditions, or causes moving him thereunto; and all to the praise of his glorious grace.
>
> Westminster Confession of Faith

It would seem that St. Paul, St. Augustine, and Calvin had reached an unimpeachable conclusion as to God's sovereignty, unchangeable will, and the inability of fallen humanity to contribute anything to its own salvation. But, as the Church had done earlier with Augustine, other Reformers would now do to Calvin and the Reformed Church; that is, find a way around this doctrine.

Jacobus Arminius (1560–1609) was a Reformed minister from Holland, who was in the vanguard of those who objected to this harsh doctrine; and in 1610, his disciples produced a document called the Remonstrance. This document, also called The Five Arminian Articles, was aimed at what they considered the most egregious articles of Calvinism. The table below, **Fig. 52**, will give the five articles of Arminianism, along with the five responses from the Calvinists.

Comparison of Arminian and Calvinistic sotereology

Arminian:

> We are saved through the joint efforts of God (taking the initiative) and man (responding); man's response being the determining factor. God has provided salvation for everyone, but His provision becomes effective only for those who, of their own free will, "choose" to cooperate with Him and accept His offer of grace. God predestines to salvation those whom he foresaw (before creation) would believe. At the crucial point, man's will plays a decisive role; thus man, not God, determines who will receive the gift of salvation.

Calvinistic:

> We are saved by the sovereign power of God. The Father chose a people, the Son died for them, the Holy Spirit makes Christ's death effective by bringing the elect to faith and repentance, thereby causing them to willingly obey the gospel. The entire process (election, redemption, regeneration) is the work of God and is by grace alone. God, not man, determines who will receive the gift of salvation. From Calvin's Institutes of the Christian Religion:
>
> > We call predestination God's eternal decree...each man...eternal life is fore-ordained for some, eternal damnation for others.

The five points of Calvinism were developed in response to the Arminian position (**Fig. 52**). They are more easily remembered if they are associated with the word T-U-L-I-P:

T—Total Depravity
U—Unconditional Election
L—Limited Atonement
I—Irresistible (Efficacious) Grace
P—Perseverance of the Saints

Calvinism	**Arminianism**
Total Depravity Man is completely a sinner, without any hope of helping himself. Since Man is fallen and totally corrupt he would be unable of his own free will to have faith for salvation. Salvation must be wholly ascribed to God, who has chosen his own from eternity in Christ.	Free Will Man, unaided by the Holy Spirit, is unable to come to God. Man is so depraved that divine grace is necessary to enable him to freely choose to repent and believe.

Calvinism	**Arminianism**
Unconditional Election God elected some people to salvation when they had no merit at all. Election is completely undeserved by man and is not based on anything a man might do. God did not foresee that some would believe and therefore elect them to salvation, but He chose to save some graciously. Unconditional election and damnation as a result of the predetermined will and decree of God whereby God softens the hearts of the elect, while he leaves the non-elect in his just judgment to their own wickedness and obduracy.	Conditional Election God elects or condemns on the basis of foreseen faith or unbelief accomplished by man's free will.
Limited Atonement The atonement is limited to the elect. Christ did not bear the sins of every individual who ever lived, but instead only bore the sins of those who were elected for salvation. "Christ should effectually redeem all those, and those only, who were from eternity chosen for salvation and that Christ should purge them from all sin, both original and actual, whether committed before or after believing and should preserve them even to the end."	General Atonement Christ died for all people, although only believers are saved. The atonement is for all, but only believers enjoy its benefits.
Irresistible Grace It is impossible for a sinner to resist salvation once the Holy Spirit calls him. God's call to someone for salvation cannot be resisted.	Holy Spirit can be Resisted The calling of the Holy Spirit can be resisted. This grace may be resisted.

Calvinism	Arminianism
Perseverance of the Saints It is not possible to lose one's salvation. A saved person will be saved forever. "…it is utterly impossible, since his counsel cannot be changed, nor his promise fail, neither can the call according to his purpose be revoked," for the elect to fall from grace.	Falling from Grace Whether all who are truly regenerate will certainly persevere in the faith is a doctrine that was left open to inquiry.

Fig. 52 Calvinism and Arminianism Compared

Thus, within a very short period of time from Luther, we have the first major split within the Protestant movement. The "priesthood of all believers" interpreting "scripture alone" would condemn the movement to fracture over and over again.

It is tempting to think that, if the various reformers had gotten their act together and cooperated, possibly the Roman Catholic Church might not have been able to recover in the face of the Protestant heresy.

But, as usual, divisiveness[302] within allowed the Catholic Church to counter with a reformation of its own.

The Counter Reformation

With the coming of the Protestant Reformation, the Church now realized its problems and attempted to fix them. The most important ecumenical council since Chalcedon was convened by Pope Paul III on December 13, 1545, in the village of *Trento* (Trent) in Northern Italy. Named for the village in which it was held, the Council of Trent (1545–1563) became the nineteenth Ecumenical Council of the Roman Catholic Church. It lasted for 25 discontinuous sessions over an 18 year period under the oversight of five different Popes.

---

302. Even within Calvinism, a debate raged between the Supralapsarians and the Infralapsarians. In the former, election and reprobation was decreed before Adam's Fall; in the latter, after the Fall. Interestingly, both groups evolved to a position more like that of Arminius and, indeed, like that of the Catholics by rejecting double predestination altogether (see **Fig. 42**Fig. 42 The First Seven Ecumenical Councils).

Its obvious purpose was to defend against the Protestant heresy, which it attempted to do by:

Condemning heresies

The council closed with the words "Anathema to all heretics, anathema, anathema." They were addressing in particular the heretics Luther, Calvin and others. Specifically, Luther's doctrine of "justification by faith alone" was condemned. It was resolved that man was inwardly justified by cooperating with the divine grace that God freely grants.

Defining doctrines

Many Protestants had denied the doctrines of the Church, so the council made a clear definition of the disputed doctrines. Among them being:

Reaffirmation of the Niceno-Constantinopolitan Creed
- Affirmed Bible—Apocrypha on par with rest of canon; Vulgate is authoritative; scripture and tradition equal authority
- Affirmed all seven sacraments
- Reaffirmed Real Presence of Christ in the Eucharist
- Affirmed the nature and consequences of Original Sin
- Affirmed purgatory and indulgences
- Affirmed veneration of images, relics and saints
- Reformed the Missal and Breviary
- Reformed the Mass
- Wrote a catechism based on the decrees of Trent

Reforming conduct and morals

Although doctrine became a major stumbling block to any further reconciliation between the Catholics and the Protestants, it was the blatant immorality of the clergy that brought the Reformation to a head. As they had tried to do three hundred years earlier at the fourth Lateran Council, the Church again made a more determined effort to clean up its own house:

- Enacted decrees on clerical morals and education
- Reformed sale of indulgences

- Affirmed excellence of celibate state
- Defined valid marriage and forbade remarriage after divorce
- Commissioned a list of forbidden books
- Obligated bishops to reside in their sees, abolishing plurality of bishoprics

Pope Pius IV closed the last session on December 4, 1563, and issued a Papal Bull on February 7, 1564, in which he enjoined strict observance of all decrees of the council.

Unfortunately, it was, as they say, too little too late...

Warring Sects

...The damage was done.

Now, Northern Europe was at war with Southern Europe. The territory of Christendom was roughly divided into the north and south, but in some countries there was a mixture of religions within the same geography.

France

The religious wars of France were fueled by two causes: a grasp for power between the king and nobles, and among the nobles for control of the king; and the struggle of the French Protestants to gain freedom of worship in the midst of an overwhelming Catholic majority.

Actually, it would be difficult to find a war of religion of any time or place that did not include both the grasp for secular power and religious idealism. This particular one became known as the Wars of Religion and, also, as the Huguenot Wars.

Between the years 1562 and 1598, there were eight distinct civil wars in France. The first three civil wars ended with some concessions to the Huguenots; they gained some religious freedom and the wardenship of four cities. On August 24, 1572, throughout France, a general slaughter of Protestants initiated the fourth civil war. This slaughter began on St. Bartholomew's Day and 3000 people were killed in Paris, with 70,000 killed in all of France. It was notably the most egregious single event of the entire period and came to be called the St. Bartholomew's Day Massacre.

From 1572 through 1594, there were four more civil wars until the Huguenot king, Henry IV, converted to Catholicism and issued the Edict of Nantes; thereby, granting religious freedom of worship throughout France and established Protestantism in 200 towns, creating a state within a state.

The wars were ended and peace settled upon France for a while. However, with the goal of making France a Catholic state, Cardinal Richelieu and King Louis XIV revoked the Edict of Nantes and by 1685 the country was returned to nominal Catholicity.

Germany

Protestantism had started in Germany with Luther's excommunication in 1520, and by 1531 a league (the Schmalkaldic League) of Protestant princes in the Holy Roman Empire was formed for mutual defense against Charles V, Holy Roman Emperor.

A treaty designed to relieve tension and establish tolerance for Lutherans in the empire, called the Peace of Augsburg, was signed between Charles V, Holy Roman Emperor, and the forces of the Schmalkaldic League on September 25, 1555 at the city of Augsburg in Germany. The aforesaid tension and toleration was only between Lutherans and Catholics in which the religion of a particular prince would be enforced on the people living in his territory. People so desiring could move to a principality more congenial to their religion, if they desired.

Calvinists and other Protestant sects were not included:

> However, all such as do not belong to the two above named religions shall not be included in the present peace but be totally excluded from it.
>
> Article 7 of the treaty

This oversight was to become the undoing of the Peace. Over the years, many princes had converted to a Calvinism, or some other sect, and were no longer protected by the treaty. In Northern Germany, Protestants continued taking over Catholic property and in the Catholic areas, the governments broke down due to distrust by the Protestant minorities.

Given all of these new tensions, it was not long before war broke out, first in Bohemia; then in Germany. The war was to last from 1618 through 1648 and was to be remembered as the Thirty Years War.

The French Wars of Religion pale to insignificance when compared to the bloodbath unleashed by the Thirty Years War. It has been estimated that eight million people perished and the land was left in ruins.

Finally, exhausted by the strife, the Peace of Westphalia was signed on October 25, 1648. The war ended with all religions in Germany being given the right of free exercise.

These two wars had ended, but many more were to continue to flare as politics and intolerance necessitated.

Christianity had long before failed to unite the Roman Empire as Constantine had hoped. Now, it had shattered all of Europe, and made it worse than when the fourth century historian had claimed:

> "No wild beasts are such enemies to mankind as are
> most Christians in their deadly hatred of one another."
> (Ammianus Marcellinus, 4th century historian)

The religion of love had turned into one of hatred—again!

To be sure, Christianity would later create pockets of unity, only to split again and yet again.

Jesus had long ago asked that his disciples love one another. Reasonable people would eventually attempt to honor that request.

Enlightenment

In the seventeenth and eighteenth centuries, there appeared an intellectual movement in Europe that came to be known as the Age of the Enlightened. In the 1780's, Immanuel Kant will look upon his preceding century, and see that an emancipation from superstition and ignorance was the essence of the Enlightenment.

The monolithic Church had been assaulted in turn by Humanism, the Renaissance and, the Protestant Reformation. The resurgence of classical rational thought, the experimental sciences, and the doubts caused by the breakdown of religious tradition allowed new modes of examining the world.

In particular, the laws of the universe discovered by Isaac Newton (1642–1727) showed the world to be a giant mechanism that could be understood by human reason, and without resort to the religious concept of a personal God managing everything behind the scenes. Indeed, a clockwork universe eliminated the need for anything but an initiator to get things started, and then leave the mechanism to its own devices.

Now the wars would be between religion and science.

Science Comes to the Fore

We must now ask if it is necessary for there to be such a war.

James Ussher (1581–1656), Archbishop of Armagh and Primate of all Ireland in 1650 declared: The world began on Sunday, October 23, 4004 B.C. Another scholar later honed this more exactly to October 23, 4004 B.C., at nine o'clock in the morning.

Science, as we shall see, is not so certain of the date, but believes it was before then...

Science, religion and philosophy—conflict or a way to meaning (essay)?[303]

> Myself when young did eagerly frequent
> Doctor and Saint, and heard great argument
> About it and about: but evermore
> Came out by the same door as in I went.
> Omar Khayyam quatrain 27

This poem from Omar Khayyam's *Rubaiyat* expresses well my sentiment toward the apparent futility of human inquiry embodied in religion, philosophy and, even science.

Science and religion in conflict?

There obviously is a conflict between religion and science. I will claim that such conflict need not exist, and that problems arise only when mythos and models are inappropriately combined, or conversely, when they fail to take each other into account because of dogmatic thinking on both sides.

Albert Einstein recognized the dangers of dogmatism:

> "...the boundless suffering which, in its end result, this mythic thought [religion] has brought upon man.... only if every individual strives for truth can humanity attain a happier future; the atavisms in each of us that stand in the way of a friendlier destiny can only thus be rendered ineffective" (Smith, foreword by Albert Einstein).

In this section, I will juxtapose Philosophy's branches of epistemology and ontology/cosmology—metaphysics with its counterparts of Science and Religion, and attempt to show why I believe that inquiry into science, religion, and philosophy is not futile; but rather, the most rewarding endeavor in which we may participate. In fact, I will claim that an appropriate combination of science and religion could lead to a meaningful philosophy of life.

---

303. This essay (to the section heading "Theodicy and Modern Science") was written, in the first person, by the author in 1995. Although slightly dated, it is included here in order to stress the importance of science in the Enlightenment. It also expresses the author's opinions and serves as a preface to my own thoughts on a rational theodicy.

Definitions—model, mythos and school of thought

Science, religion, and philosophy all attempt to explain ultimate reality by a process of "model" building. Disastrous effects occur when the model is mistaken for reality itself. Some definitions follow:

> Model—a scientific device that attempts to approximate reality in such a way as to allow for describing present and predicting future events. It is usually built and validated by empirical evidence and accuracy of prediction. (Examples: Ptolemy cosmology, Bohr atom, celestial mechanics, quantum theory).
>
> Mythos—also an attempt to describe reality, but with emphasis on why reality is as it is. Myths are usually built on accumulated tradition and validated by authority and internal consistency. (Examples: special creation, sky god, Dionysian death/resurrection, question of evil).
>
> Schools of Philosophical Thought—may be viewed as similar to models and myths in that they attempt to explain reality. In epistemology and metaphysics, the major conflicts arise between the movements of realism and anti-realism. (Examples: Plato's Ideas, Phenomenalism, Positivism).

Conflicts can take place not only between the models of science and the mythos of religion, but also between mutually conflicting models of science and mutually conflicting religious myths. Over a long history, science (and to some extent philosophy), has learned to deal with these conflicts. In this regard, religion would do well to emulate the success of science.

All is not well with these areas of inquiry, as I will show. Philosophy in the twentieth century seems to have put itself out of business. Religion has made itself look irrelevant with its adherence to obsolete myths, and dangerous because of the attendant violence created by fundamentalism. And, science has ignored the other two to the detriment of the hopes of people depending on something that offers purpose to their lives. I will look at all three disciplines: first, philosophy.

When philosophy abdicates its historic role

Stephen Hawking claims in his popular book, *A Brief History of Time*: "...in the nineteenth and twentieth centuries, science became too technical and mathematical for the philosopher, or anyone except a few specialists. Philosophers reduced the scope of their inquiries so much that Wittgenstein, the most famous philosopher of this century, said "the sole remaining task for philosophy is the analysis of language." What a come down from the great tradition of philosophy from Aristotle to Kant" (Hawking 174–5).

Contemporary philosophy has come across as not having much to say on the great "Why" questions that have always haunted mankind. Recently, there have been attempts to get back into these historic inquiries; and I believe this is good and necessary, for: "If philosophy does not aim at answering such questions, free will, why we exist, mind/body, etc.] it is worth nothing" (Dummett 1).

Man appears to be the only animal that can ask "why". The earliest records of humankind show this proclivity successively through religion, philosophy; and science. It would seem that the most recent development, that of science, would offer the best vehicle to provide answers to these questions that we continue to ask.

I will argue that I do not believe this to be true; science is necessary but not sufficient to the task. Perhaps the oldest of these disciplines, religion, may provide the surest method to address these "why" questions. I will claim that this is also not the case.

In fairly modern times, there have arisen movements within philosophy that could do irreparable damage to philosophy itself if unchallenged: skepticism and logical positivism. The Skeptics would divorce us from the external world to the extent that:

- we can have no knowledge of the external world

The Logical Positivists would claim that all metaphysical utterances are nonsense:

- because metaphysical utterances are, in general, empirically unverifiable; they are either trivially analytic or meaningless

So much for epistemology and metaphysics!

To further exacerbate the difficulties, no less a philosopher than the great Wittgenstein seems to make the nihilistic claim about philosophy that:

> there is no proper role for the philosopher beyond the dissolution of linguistic confusion (qtd. in Ammerman 11).

In the face of these claims, I would say that philosophy (as a meaningful enterprise for knowing and being) would certainly not be very useful in providing humans with answers to the big questions of "Why'; or providing meaning to our lives.

Let us look more closely, but briefly, at some of the competing schools of philosophical thought (the philosophical counterpart to models and mythos), with the intent to arrive at a greater understanding of, if not the Universe, at least some interesting thinking about it. Then we will see what science, then religion, has to offer in our search for meaning.

Philosophical movements

Realism is "the attempt to see things as they are without idealization, speculation, or idolization" (Angeles 253).

The naive realist believes that the world exists as we perceive it; that is, appearance and reality are the same thing. The senses actually present true and accurate information to the perceiver about things.

The Greek philosophers, particularly Plato, believed that universals (their "Ideas" and "Forms') exist in the external world, independently of perception.

In modern philosophy, the realist holds that material objects exist externally to the perceiver, and independently of their sense experiences or perceptions. This common sense approach "works" quite well with ordinary macro-world objects, like tables and chairs; but fails, as we shall see, in science's quantum-world of indeterminacy.

It is this belief in independent existence that can open the modern realist up to the skeptic's charge—that one can't possibly know what the realist claims to know.

"**Skepticism** ranges from complete, total disbelief in everything, to a tentative doubt in a process of reaching certainty" (Angeles 276).

Skepticism reached its zenith in the philosophy of David Hume. Hume claimed that no truths about matters of fact could be established deductively or inductively. Inductive reasoning rests on unjustifiable assumptions that nature is uniform and that the future will resemble the past. Since these assumptions are not supported by evidence, Hume cannot allow induction. On the other hand, deductive reasoning operates with the necessary connections among events; but there is no evidence that such connections actually exist, therefore, deduction is also not allowed.

Thus, if one is denied any form of reasoning about the world and the only knowledge one can have is of what one has direct experience (namely perceptions), then one can never get to the reality existing behind those perceptions.

The skepticism of the Greek philosopher, Carneades, offers a bit more hope. His claim is also that all we can ever have are images of an external world, but are never sure about which images are accurate and which are inaccurate, since the mind influences the way these images are interpreted. Therefore, he claims that truth does not exist, and all we can rely on are degrees of probability.

This concept of probability will figure heavily in the later discussion of quantum mechanics.

Phenomenalism is an anti-realistic view of the world. Its principle claims are that only phenomena (sense-data) can be known to conscious perceivers, and that we cannot know anything about the ultimate nature of reality itself, because all we have is the sense-data (and not the actual objects we are perceiving). Indeed, the physical world cannot even be said to exist apart from the actual or possible sense-data of some perceiver. This latter idea will figure prominently in my later discussion of quantum mechanics.

Therefore, science can never ask questions about how things "really are"; it can only examine the observations (sense-data) and build models of the universe, restricting them to what is, in fact, knowable.

This harkens back to the proclamations of the Vienna Circle (and the logical positivists), who declared meaningless all statements that cannot be empirically verified. If, indeed, all we can know depends on observation; then it makes no sense to declare the world to really be this way or that independently of observation.

Wittgenstein would famously declare: "What we cannot speak about we must pass over in silence" (Wittgenstein para 7).

"Phenomenalism is a metaphysical doctrine par excellence, being one version of a rejection of realism about the external world; and Phenomenalism was strongly supported by the positivists" (Dummett 10).

Positivism's characteristic theses "are that science is the only valid knowledge and facts the only possible objects of knowledge; that philosophy does not possess a method different from science; and that the task of philosophy is to find the general principles common to all the sciences and to use these principles as guides to human conduct and as the basis of social organization" (Edwards 6: 414).

The main tenet of the logical positivists is that a statement has cognitive meaning if, and only if it is (at least in principle), empirically verifiable. A foundation of sense experience (positive knowledge) must be reached before a statement can have cognitive meaning.

Metaphysical statements are meaningless, since it is impossible to empirically verify them, nor are they analytic tautologies as are statements about mathematics and logic.

At its most extreme, logical positivism claims that statements about the external world and about other minds are meaningless because there is no empirical way of verifying them.

Wittgenstein, in his *Tractatus*, also influenced the logical positivists in that they finally came to the conclusion that has Carnap asking: "what, then, is left over for philosophy, if all statements whatever that assert something are of an empirical nature and belong to factual science" (Carnap 77)?

Wittgenstein had earlier said that the only function of philosophy is to clarify meaningful concepts and propositions. So, indeed, what would be left over for philosophy?

Instrumentalists "regard theoretical entities as useful fictions enabling us to predict observable events; for them, the content of a theoretical statement is exhausted by its predictive powers" (Dummett 6).

This school of thought is the essence of scientific inquiry into the world of quantum physics.

A case in point: The theory of quarks was developed by Murray Gell-Mann in the 1960's to explain the likely building blocks of sub-atomic particles of the atom's nucleus. Protons were originally thought to be elementary particles (not being further reducible). Experiments in which protons were collided at very high speeds showed this not to be the case, but that they were reducible to smaller particles. These were named quarks by Gell-Mann after a line from James Joyce's Finnegan's Wake: "Three quarks for Muster Mark "—a reference to the fact that he believed there to be three different sub-proton particles involved. This "fiction" turns out to be true if one allows for the corresponding anti-quarks, which totaled six.

Even though they were mathematical "fictions" at the time of their being postulated, the strangest thing happened on the way to their actual discovery—they became real (if by real one means their effects can be observed in particle physics experiments).

Neutralism is an anti-realist school of thought concerning time, in particular, the future. The realist would say that time is real and that the future, in fact, exists already in some determinant form. The neutralist would agree with Kant, "the temporal character of our existence is itself something imposed upon it by the mind; and post-Kantian idealists have concurred in regarding time as unreal" (Dummett 6).

In this area of philosophy, Einstein, usually a realist, may have thought as a non-realist by saying: "The distinction between past, present and future is only an illusion, even if a stubborn one" (Davies, Time 70).

Science models can change.

Scientific models should be accepted by religions—but not as dogmas—for scientific models will change. Some examples of science models that have changed radically are those of creation/cosmology and time.

Creation/Cosmology:

Findings in particle physics have allowed scientists to delve deeply into the origins of the universe.

In recent decades, there have been two main competing theories of the universe's origin: the "steady state" and the "big bang" theories. (I have personally always thought the steady state model was more esthetically pleasing with its claim to the infinity of the universe in both time and space—and still hold out against the big bang even against all the current evidence.)[304] The steady staters disparaged the alternate theory with the derisive name of "big bang" (from the observed expansion from a long ago point) and the name stuck. So did the theory!

Keep in mind, it is only a model (paradigm) of how things might have happened. It's a model that works so far (the philosophical school of pragmatism performs very well in science).

At any rate, using this cosmological model, physicists have been able, over the years, to apply quantum physics to it and worked out remarkable details of what happened in the first instants of creation. One of the first discoveries of quantum physics was that energy is released in tiny packets (or quanta). This implies that the universe is not made up of a continuous substance but is built of these discreet quanta.

Since the smallest quanta of time that can exist is the Planck time of 10^{-43} seconds (10 raised to the minus 43 power), the laws of physics hold down to that time, and we can know what happens to matter, energy, time, and space in that instant, so we can successfully model the universe from 10 to the minus 43 seconds onward.

At less than 10^{-43} seconds, physics does not obtain, and we are left totally devoid of knowledge in that realm. With this model, it is complete nonsense to ask what happened before the big bang since, in our universe, not only space but time began with it.

---

304. Since I originally wrote my parenthetical thoughts nine years ago, the Cosmologists have enlarged their view and "the infinity of the universe in both time and space" has come back around with the concept of a multi-verse. So any religion that hitched its wagon to the Big Bang science model committed one of the errors I described in this essay.

Any statements about the universe "before" the big bang are, even in principle, unverifiable with the current model. Thus, science cannot even answer "what" at the sub-quantum level. And, even though many have thought science could provide all our answers, it certainly can not explain "Why".

Time:

Although he was a solid classical physicist to the end, Albert Einstein, in his theory of special relativity, forever destroyed the notion of "now" (simultaneous events). Because of the finite speed of light (and, therefore, the speed of information propagation) the time of an event is totally dependent upon the relative position and velocity of the observers. From the point of view of a third observer, the same event could be in one person's past and in another's future.

There is nothing magical here, nor does it depend on the consciousness of an observer, as a realist quantum mechanical interpretation would claim. It is, however, a fact that seems to question our normal notions of time. In quantum theory and with Bell's Theorem, we shall see that both time and space are not as they would seem to be.

Before time became relative, it was considered absolute (a major shift in belief). Before the "Big Bang" theory and its predecessors came about, the universe was thought to be just the solar system surrounded by the Milky Way, and well before that, it was just the Earth-centered universe of Ptolemy.

When religion appropriates a scientific model into its world view.

Consider the case of the Ptolemaic model of the universe. Ptolemy, Aristotle, and others had conceived of the universe as a series of concentric spheres with the Earth at the center, with the planets, moon and sun orbiting it; and finally surrounded by the outermost fixed sphere of the stars. Of course, over the centuries, the model had to be modified in order to accommodate observed motions in the heavens (e.g., epicycles, equants, etc.) and to make the model "work;" that is, predict events.

Even with these alterations in the model, the spheres were maintained, and the Church accepted Ptolemy's world view. This view was incorporated into the Christian faith as part of its teachings, giving to God the Realm beyond the outermost sphere.

This placed the "scientific" explanation of reality into Church teaching with the full force of authority. Significant changes to, or abandonment of, the geo-centric sphere model would eliminate the Realm of God and undermine the authority of the Church; therefore, there could be no change. People who realized the need for a more accurate view of reality demanded change, and the Church burned them at the stake for their effort. One would think that the eventual victory of the new model of reality (in the face of dogmatic "truth") would have destroyed the keepers of that dogma. One would have to think again.

What actually happened was that progress in knowledge and understanding of reality was thwarted for centuries, and the betterment of mankind was retarded. This kind of drag on the improvements to man's lot almost certainly has been responsible for the continued ignorance that resulted in the plagues and famines that have killed or made life miserable for millions. And, it continues…

When the scientific world-view changed, conflict arose. Religion would be advised to stay out of the scientific business of "how".

<u>When religion fails to recognize a reasonable scientific model.</u>

When a scientific model, such as evolutionary theory (which is recognized as tentative and incomplete), is established as a reasonable description of reality; but collides with the established creation mythos of religion, somebody will have to admit to being wrong. When religion tenaciously hangs on to an obsolete myth, there is indeed a conflict between religion and science. But, this is only because religion failed to remember that it is in the "why" business, and creation myths were meant to describe "how" in a pre-scientific world.

Richard Leakey speaks on human evolution:

> Until many more relics of human prehistory have been unearthed and analyzed, no anthropologist can stand up and declare, This is how it was in every detail. There is, however, a great deal of agreement among researchers about the overall shape of human prehistory.... four key stages…bipedal apes…adaptive radiation…large brain…modern humans (Leakey xv).

Few claim that evolution is <u>the</u> description of reality, but that it is a good working model of what most likely took place with life over the millions of years, in which it has developed from molecular components to the complex being which is us. It is empirically far superior to the ancient stories of how life came to be. Religions only make themselves look foolish when they deny the possibility of such a reasonable model.

It is understandable that religion would rebel at man being just another amoral animal, as the principle of evolution implied.

> The theologians were never more right than when they asserted that under the principle of evolution there would be no justification for ethics, meaning nineteenth century middle-class English ethics as opposed to other possible codes…(all codes or none would be equally justified)…the only standard of reference being its practical utility for those who use it (Smith 433).

The problem is that what the religion of the time of Darwin (and some still today) failed to see was that by insisting that an obsolete myth prop up their religion; that religion (and its dependent ethics) would topple when the prop finally failed. Tying absolute truth to a shaky story tends to make that truth seem a bit fallible.

<u>When science uses a dogmatic world view.</u>

Unfortunately, at times, science has also succumbed to dogmatism.

Mechanistic World View:

A similar situation to that of religion exists within science and philosophy in that theories and schools of thought may contradict each other, and the answers you get may depend on who you ask. The big difference is that theories are just that; models of the world that help us look at it. The quantum theory "works" in that we are able to predict the behavior of sub-atomic particles and build electronic devices. The Big Bang theory works in that it meets the tests to support it, and also predicts further findings in astro-physics.

Few would claim that these models actually depict reality and, furthermore, it is recognized that they will have to be changed or replaced, as new information warrants. This open-minded attitude gives us the hope for new and more refined facts about the world, which is good in itself. However, it does not offer, nor claim to offer, ultimate truth—except when science becomes dogmatic as the post-Newtonian era showed.

The scientific method (that is, the insistence on verifying or falsifying a proposition based on empirical evidence by repeatable experiment, where possible, under controlled conditions) has proved to be one of the most important concepts ever devised by man. It has delivered us from doubt and dogma and has provided the way for the ordinary person's physical comfort, undreamed of by the kings of antiquity. It has been so successful that we have incorporated it into our being, and have come to believe that it holds the key to all of our big questions.

With the advent and development of classical physics, many intelligent people, including scientists and philosophers, believed that if we but knew the positions and velocities of all material bodies, we could predict what would happen into the infinite future. Since this was theoretically (not practically) possible, all that the universe needed was an initial start; and all events were pre-determined from then on. This classical mechanistic view of the universe lulled us into believing that all physical things were knowable; since they were determinant.

The sixteenth century mechanistic universe was believed to have eliminated the need for religion, and this belief is still around. It shouldn't be, because the mechanistic and materialistic universe has been utterly destroyed by the new physics. Physicist Paul Davies claims in *The Matter Myth* that:

> …deep divisions in the scientific community, concerning the nature of reality, point up the shakiness of any claim that science deals with the whole truth. Quantum mechanics seems to impose an inherent limitation on what science can tell us about the real world, and it reduces to mere models entities that we used to regard as real in their own right (Davies Matter 28).

So, the classical world has been shattered by a new way of thinking about the universe and nothing is so certain anymore.

<u>When myths collide.</u>

If you want the answers to the really big "Why" questions, religion is where you'll find them! If you want to know "why am I here?', "why is the universe here?", "what happens when I die?"—you can get rock-solid answers from religion.

The problem is that you get too many "right" answers to the same question, but the answers do not agree and, in some cases, are downright antagonistic to one another.

As in science and philosophy, if the answer to my religious question depends on who I ask, then I have, in all probability, not gotten the correct answer.

A particular religion may be totally internally consistent and, therefore, "true" within its own bounds (paradigm). This form of truth has and will continue to suffice for the vast majority of mankind and may continue to offer people needed salvation. But, when dogmas collide, the whole of mankind is worse off, because religious mythos generally has the authority of received or revealed truth; these collisions are usually explosive. Witness the Crusades, the wars of the Reformation, and the fundamentalists' religious wars around the globe.

This is where the example of resolving scientific model collisions would be instructive to those involved in religion. One might accept the validity of mythos to describe the "why" of the universe. But, when myths collide, one must have the intellectual honesty to recognize that they are just human attempts to understand that which lies outside the realm of science, and are not absolute truth. Accept the best as metaphors for reality and keep looking.

Keep the myths as poetry. Incorporate science to explain the "what" and the "how" as appropriate.

<u>Combining science and religion into a philosophy of meaning.</u>

This is the Grand Challenge of Philosophy today. Can we forge the models of science and the mythos of faith into a viable philosophy that gives meaningfulness to our lives? Of course, I believe the answer to be yes.

So do some physicists who have pushed the new physics to its limit and beyond, such as Frank Tipler:

> ...near the Omega Point (the end of space/time), life must have engulfed the entire physical cosmos...control all matter and energy...the information stored becomes infinite...(Tipler 154).

Therefore, Tipler claims that the Omega Point itself has become omnipresent, omnipotent, and omniscient (i.e., God)! I agree that his Omega Point could be viewed as God, but Tipler's other claims that it is Personal (and will cause a general Resurrection) do not logically follow.

Leon Lederman would not think much of Tipler's ideas, but admits that the revolutions in science can have an impact on our worldview:

> Newton created not only the universal laws of gravitation but also a deterministic philosophy that caused theologians to place God in a new role. Newtonian rules...determine the future...quantum physics...softens the deterministic view, allowing individual atoms the pleasure of uncertainty (Lederman 1981).

"The paradigm shift that we are now living through is a shift away from reductionism and toward holism; it is as profound as any paradigm shift in the history of science" (Davies 291). I believe that the models of the "new physics" may very well impact epistemology and metaphysics and, indeed, our cherished myths.

Holism has always been the keystone of Eastern metaphysics. As Chuang Tzu said: "Heaven and Earth came into being with me together, and with me all things are one." Physics is not the same thing as Eastern philosophy, but they share a common idea—that of holism, as witnessed by quantum mechanics and, especially, Bell's Theorem.

Quantum Mechanics, Bell's Theorem and Holism:

> The essence of (**Niels Bohr's Principle of Complementarity**) is that, even though the wave and particle descriptions [of light] seem to be mutually exclusive, we are never forced to choose between them because they cannot be simultaneously revealed. The two descriptions—wave and particle—are complementary (Resnick 209).

Heisenberg's Uncertainty Principle "states that it is not possible to measure simultaneously the exact component of momentum...of a particle and its exact corresponding position" (Resnick 213).

The "momentum versus position" uncertainty is not simply a problem of measurement precision. It actually exists, as do other uncertainties, such as "time versus energy' which allows the creation of matter/energy out of nothing, if it is observed within the quantum fluctuation time allowed by uncertainty. One might say that the universe will trade a little time for a little matter, and that "may-fly" of the sub-nuclear world, the virtual particle, is, thereby, allowed its bit of existence.

The complementarity and uncertainty concepts taken together became—

The Copenhagen Interpretation of Quantum Mechanics:

The essence of the Copenhagen interpretation is that the world must be observed to be objective. It makes no sense to claim that quantum entities possess attributes (such as momentum, spin, etc) until an actual measurement has taken place. This interpretation "works", but at the expense of determinism and of the objective reality of the world.

Bohr vs. Einstein:

Einstein believed in realism—that an objective world exists independently of any observation process and, therefore, claimed, "I still believe in the possibility of giving a model of reality which shall represent events themselves and not merely the possibility of their occasion" (qtd. in Resnick 224). He claimed that quantum theory is incomplete.

Einstein was upset with the indeterminism and lack of objective reality, but finally admitted defeat and agreed that the Copenhagen interpretation was, indeed, consistent and "worked." But, not to give up, he claimed that the quantum theory was an incomplete theory because it violated local causality—that events far away cannot instantaneously influence objects here.

The great debate, over the reality of the world implied by quantum theory (between Niels Bohr and Albert Einstein) began in 1927 and continued for years. At one point in the debate, in order to defeat quantum theory, Einstein, Podolsky and Rosen proposed a thought experiment (the famous EPR paradox).

The EPR Experiment:

The EPR experiment is a test for orthodox quantum measurement. The idea was to use experimental information gathered on one particle to determine the complementary properties of another particle. Einstein tried to demonstrate that it was theoretically possible to determine precise values for complementary constructs in quantum theory (such as position and momentum), thereby, proving Heisenberg wrong.

Imagine two particles (electrons) originating from a definite quantum state, and then moving apart. There is no apparent communication between them until at some time we choose to measure <u>one</u> of them.

EPR chose the simplest case to prove the Heidelberg Uncertainty Principle to be wrong. They determined the initial momentum of the electron pair, and then allowed them to separate. Due to the conservation of momentum, the two particles are correlated (each having the same momentum). When one particle's momentum is finally measured, we can be assured that the other's will be the same. If we measure the second electron's position and since we know its momentum must be identical to the first electron's—we now know its momentum and position exactly—violating the Uncertainty Principle.

That sounded good, but Bohr was unimpressed. He claimed that measurements by proxy did not count; that one must be measuring the complementary attributes of a single particle, since, according to the Copenhagen Interpretation, the objectivity (or independent reality) of the world is denied until it is actually measured. Electrons do not "possess" position or momentum until an actual measurement is performed.

EPR emphasized a very important principle in classical physics—the principle of local causes—that one event cannot influence another event without a direct mediation (i.e., a signal). Space-like separation of events forces a certain amount of time to separate cause/effect, due to the limitation of the speed of light. This fact would be very important years later when John Bell was thinking about the EPR experiment.

Bell's Theorem:

The EPR paradox caused quite a stir for many decades until John Bell, in 1964, showed by thought experiment that only two "realities" were possible: either the world was non-objective, or it was non-local, allowing instantaneous action-at-a-distance. In all the actual experiments done since 1965, "they agree with the quantum theory, clearly violating the alternate predictions made by local reality. Quantum theory has been confirmed" (Peat 85–127).

John Bell derived his famous inequality by using a variation of the EPR experiment and depending on the two fundamental assumptions of the EPR experiment: the objective reality of the world and the impossibility of faster-than-light mediation.

Assume we have two particles in a paired system (if electrons, we know they have equal and opposite spin). The electrons are spin-correlated, and even if they were to move away from each other, that correlation would continue. The same is true for any other pair of quantum particles, like a photon, where polarization is the attribute used instead of spin.

Experiments on Bell's inequality have been done on polarized photons, where a pair of photons is "fired" in opposite directions where they encounter polarized lenses with photon detectors behind them. As anyone familiar with polarized sunglasses knows, light "waves" oriented in one direction will pass through the lens, where light waves in the perpendicular direction are blocked.

Two photons (that originate from a single quantum state and propagate in opposite directions) are perfectly correlated, and each will either pass through the lens and hit the detector or not. If the lenses are oriented in the same direction, the results will be identical; if the lenses are oriented at 90 degrees to each other, the results will be exactly opposite. These two orientation's results are predicted by both classical and quantum physics.

Classical physics claims that the correlation probabilities for all angles between 0 and 90 degrees lie between -2 and + 2; whereas, quantum physics allows for a value greater than 2 (e.g., for 45 degrees it is 2.83). Actual experiments were to prove the quantum values correct!

Saying that the classical (local reality) case for correlation lies between -2 and +2 is saying that classical physics predicts Bell's inequality: $-2 < P < +2$. However, quantum theory predicts a trigonometric equation, which allows probability values to exceed 2.

The Aspect Experiments:

The predictions of quantum theory accounted for the probability distribution that actually occurred, but this does not entirely dismiss the idea that, somehow, information was carried in some manner between the two particles. It fell to the team led by Alain Aspect, in 1982, to prove that Einstein's classical view of the world is not compatible with quantum physics.

Aspect used a delayed decision experiment (emulating Wheeler's two slit, particle/wave, setup) where the choice of orientation of the polarized lens would be made after the photons were in flight. His apparatus was 13 meters apart (at that distance light takes 40 nanoseconds to cross) and the lens orientation could be switched in 10 nanoseconds. Therefore, the photon gun would "fire" two photons in opposite directions; and while they were traveling toward the lenses, one lens would be rotated a few degrees.

Remember, the photons are correlated by polarity when they leave the gun, and when the photon hits the changed lens, the other photon "knows" that it has happened and stays correlated! As in the delayed decision of the two slit experiment, this appears to "cause" a change to have been made in the past.

How did the second photon know about the change? It was way too far away for a light signal to tell it. Is there a signal faster-than-light? There may be, but it's not likely. What is more likely is that non-locality is a real fact of nature.

Quantum Wholeness and Non-locality:

"In Bohr's words, there is "an indivisible wholeness', an unanalyzable wholeness. At the moment of observation, the observer and the observed make a single unified whole (qtd. in Peat 62)." Classical science reduced the whole to its analyzable parts; whereas, quantum theory, shown by Bell, says that "the part can never be finally isolated from the web of relationships which disclose the interconnectedness with the whole (Kafatos 176.)"

Roger Penrose later claimed that "any kind of realistic description of the quantum world which is consistent with the facts must apparently be non-causal, in the sense that effects must be able to travel faster than light" (Penrose 279–87)!

The Tao:

The "holistic nature of the atomic world was key to Bohr's Copenhagen interpretation. It was something totally new to physics although similar ideas had long been taught in the East. For more than two thousand years, Eastern philosophers had talked about the unity that lies between the observer and that which is observed (Peat 62I)."

Even the great classical physicist, Albert Einstein, said in *Albert Einstein: Philosopher—Scientist,* "Autobiographical Notes" that "'A human being is a part of the whole, called by us the "Universe', a part limited in time and space. He experiences himself, his thoughts and feelings as something separate from the rest—a kind of optical illusion of his consciousness', or as paraphrased "the sense of ourselves as separate from the whole is merely another macro-level illusion" (qtd. in Kafatos 113)."

Now modern physics has claimed a similar idea to that of the Eastern philosophies. "...experiments testing Bell's theorem suggest that all the parts, or any manifestation of "being" in the vast cosmos, are seamlessly interconnected in the unity of "Being" (Kafatos 180).

It would seem that Chuang Tzu, for whatever reason, was right; that all things are one.

In response to a question on how we humans are able to create sublime religious art, Joseph Campbell claimed: "that's what art reflects—what the artist thinks about God, what people experience of God. But the ultimate mystery is beyond human experience" (Campbell 228).

Maybe so, but we want to know more.

Theodicy and Modern Science

We want to know more...And, maybe we can with the assistance of modern scientific concepts. In Part II we discussed the various theodicies that religions have developed in order to save the goodness of God, in spite of the fact of moral and natural evil in the world. The last one on the list was taken from chapter nine of the ancient book of Ecclesiastes. This is the same chapter that says:

> For a living dog is better than a dead lion. The living know that they will die, but the dead know nothing; they have no more reward, and even the memory of them is lost.
>
> Eccl 9:4–5

Time and chance

Even at the supposed late composition date of ca. 300 BCE, in these verses, the author has retained the very bleak eschatology of the earlier Israelites. Death is the end and "there is no work or thought or knowledge or wisdom in Sheol, to which you [everyone alike] are going."

Just a few verses later the author offers an explanation for the injustice that occurs in the world:

> Again I saw that under the sun the race is not to the swift, nor the battle to the strong, nor bread to the wise, nor riches to the intelligent, nor favor to the skillful; but time and chance happen to them all.
>
> Eccl 9:11

This puts the lie to the promises of Deuteronomy where goodness is said to be rewarded. Here, the good things that people do are insufficient for guaranteeing a reward. Indeed, even badness may well be rewarded depending on time and chance!

It would seem that Jesus acknowledged that natural evil in the form of accidents bears no relationship with the righteousness of the victims. When asked:

> Or those eighteen who were killed when the tower of Siloam fell on them—do you think that they were worse offenders [sinners] than all others living in Jerusalem?
>
> Luke 13:4–5

His reply was, no. Jesus didn't think the accident was a punishment for sin. He also didn't question why God would allow such an evil to befall his children. He simply assumed that the world worked that way and God was not involved for either good or ill.

Most theodicies reasonably address moral evil in which a person's free will allows bad things to affect others. These theodicies fail to convince when natural evil is involved, such as the case of an inanimate object (the Siloam tower) killing innocent bystanders.

Quantum physics and chaos theory

Plato had offered a way out of making God the author of evil that had been further expanded on by the neo-Platonists. In Greek philosophy, evil was thought to have no real being; it was simply the absence of good. Plotinus claimed that:

> If such be the Nature of Being and of That which transcends all the realm of Being, Evil cannot have a place among Beings or in the Beyond-Being;

> these are good. There remains, only, if Evil exists at all, that it be situate in the realm of Non-Being.
>
> Enneads I.8.3

For Plotinus, evil was the privation of good (*privatio boni*), a negative theory of evil that was accepted by the great Christian thinkers, St. Augustine and St. Thomas Aquinas, and incorporated into the Church's Theodicy doctrine.[305]

But, not everyone has been satisfied with that reasoning. Evil seems quite real when it is happening to you, so anyone refusing to buy into the *privatio boni* theory is still left with the problem of evil—why does God allow evil to befall good people?

Determinism

Predestination should be seen as the despicable doctrine it is. Despite all arguments to the contrary, it eliminates human free will and condemns everyone to a fate that was predetermined before the creation of the world. St. Augustine was troubled by this doctrine but, in his zeal to counter the Pelagian heresy, he came down firmly on the side of double predestination: God elects some people for salvation and the masses are elected for damnation.[306]

That the future is thus determinant has been supported by many philosophies (i.e., Stoics) and many churchmen (i.e., Augustine and Calvin). As we've seen in the science section above, it was also supported by Newtonian science. With both science and religion working against indeterminism, free will did not stand much of a chance.

Modern physics has completely changed that mindset and has established that indeterminism is a fact of the natural world. This has elevated free will once again to its proper place, and it has also allowed for a positive theology of evil that is real and exists in the realm of being.

---

305. Note the conflict between the negative privation of good and the positive acts of Satan as explanations for the problem of evil.

306. The conundrum is, how is man's will to acts free if God already knows everything. Augustine would say that the will is free and we act by voluntary necessity. This logically difficult theology would allow the Reformers (especially Calvin) to revive double predestination.

Indeterminism

Totally random and uncaused events happen at the quantum level, and chaos theory states that minute initial conditions of any system are enormously amplified in the course of time that the system is in operation. The famous example of chaos theory is: a butterfly flaps its wings in Brazil and causes a later massive storm in America. The slight movement of air from the butterfly's wings results, over time, in a storm. Any slightly different flapping would have caused a completely different effect.

An example of a natural evil

A quantum event, such as the emission of radiation, might possibly affect the macro world by making a tiny modification to the trajectory of a distant comet. After billions of years have passed, the comet strikes the earth, destroys a major city, and kills millions of innocent people. Here we have a chance event that, in time, creates a natural evil. Satan didn't do it, God didn't do it, a privation of good didn't do it—time and chance did it.

Toward a rational theodicy

So, how does science help in offering a rational theodicy? After all, God could have intervened and saved the people by turning aside the comet at any time during its flight. He could have changed the initial conditions by having the radiation affect the comet differently. Or, the best prevention would be to not allow the random quantum event to happen in the first place. Notwithstanding what God could have done, we know that natural disasters actually happen all the time and, therefore, that He has done none of the necessary preventive measures.

So, are we not back to the same ancient Israelite belief that God is the maker of both good and evil? On the one hand, yes, in that He could intervene in natural evils. On the other hand, no, in that he did not cause the natural evil—it was truly random. But still, why would God make a universe that works in an evil way? Well, consider the alternative.

A universe made another way means that everything would either be totally predetermined, or that it would be totally micro-managed. Either of these scenarios obviates any possibility of independent action, or choice for any sentient beings, including us. And, a God who would predetermine our eternal fate, or who would micro-manage events that lead to the punishment of the righteous, is not worthy of consideration. Of course, God may do either, or both, of these things and not really care about our consideration. In that case, God is not only the maker of evil; He is evil.

No, it is better to accept the wisdom of Ecclesiastes (buttressed with the findings of modern science), and assign the natural evils of the world to the vagaries of time and chance.

Ecumenism[307]

> Now I beseech you...that ye all speak the same thing, and **that there be no divisions among you**; but that ye be perfectly joined together in the same mind and in the same judgment.
>
> St. Paul, 1 Corinthians 1:10.

The Enlightenment age brought reason back to people's thinking and managed to oust some of the superstitions of the dark past. In the early twentieth century a different kind of enlightenment entered the thought processes of rational people—maybe our side isn't the sole bearer of all that is good and moral in the world. Just maybe, some others have access to an equal righteousness. Maybe we should stop hating the others and join together as partners.

Would that everyone managed to grasp this concept, but only a small number did so. Most could not face the possibility that another faith might possess the truth because if they do, we don't.

Past arrogations to sole truth

The following is a *De Fide* teaching of the Catholic Church:

> "OUTSIDE THE CHURCH THERE IS NO SALVATION"

This teaching has been solemnly defined by the Fourth Lateran Council (1215) and affirmed by the Union Council of Florence (1438), and by Popes Innocent

---

307. The term comes from the Greek, and means "the inhabited world." It had been used for centuries to define the Universal Councils of the Church. Now it was being used to describe the unitive forces at work among the various denominations.

III (1160–1216), Boniface VIII (1235–1303), Eugene IV (1383–1447), Pius IX (1792–1878), Leo XIII (1810–1903), Pius XII (1876–1958)...and others.

It is also the unanimous conviction of the Church Fathers that salvation cannot be achieved outside the Church.

These assertions and other past abuses are hard to overcome. However, there have been, and still are, many good people who attempt to do so.

Can we ever get to a single Christianity?

Was there ever a single Christianity at any time in the past? We know that by the time Christians were so called at Antioch, there were at least two strains of Christianity. We know that during the peak of the monolithic Church, there were numerous other sects vying for recognition. At the height of the Medieval Church in Europe, there were the great Orthodox Churches in the East and numerous "heretical" sects in the West.

I believe we can safely say that there was never a time in the past when there was a single Christianity. The questions are now: can we get to one in this present or future time? And, do we want to?

Protestant attempts at ecumenism

Even before the twentieth century, there was some movement toward unity. The Evangelical Alliance was founded in England in 1846, and in America in 1867. In 1908, the Federal Council of Churches was founded by some of the larger Protestant denominations in the US, followed by Christian Unity in 1910.

Internationally, the ecumenical movement started with the World Missionary Conference in Edinburgh (1910), the Universal Christian Conference on Life and Works in Stockholm (1925), and the World Conference on Faith and Order in Lausanne (1927). The later two organizations joined together in 1937.

The World Council of Churches formed at Amsterdam in 1948 united Protestants and some Eastern Orthodox and Old Catholic groups. It was joined by the International Missionary Conference in 1961.

In 1961, Roman Catholics were invited to attend the World Council and, since 1965, the Council has hosted a joint working group with Catholics.

Anglican and Catholic contact was restored in 1966.

Catholic and Orthodox attempts at ecumenism

Catholic ecumenism came late in this latest round of attempts.

To be sure, after the confrontations between the Patriarch of Constantinople and the Pope, which resulted in mutual excommunication in 1054, and the sack of Constantinople by the Fourth Crusade in 1204, there was little interest in reunion. Nevertheless, wounds heal and attempts were made at the Councils of Lyon (1274) and Florence (1438). These attempts appeared to work temporarily, but failed due to the insistence on papal primacy.

Even in the twentieth century, Pope Pius XI, in his *Mortalium Animos* (1928), condemned the ecumenical endeavors of the Protestants, and warned against doctrinal compromises and entertaining the concept of a united church made up of independent bodies holding different beliefs.

This attitude was to slowly change as some commended a spiritual ecumenism that appealed to the Catholic Church, as a means of attaining a degree of unity. By the time of Pope John XXIII, an ecumenical fervor had attached itself to the Church and his Second Vatican Council (1962–1965) initiated a series of contacts with many non-Catholic groups in the interest of reconciliation.

The Vatican gave formal recognition to the ecumenical movement in 1960, when it formed the Secretariat for Promoting Christian Unity. Since then, several things have happened toward attaining that unity:

The Second Vatican Council (1962–1965) under the direction of Pope John XXIII (to which both Protestant and Orthodox observers were invited), made some serious attempts to heal the wounds of the past. The Decree on Ecumenism produced by the Council encouraged dialog with Orthodox and Protestant churches.

In 1965, Rome and Constantinople lifted the reciprocal excommunications of 1054.

In 1969, Pope Paul VI visited the World Council of Churches and the Catholic Church now has membership on some of its committees.

The Pope and Patriarch of Alexandria reached some agreements in 1973.

Pope John Paul II visited some Orthodox churches in 1999.

Lutheran and Catholic joint declaration on "justification by faith" was signed in 1999.

Orthodox and Lutheran churches made contact in 1967.

Orthodox churches created the Pan-Orthodox Conference.

Valiant efforts at reconciliation

In the *Catechism of the Catholic Church*, there is an effort to explain the meaning of the affirmation: "Outside the Church there is no salvation." In sections 846 and 847 it states:

> Re-formulated positively, it means that all salvation comes from Christ the Head through the Church which is his Body:
>
> > ...the Council teaches that the Church, a pilgrim now on earth, is necessary for salvation: the one Christ is the mediator and the way of salvation; he is present to us in his body which is the Church. He himself explicitly asserted the necessity of faith and Baptism, and thereby affirmed at the same time the necessity of the Church which men enter through Baptism as through a door. Hence they could not be saved who, knowing that the Catholic Church was founded as necessary by God through Christ, would refuse either to enter it or to remain in it.
>
> This affirmation is not aimed at those who, through no fault of their own, do not know Christ and his Church:
>
> > Those who, through no fault of their own, do not know the Gospel of Christ or his Church, but who nevertheless seek God with a sincere heart, and, moved by grace, try in their actions to do his will as they know it through the dictates of their conscience—those too may achieve eternal salvation.

Fearing that the members of the Church were becoming too accepting of relativism and pluralism, the Church promulgated the document *Dominus Iesus*, some of which is reproduced below:

> ...
>
> The Catholic faithful *are required to profess* that there is an historical continuity—rooted in the apostolic succession—between the Church founded by Christ and the Catholic Church: "This is the single Church of Christ...which our Saviour, after his resurrection, entrusted to Peter's pastoral care (cf. *Jn* 21:17), commissioning him and the other Apostles to extend and rule her (cf. *Mt* 28:18ff.), erected for all ages as "the pillar and mainstay of the truth" (*1 Tim* 3:15). This Church, constituted and organized as a society in the present world, subsists in [*subsistit in*] the Catholic Church, governed by the Successor of Peter and by the Bishops in communion with him". With the expression *subsistit in,* the Second Vatican Council sought to harmonize two doctrinal statements: on the one hand, that the Church of Christ, despite the divisions which exist among Christians, continues to exist fully only in the Catholic Church, and on the other hand, that "outside of her structure, many elements can be found of sanctification and truth", that is, in those Churches and ecclesial communities which are not yet in full communion with the Catholic Church. But with respect to these, it needs to be stated that "they derive their efficacy from the very fullness of grace and truth entrusted to the Catholic Church".
>
> ...
>
> On the other hand, the ecclesial communities which have not preserved the valid Episcopate and the genuine and integral substance of the Eucharistic mystery, are not Churches in the proper sense; however, those who are baptized in these communities are, by Baptism, incorporated in Christ and thus are in a certain communion, albeit imperfect, with the Church. Baptism in fact tends per se toward the full development of life in Christ, through the integral profession of faith, the Eucharist, and full communion in the Church.
>
> "The Christian faithful are therefore not permitted to imagine that the Church of Christ is nothing more than a collection—divided, yet in some way one—of Churches and ecclesial communities; nor are they free to hold that today the Church of Christ nowhere really exists, and must be considered only as a goal which all Churches and ecclesial communities must strive to reach".

> "Therefore, these separated Churches and communities as such, though we believe they suffer from defects, have by no means been deprived of significance and importance in the mystery of salvation. For the spirit of Christ has not refrained from using them as means of salvation which derive their efficacy from the very fullness of grace and truth entrusted to the Catholic Church".
>
> . . .
>
> *Equality,* which is a presupposition of inter-religious dialogue, refers to the equal personal dignity of the parties in dialogue, not to doctrinal content, nor even less to the position of Jesus Christ—who is God himself made man—in relation to the founders of the other religions.

Backlash

I applaud the sincere attempts at reconciliation and hope that there can be a reunion in the spirit of mutual respect and understanding, instead of the destructive historical anathemas. However, the language of *Dominus Iesus* would certainly chill any ardent desire for unity on the part of non-Catholics. Who would really want to subsist in another's shadow? As I stated before—and will again—if you have the truth, why would you compromise?

Understandably then, there has been a serious backlash to the attempts at ecumenism on the part of many who fear losing their identity and their understanding of the truth.

Much of the criticism comes from Protestants who cannot accept the terms they perceive as coming from the Catholics. They see the historical statements about "no salvation outside the church" and, the new Catechism aside, take it to mean that unity will only come as absorption into the papacy. Many Lutherans have condemned the joint declaration between their church and Rome as denying the Gospel truth of justification. And on it goes. After all, if we indeed have the truth of God in hand, how can we possibly admit of another's claim to a divergent truth? If one takes his particular faith literally, can there be any compromise?

Is there a good solution to this impasse? The very unlikely elimination of literalization would help. But, our next question is—

Do we even want to have a united Christianity?

The goal seems admirable and, perhaps, it would help unite instead of divide people. However, this has been tried before with dire consequences to the Christian religion and humanity in general. It has been tried in other religions with equally bad results.

As I see it, the problem is that a unified religion is a powerful religion, which inevitably combines with the power of the state to enforce its dogmas. The absolutely powerful, thus corrupted, state then becomes a theocracy.

Name a good theocracy…

Our final graphic, **Fig. 53**, shows the development of Christianity from the end of the Middle Ages to the present time.

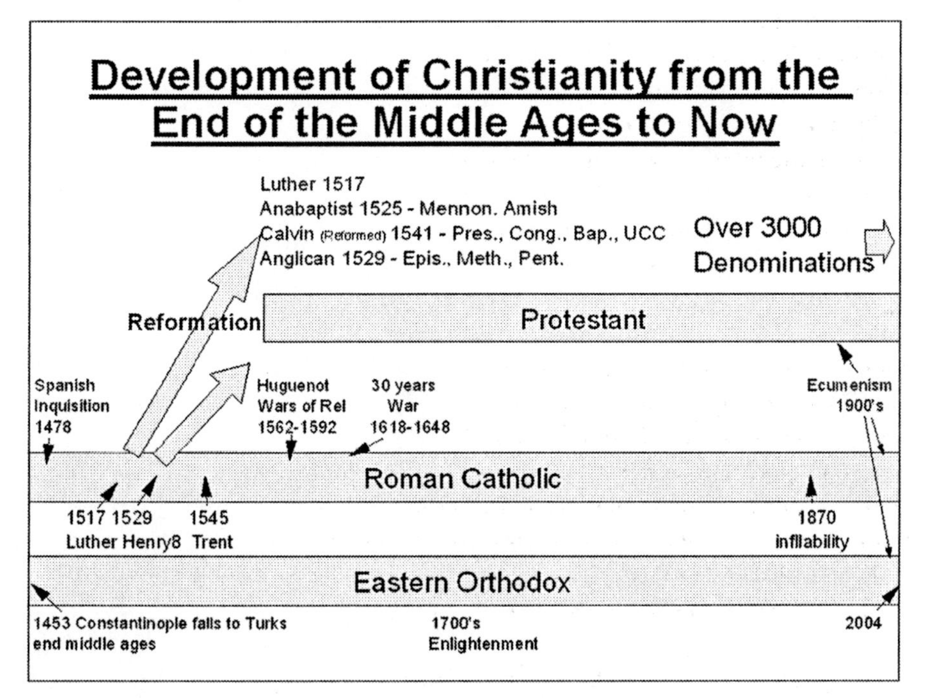

Fig. 53 Development of Christianity to the Present

EPILOG

> The time is fulfilled, and the Kingdom of God has come near; repent, and believe in the gospel (Mark 1:14–15)...
>
> To you has been given the secret of the kingdom of God, but for those outside, everything comes in parables; in order that they may indeed look but not perceive, and may indeed listen but not understand; so that they may not turn again, and be forgiven (Mark 4:11–12).

These are the quotes which opened the Preface of this book.

The first of the quotes raised the question of: What is the gospel and what is the Kingdom of God? Those questions have been discussed sufficiently; the ambiguities of scripture do not allow for a definitive conclusion. However, if we look at only the texts of Q1, we find that the good news is that of the Kingdom of God in our midst. And, we see that the Kingdom is not the apocalyptic vision held by the sectarians of the Dead Sea, nor that of the early Church.

The apocalyptic vision would certainly arise in varying degrees with later Q2 and the canonical Gospels and, especially, with Revelations. This vision would also fade in the succeeding centuries as the Church became organized and took the mantel of Kingdom upon itself.

As to the "secret" given to some but not to others, can we still see the residual effects of a Christianity now vanished? Elsewhere, it is said that the way to salvation is narrow and that few would be chosen. Mark 4:11–12 might be an echo of a defeated sect which claimed those few to be the recipients of the secret teaching of gnosis.

APPENDIX—
STATISTICS ON RELIGION IN THE USA

The facts in the following tables (**Fig. 54, Fig. 55** and **Fig. 56**) are mostly from the ARIS study as delivered by the web site Adherents.com.[308]

Top Twenty Religions in the United States, 2001

Top Twenty Religions in the United States, 2001
(self-identification, ARIS)

Religion	1990 Est. Adult Pop.	2001 Est. Adult Pop.	% of U.S. Pop., 2000	% Change 1990–2000
Christianity	151,225,000	159,030,000	76.5%	+5%
Nonreligious/ Secular	13,116,000	27,539,000	13.2%	+110%
Judaism	3,137,000	2,831,000	1.3%	-10%
Islam	527,000	1,104,000	0.5%	+109%
Buddhism	401,000	1,082,000	0.5%	+170%
Agnostic	1,186,000	991,000	0.5%	-16%
Atheist		902,000	0.4%	
Hinduism	227,000	766,000	0.4%	+237%
Unitarian Universalist	502,000	629,000	0.3%	+25%
Wiccan/Pagan /Druid		307,000	0.1%	

308. The document from which the ARIS tables are taken is copyright © 2002 by Adherents.com. Their permission to use: "Any list shown here may be copied and used, without prior permission, if a link to this page is included and the list is not changed." Created April 1999. Last updated 23 April 2004. See web site http://www.adherents.com/rel_USA.html.

Religion	1990 Est. Adult Pop.	2001 Est. Adult Pop.	% of U.S. Pop., 2000	% Change 1990–2000
Spiritualist		116,000		
Native American Religion	47,000	103,000		+119%
Baha'i	28,000	84,000		+200%
New Age	20,000	68,000		+240%
Sikhism	13,000	57,000		+338%
Scientology	45,000	55,000		+22%
Humanist	29,000	49,000		+69%
Deity (Deist)	6,000	49,000		+717%
Taoist	23,000	40,000		+74%
Eckankar	18,000	26,000		+44%

Fig. 54 Top Twenty Religions in the United States
(Source: ARIS—American Religious Identity Survey, 2001). Table is from http://adherents.com

The non-religious were included in the preceding table under the headings of nonreligious/secular, agnostic, and atheist. At first glace, one wonders why there is a differentiation among them. It is essentially a mindset that has atheists caring a great deal about the non-existence of God; where agnostics just don't know, and the secular just don't care.

Largest Denominational Families in the U.S., 2001

The **Fig. 55** below illustrates the difference between religion identification and attendance.

Largest denominational families in U.S., 2001
(self-identification, ARIS)

ARIS: Total number of adults, U.S., 2001: 207,980,000

Denomination/ Denominational Family	# of Adults self-identification 2001	% of U.S. pop. self-identification 2001	% weekly church attendance this denom. 2001	% of U.S. pop. in attendance at this denom. during a given week
Catholic	50,873,000	24.5%	48%	11.74%
Baptist	33,830,000	16.3%	50%	8.13%
Methodist	14,150,000	6.8%	49%	3.33%
Lutheran	9,580,000	4.6%	43%	1.98%
Pentecostal/ Charismatic/ Foursquare	4,407,000	2.1%	66%	1.40%
Presbyterian	5,596,000	2.7%	49%	1.32%
Mormon/ Church of Jesus Christ of Latter-day Saints	2,697,000	1.3%	71%	0.92%
Non-denominational Christians	2,489,000	1.2%	61%	0.73%
Church of Christ	2,593,000	1.2%	58%	0.72%
Episcopal/ Anglican	3,451,000	1.7%	30%	0.50%
Assemblies of God	1,106,000	0.5%	69%	0.37%
Congregational/ United Church of Christ	1,378,000	0.7%	* 30%	0.20%
Seventh-Day Adventist	724,000	0.3%	47%	0.16%

Fig. 55 Largest Denominational Families in the US

Charts are from http://adherents.com. Based on church attendance, ARIS/Barna. Barna asked about actual attendance versus a claimed identification. *The Barna poll did not report attendance figures for the United Church of Christ/Congregationalists. Figure used here is from the sociologically similar Episcopalians.

Graphic of Largest Denominations in the USA

Fig. 56 graphically shows the relative sizes of US Denominations (all members).

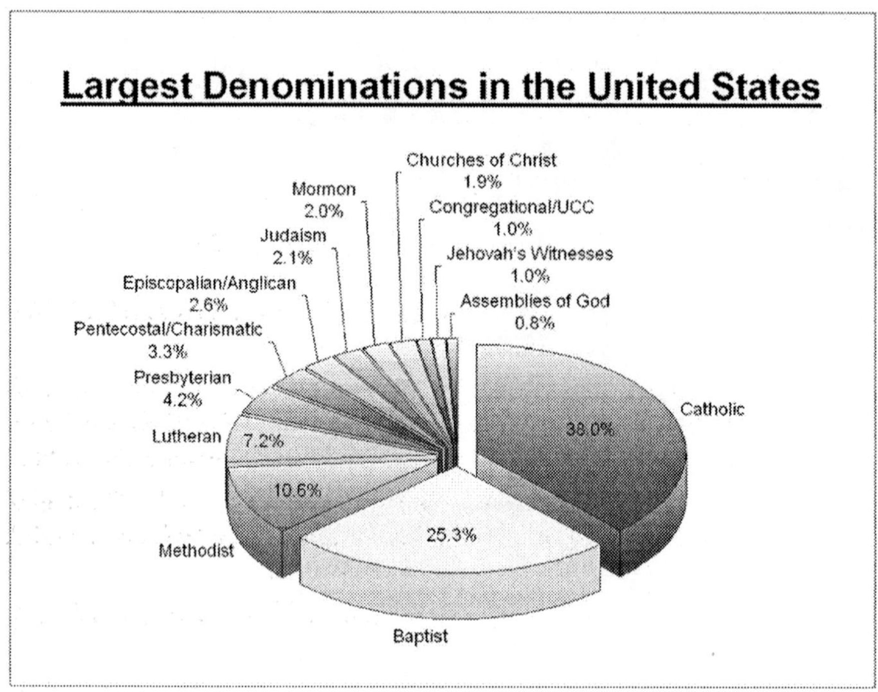

Fig. 56 Graphic of Largest Denominations in the USA

BIBLIOGRAPHY

Works recommended by the author (to provide a more detailed presentation on a particular topic) are identified below by a: *See comment in italics.*

Works cited in St. Augustine essay

The Doctrine of *Creatio Ex Nihilo* (Essay) starting on page 223.

Ambrose. *Hexameron.* Trans. John J. Savage. *The Fathers of the Church* 42. New York: Fathers of the Church, Inc., 1961.

________, *Of the Christian Faith, In A Select Library of the Christian Church. Nicene and Post-Nicene Fathers.* Second Series, Vol. 10: *Select Works and Letters. Ed Philip Schaff and Henry Wace.* New York: Christian Literature Co., 1896.

Anderson, Bernhard W. "Introduction: Mythopoetic and Theological Dimensions of Biblical Creation Faith." In *Creation in the Old Testament,* Ed. Bernhard W. Anderson. London: Fortress Press, 1984.

Archer-Hind, R.D. Introduction and annotations to *The Timaeus of Plato, by Plato.* New York: Arno Press, 1973.

Augustine, *Acts or Disputations Against Fortunatus the Manichaean, In A Select Library of the Christian Church. Nicene and Post-Nicene Fathers.* First Series, Vol. 4: *The Writings Against the Manichaeans and Against the Donatists. Ed Philip Schaff.* Edinburgh: T&T Clark, 1887; repr. Grand Rapids: Eerdmans Publishing Co., 1996.

________, *Against the Epistle of Manichaeaus called Fundamental, In A Select Library of the Christian Church. Nicene and Post-Nicene Fathers.* First Series, Vol. 4: *The Writings Against the Manichaeans and Against the Donatists. Ed Philip Schaff.* Edinburgh: T&T Clark, 1887; repr. Grand Rapids: Eerdmans Publishing Co., 1996.

________. *City of God.* Trans. by Henry Bettenson. London: Penguin Books, 1972.

________, *Concerning the Nature of Good, Against the Manichaeans, In A Select Library of the Christian Church. Nicene and Post-Nicene Fathers.* First Series, Vol. 4: *The Writings Against the Manichaeans and Against the Donatists. Ed*

Philip Schaff. Edinburgh: T&T Clark, 1887; repr. Grand Rapids: Eerdmans Publishing Co., 1996.

________. *Confessions.* Trans. by R. S. Pine-Coffin. London: Penguin Books, 1961.

________. *On the Literal Interpretation of Genesis: An Unfinished Book.* Trans. Roland J. Teske. The Fathers of the Church 84. Washington: Catholic University of America Press, 1991.

________, *On Two Souls, Against the Manichaeans, In A Select Library of the Christian Church. Nicene and Post-Nicene Fathers.* First Series, Vol. 4: *The Writings Against the Manichaeans and Against the Donatists. Ed Philip Schaff.* Edinburgh: T&T Clark, 1887; repr. Grand Rapids: Eerdmans Publishing Co., 1996.

________, *Reply to Faustus the Manichaean, In A Select Library of the Christian Church. Nicene and Post-Nicene Fathers.* First Series, Vol. 4: *The Writings Against the Manichaeans and Against the Donatists. Ed Philip Schaff.* Edinburgh: T&T Clark, 1887; repr. Grand Rapids: Eerdmans Publishing Co., 1996.

Barbour, Ian G. "Creation and Cosmology." In *Cosmos as creation*. Ed. Ted Peters, Nashville: Abringdon Press, 1989.

Drees, William B. *Beyond the Big Bang*. LaSalle: Open Court Publishing Company. 1990.

Goldstein, Jonathon A. "The Origin of the Doctrine of Creation Ex Nihilo." *Journal of Jewish Studies* 35 Aug, 1984.

Irenaeus of Lyon, Against the Heresies. In *The Ante-Nicene Fathers. Vol. 1: The Apostolic Fathers.—Justin Martyr.—Irenaeus. Eds Alexander Roberts and James Donaldson.* Buffalo: Christian Literature Co., 1886.

Justin Martyr. *The First and Second Apologies.* Trans. Leslie William Barnard. Ancient Christian Writers 56. New York and Mahwah: Paulist Press, 1997.

Lilla, Salvatore R. C. *Clement of Alexandria.* Oxford: Oxford University Press, 1971.

May, Gerhard. *Creation Ex Nihilo: The Doctrine of "Creation out of Nothing" in Early Christian Thought*. Trans. by A.S. Worrall. Edinburgh: T&T Clark, 1994.

Metzger, Bruce M. and Roland E. Murphy, Eds. *The New Oxford Annotated Bible: NRSV.* New York: Oxford University Press, 1994. ***See** for text and comments on the Bible.*

Niemeyer, Gerhart. "History and Civilization." *Anglican Theological Review: Supplementary Series* 7 Nov, 1976.

Origen. *On First Principles.* Trans. by G.W. Butterworth. New York: Harper Tourchbooks, 1966.

Peters, Ted. "On Creating the Cosmos." In *Physics, Philosophy, and Theology: A common quest for understanding.* Eds. Robert J. Russell, William R. Stroeger, S.J. and George V. Coyne, S.J. Vatican City: Vatican Observatory, 1988.

Plato. *Timaeus.* Trans. Desmond Lee. Plato: Timaeus and Critias. London: Penguin Books, 1977.

Tatian. *Oratio Ad Graecos.* Trans. Molly Whittaker. Oxford Early Christian Texts. Oxford: Clarendon Press, 1970.

Tertullian. *The Treatise Against Hermogenes.* Trans. and annotated J.H. Waszink. *Ancient Christian Writers* 24. New York and Ramsey: Neuman Press, 1956.

Theophilus of Antioch. *Ad Autolycum.* Trans. Robert M. Grant. *Oxford Early Christian Texts.* Oxford: Clarendon Press, 1970.

Ward, Keith. *Religion and Creation.* Oxford: Clarendon Press, 1996.

Works cited in Eschatology essays

Evolution of Jewish eschatology: a recapitulation with Biblical examples (essay) starting on page 131.
Eschatology in Early Christianity (Essay) starting on page 266.

Bayliss, Miranda. "The Cult of Dead Kin in Assyria and Babylonia," Iraq 35, no. 2 autumn, 1973.

Borg, Marcus J. "Thinking About the Second Coming." Bible Review no. 10 Aug. 1994.

Burkill, T.A. *The Evolution of Christian Thought*, Ithaca: Cornell University Press, 1971. *See for Christian development.*

Clifford, Richard J. "Creation in the Hebrew Bible." In *Physics, Philosophy, and Theology: A common quest for understanding.* Eds. Robert J. Russell, William R. Stroeger, S.J. and George V. Coyne, S.J. Vatican City: Vatican Observatory, 1988.

Filoramo, G. "Hell-Hades," In *Encyclopedia of the Early Church*, edited by Angelo DiBeradino, Trans. Adrian Walford. New York: Oxford University Press, 1992.

_______. "Judgment." In *Encyclopedia of the Early Church*, edited by Angelo DiBeradino, Trans. Adrian Walford, New York: Oxford University Press, 1992.

Greenspoon, Leonard J. "The Origin of the Idea of Resurrection," in *Traditions in Transformation: Turning Points in Biblical Faith*, eds. Baruch Halpren and Jon Levenson Winona Lake: Eisenbrauns, 1981.

Heidel, Alexander. *The Babylonian Genesis*. Chicago: University of Chicago Press, 1951.

Hill, Charles E. Reanum Caelorum. Oxford: Clarendon Press, 1992.

Hinnells, John, "The Zoroastrian doctrine of salvation in the Roman world." In *Man and his salvation*, edited by Eric J Sharpe and John Hinnells. Manchester: Manchester University Press, 1973.

Jacobsen, Thorkild. *The Treasures of Darkness* New Haven: Yale University Press, 1976. *See for Mesopotamian religions.*

James, E.O. "Professor Brandon's Contribution to Scholarship," in *Man and his salvation*, eds. Eric J. Sharpe and John R. Hinnells. Manchester: Manchester University Press, 1973.

LeGoff, Jacques. *The Birth of Purgatory*. Trans. Arthur Goldhammer. Chicago: University of Chicago Press, 1984.

Lewis, T.J. *Cults of the Dead in Ancient Israel and Ugarit*. Atlanta: Scholars Press, 1989.

Lloyd, Alan B., "Psychology and Society in the Ancient Egyptian Cult of the Dead." In *Religion and Philosophy in Ancient Egypt*, Ed. William Kelly Simpson. New Haven: Yale University Press, 1989.

Margalit, Baruch. "Death and Dying in the Ugaritic Epics," in Bendt Alister, ed., *Death in Mesopotamia*. Copenhagen: Akademisk Forlag, 1980.

Pelikan, Jaroslav. *Development of Christian Doctrine*. New Haven: Yale University Press, 1969.

_______. "The Eschatology of Tertullian." *Church History* 21 (Je 1952.

_______. *The Emergence of the Catholic Tradition (100–600). Vol. 1 of The Christian Tradition: A History of the Development of Doctrine.* Chicago: University of Chicago Press, 1971. *See for Christian development.*

Quasten, Johannes. *The Ante-Nicene Literature after Irenaeus. Vol. 2 of Patrology.* Westminster, Maryland: Christian Classics, Inc., 1986.

Sachs, John R. "Apocatastasis in Patristic Theology." *Theological Studies* no. 54 D 1993.

Seeberg, Reinhold. *Text-Book of the History of Doctrines*. Trans. Charles E. Hay. Grand Rapids, Michigan: Baker Book House, 1966.

van Uchelen, Nico. "Death and the Afterlife in the Hebrew Bible of Ancient Israel," in *Hidden Futures: Death and Immortality in Ancient Egypt, Anatolia, the Classical, Biblical and Arabic-Islamic World*, eds. J. M. Bremer et al. Amsterdam: Amsterdam University Press, 1994.

Von Campenhausen, Hans. *Men Who Shaped the Western Church*. Trans. Manfred Hoffmann. New York: Harper & Row, Publishers, 1964.

Yamauchi, Edwin. *Persia and the Bible*. Baker Pub Group, 1990.

Zaehner, R. C. *The Teachings of the Magi*. New York: Macmillan Company, 1956.

Works cited in Science, religion and philosophy essay

Science, religion and philosophy—conflict or a way to meaning (essay)? Starting on page 301.

Ammerman, Robert R., ed. *Classics of Analytic Philosophy*. Indianapolis: Hackett Publishing Co., 1990.

Angeles, Peter A. ed. The *HarperCollins Dictionary of Philosophy*. New York: HarperCollins, 1992.

Campbell, Joseph. *The Power of Myth*. New York: Doubleday, 1988.

Carnap, R. "The Elimination of Metaphysics Through Logical Analysis of Language". Trans. Authur Pap.

_______. *Logical Positivism*. Ed. A. J. Ayer Glencoe, III: The Free Press, 1959. 60-81.

Davies, Paul and John Gribbon. *The Matter Myth*. New York: Simon and Schuster, 1992.

Davies, Paul. *About Time*. New York: Simon and Schuster, 1995.

Dummett, Michael. *The Logical Basis of Metaphysics*. Cambridge: Harvard University Press, 1991.

Edwards, Paul, ed. *Encyclopedia of Philosophy* 8 vols. New York: MacMillan, 1972.

Hawking, Stephen W. *A Brief History of Time*. London, etc.: Bantam Books, 1988. *See for modern physics.*

Kafatos, Menas and Robert Nadeau. *The Conscious-Universe*. New York: Springer-Verlag, 1990.

Khayyam, Omar. *The Rubaiyat of Omar Khayyam*. Trans. Edward Fitzgerald, version 5. New York: Walter J. Black, Inc. 1942.

Lederman, Leon. *The God Particle*. New York: Doubleday, 1994.

Peat, F. David. *Einstein's Moon*. Chicago: Contemporary Books, 1990.

Penrose, Roger. *The Emperor's New Mind*. Oxford: Oxford University Press, 1990.

Resnick, Robert and David Halliday. *Basic Concepts in Relativity and Early Quantum Theory*. New York: John Wiley & Sons, 1985.

Smith, Homer W. *Man and His Gods*. New York: Grosset and Dunlap, 1952.

Tipler, Frank. *The Physics of Immortality*. New York: Doubleday, l994.

Wittgenstein, Ludwig. *Tractatus Logico-Philosophicus*. London: R. & Kegan Paul, 1988.

General Bibliography

Anthes, Rudolf. "Egyptian Theology in the Third Millennium B.C." *Journal of Near Eastern Studies* 18, no. 3, 1959.

_______. "Mythology in Ancient Egypt." In *Mythologies of the Ancient World*. Ed. Samuel Noah Kramer, 17–92. Garden City, New York: Anchor Books, 1961.

_______. "The Original Meaning of maa kheru" *Journal of Near Eastern Studies* 13 (Jan-Oct 1954): 21–51.

Baines, John, "Society, Morality, and Religious Practice." In *Religion in Ancient Egypt: Gods, Myths and Personal Practice*, Ed. Byron E. Shafer, 123–200. Ithaca, New York: Cornell University Press, 1991.

_______. "Origins of Egyptian Kingship." In Ancient Egyptian Kingship. Eds. David O'Conner, and David Silverman. Leiden: E.J. Brill, 1995.

Barnstone, Willis ed. *The Other Bible*. HarperSanFrancisco, 1984. ***See for other ancient scriptures.***

Barnes, Jonathon. *The Presocratic Philosophers*. Vol 2. London: Routledge & Kegan Paul, 1979.

Bettenson, Henry. *The Early Christian Fathers*. London: Oxford University Press, 1956.

Bhaktivedanta Swami, A.C. *Bhagavad-Gita: As It Is*. Los Angeles: Bhativedanta Book Trust, 1977.

Boyce, Mary. *Zoroastrians. Their Religious Beliefs and Practices*. London: Routledge & Kegan Paul. 1979. ***See for Zoroastrianism.***

_______. *Zoroastrianism*. Totowa: Barnes & Noble Books, 1984

Brandon, S.G.F. *Man and His Destiny in the Great Religions.* Toronto: University of Toronto Press, 1962.

_______. *The Judgment of the Dead: The Idea of Life After Death in the Major Religions.* New York: Charles Scribner's Sons, 1967.

_______. "The Origin of Death in some Ancient Near Eastern Religions." *Religious Studies* I, no. 2, 1966.

Breasted, James Henry. *The Dawn of Conscience.* New York: Charles Scribner's Sons, 1934.

_______. *Development of Religion and Thought in Ancient Egypt.* London: Charles Scribner's Sons, 1912.

Bremmer, Jan. *The Early Greek Concept of the Soul.* Princeton: Princeton University Press, 1983.

Brown, Peter. *Augustine of Hippo: a biography.* Berkley: University of California Press, 1967. *See for St. Augustine.*

Brown, Raymond E. An Introduction to New Testament Christology. New York: Paulist Press, 1994.

Bruce, F.F. *The Spreading Flame.* Exeter: Paternoster Press, 1964.

Burkert, Walter. *Ancient Mystery Cults.* Cambridge: Harvard University Press, 1987.

_______. *Greek Religion.* Trans. John Raffan. Cambridge: Harvard University Press, 1985. *See for Greek religion.*

Burnet, John. *Plato's Phaedo.* 1911. Reprint, Oxford: Clarendon Press, 1959.

Cooper, John M. *Plato: Complete Works.* Cambridge: Hackett Publishing Company, 1997. *See for works of Plato.*

Coleman, John E. "Did Egypt Shape the Glory that was Greece?" *Archaeology* (Sep/Oct 1992): 48–86.

Crossan, John Dominic. *The Historical Jesus: the Life of a Mediterranean Jewish Peasant.* San Francisco: Harper Collins, 1992.

Cullman, Oscar. *The Christology of the New Testament.* Philadelphia: Westminster, 1963.

Damascius. *The Greek Commentaries on Plato's Phaedo.* Ed. L.G. Westerink. Amsterdam: North-Holland Publishing Company, 1977.

Darmesteter, James. *The Zend-Avesta part 1, in Sacred Books of the East,* IV 2nd ed.; Oxford: Claredon Press, 1895.

Dieterich, Albrecht. *Nekyia.* Stuttgart: B.G. Teubner, 1969.

Dietrich, B. C. *The Origins of Greek Religion.* Berlin and New York: Walter De Gruyter, 1974.

Dodds, E.R. *Euripides: Bacchae.* Oxford: Clarendon Press, 1960.

_______. *Plato: Gorgias.* Oxford: Clarendon Press 1959.

_______. *The Greeks and the Irrational.* Berkley: University of California Press, 1951.

Ehrman, Bart D. *Lost Christianities: The Battles for Scripture and Faiths We Never Knew.* Oxford: Oxford University Press, 2003. ***See** for other Christian scriptures.*

Epiphanius. *Against Heresies.* Louis Berkhof, *The History of Christian Doctrines.* London: Banner of Truth, 1978.

Erman, Adolf. *Life in Ancient Egypt.* Translated by H.M. Tirard. New York: Benjamin Blom, 1969. First published as *Aegypten* in 1885 and translated into English in 1894.

_______. *The Ancient Egyptians: A Sourcebook of their Writings.* New York: Harper and Row, 1966.

Eusebius. *The History of the Church.* Trans. G. A. Williamson. London, 1965.

Fagles, Robert. *Bacchylides: Complete Poems.* New Haven: Yale University Press, 1961.

Faulkner, Raymond O. *The Ancient Egyptian Book of the Dead.* Austin: The University of Texas Press, 1993.

_______. *The Ancient Egyptian Coffin Texts.* 3 vols. Warminster: Aris & Phillips 1973, 1977, 1978.

_______. *The Ancient Egyptian Pyramid Texts.* Oxford: Clarendon Press, 1969.

Forman, Werner and Stephen Quirke. *Hieroglyphics and the Afterlife.* Norman: University of Oklahoma Press, 1996.

Frankfort, Henri. *Kingship and the Gods.* Chicago:, 1948.

_______. *Ancient Egyptian Religion.* New York: Harper & Brothers, 1948.

Foley, Helene P. *The Homeric Hymn to Demeter.* Princeton: Princeton University Press, 1994.

Fredriksen, Paula. *From Jesus to Christ: the Origin of the New Testament Images of Jesus.* New Haven: Yale University Press, 1988. ***See** for Christian development.*

Freeman, Kathleen. *The Pre-Socratic Philosophers.* Oxford: Basil Blackwell, 1949.

_______. *Ancilla to the Pre-Socratic Philosophers.* Oxford: Basil Blackwell, 1948.

Frend, W. H. C. *The Rise of Christianity*. Philadelphia: Fortress Press, 1984. ***See for early Christian development.***

Friedman, Richard Elliott. *Who Wrote the Bible?* New York: Summit Books, 1987. ***See for the making of the Old Testament.***

Graf, Fritz. "Dionysian and Orphic Eschatology: New Texts and Old Questions." In Thomas H. Carpenter and Christopher A. Faraone, *Masks of Dionysis*. Ithaca: Cornell University Press, 1993.

Griffiths, J. Gwyn. Atlantis and Egypt. Cardiff: University of Wales Press, 1991.

_______. *The Divine Verdict: A Study of Divine Judgement in the Ancient Religions*. Leiden: E.J. Brill, 1991.

_______. *The Origins of Osiris and His Cult*. Leiden: E.J. Brill, 1980.

Guthrie, W. K. C. *Orpheus and Greek Religion*. London: Methuen, 1935.

Gunkel, Hermann. "The Influence of Babylonian Mythology upon the Biblical Creation Story." In *Creation in the Old Testament*. Ed. Bernhard W. Anderson. Oxford: Fortress Press, 1984.

Herodotus. *The Histories*. Trans. Aubrey de Selincourt. Baltimore: Penguin Books, 1966.

Homer. *The Iliad*, Trans. Robert Fagles New York: Penguin Books, 1990.

Hornblower, Simon and Anthony Spawforth, Eds. *The Oxford Companion to Classical Civilization*. Oxford: Oxford University Press, 1998.

Hornung, Erik. *Akhenaten and the Religion of Light*. Ithaca: Cornell University Press, 1999.

_______. *Idea into Image: Essays on Ancient Egyptian Thought*. Trans. Elizabeth Bredeck. Timkin Publishers, 1992. First published as *Geist der Pharaonenzeit*. Zurich and Munich: Artemis, 1989.

Iamblicus. *On The Pythagorean Life*. Clark, Gillian. Trans. Liverpool: Liverpool University Press, 1989.

Jafarey, Ali A. *The Gathas Our Guide*. Ushta Publications. 1989

Johnson, Paul. *A History of Christianity*. New York: Atheneum, 1987. ***See for 2000 year history of Christianity.***

Kirk, G.S., J.E. Raven and M. Schofield. *The Presocratic Philosophers*. Cambridge: Cambridge University Press, 1983.

Kloppenborg, John S. *Q parallels*. Polebridge Press, 1988.

Kraut, Richard. Ed. *The Cambridge Companion to Plato*. Cambridge: Cambridge University Press, 1992.

Layton, Bently. *The Gnostic Scriptures*. New York, Doubleday, 1987.

Lesko, Leonard H. "Ancient Egyptian Cosmogonies and Cosmology." In *Religion in Ancient Egypt: Gods Myths and Personal Practice*, Ed. Byron E. Shafer, 88–122. Ithaca, New York: Cornell University Press, 1991.

_______. "Death and the Afterlife in Ancient Egyptian Thought." In *Civilization of the Ancient Near East*, Ed. Jack M. Sasson, vol. III. New York: Charles Scriebner's Sons, 1995.

Lichtheim, Miriam. *Ancient Egyptian Autobiographies Chiefly of the Middle Kingdom*. Gottingen: Vandenhoeck & Ruprecht, 1988.

_______. *Ancient Egyptian Literature: A Book of Readings, 3 Vols.* Berkeley: University of California Press, 1973, 1976, 1980. ***See** for Egyptian religious texts.*

Lieth, John H., ed. *Creeds of the Churches*. Garden City, New York: Doubleday & Company, 1963.

Lyman, Rebecca. *Christology and Cosmology: Models of Divine Activity in Origen, Eusebius and Athanasius*. New York: Clarendon Press, 1993.

Mack, Burton L. *The Lost Gospel: The Book of Q & Christian Origins*. HarperSanFrancisco, 1993. ***See** for explanation of Q.*

Maspero, Gaston. *New Light on Ancient Egypt*. London: T. Fisher Unwin, 1908.

McBrien, Richard P. *Lives of the Popes*. HarperSanFransisco, 1997. *See for the Papacy.*

McMullen, Ramsay. *Christianizing the Roman Empire, A.D. 100–400*. Yale University Press, 1984.

Morenz, Siegfried. *Egyptian Religion*. Translated by Ann E. Keep. London: Methuen; Ithaca: Cornell University Press, 1973. First published as *Agyptische Religion*. Religionen der Menschheit 8. Stuttgart: Kohlhammer, 1960. ***See** for Egyptian religion.*

Moret, Alexander. *The Nile and Egyptian Civilization*. Trans. M. R. Dobie. London: Kegan Paul, Trench, Tubner & Co.; New York: Alfred A. Knopf, 1927.

Nichelsburg, George W. E., Jr., *Resurrection, Immortality, and Eternal Life In Intertestamental Judaism*. Cambridge: Harvard University Press, 1972.

Nilsson, Martin P. *Minoan-Mycenaean Religion and its Survival in Greek Religion*. Lund: C.W.K. Gleerup, 1950.

Noll, Mark A. *Turning Points: decisive moments in the history of Christianity*. Grand Rapids: Baker Book House, 1997.

O'Grady, Joan. *Early Christian Heresies*. New York: Barnes & Noble Books, 1994. ***See** for Christian Heresies.*

Olympiodorus. *Commentary on Plato's Gorgias.* Trans. Robin Jackson, Kimon Lycos, Harold Tarrant. Leiden: Brill, 1998.

Pagels, Elaine. *The Gnostic Gospels.* New York: Random House, 1979. ***See for** Gnosticism.*

Petrie, W.M. Flinders. *Religion and Conscience in Ancient Egypt.* New York: Benjamin Blom, 1972. First published in 1898.

Piankoff, Alexandre. *The Pyramids of Unas.* Princeton: Princeton University Press, 1968.

Plato. *Complete Works.* Ed. John M. Cooper. Indianapolis: Hackett Publishing Company, 1997.

_______. *Loeb Classical Library.* Eds, E. Capps, T.E. Page, W.H.D. Rouse. 12 Vols. New York: G.P. Putnam's Sons, 1913.

Plutarch. *Plutarch's Moralia.* Trans. Frank Cole Babbitt. Cambridge: Harvard University Press, 1949.

Porphyry, *Life of Plotinus.* 23.1–28, trans. A. H. Armstrong. Loeb Classical Library, London: Heineman, 1966.

Pritchard, James B. *The Ancient Near East* Vol 1. Princeton University Press, 1958. ***See** for ancient religions.*

Quirke, Stephen. *Ancient Egyptian Religion.* London: British Museum Press, 1992.

Rohde, Erwin. *Psyche.* Trans. W.B. Hillis. New York: Harcourt, Brace & Company, 1925.

Romano, James A. *Death, Burial, and the Afterlife in Ancient Egypt.* Pittsburg: The Carnegie Museum of Natural History, 1990.

Rowe, C.J. *An Introduction to Greek Ethics.* New York: Barnes & Noble, 1976.

_______. *Plato: Phaedrus.* Wiltshire: Aris & Phillips, 1986.

_______. *Plato: Phaedo.* Cambridge: Cambridge University Press, 1993.

Rubenstein, Richard E. *When Jesus Became God.* Harcourt Brace & Company, 1999.

Schoeps, Hans-Joachim. *Jewish Christianity.* Philadelphia: Fortress Press, 1969. ***See** for Jewish-Christians.*

Schubert, Kurt. "A Divided Faith." In *The Crucible of Christianity,* edited by Arnold Toynbee, 77–98. New York: World Publishing Company, 1969.

Sheehan, Thomas. *The First Coming.* New York: Random House, 1986.

Smith, Jonathan Z. *Imagining Religion.* Chicago: University of Chicago Press, 1982.

_______. *Map is not Territory.* Leiden: E.J. Brill, 1978.

Speiser, E. A. *Ancient Near Eastern Texts.* Princeton, 1950.

_______. *Ancient Near Eastern Texts Relating to the Old Testament,* edited by James B. Pritchard. Princeton: Princeton University Press, 1969.

Stilwell, Gary A. *Conduct and Behavior as Determinants for the Afterlife: A Comparison of the Judgments of the Dead in Ancient Egypt and Ancient Greece.* Dissertation.com, 2000.

Taylor, C.C.W. *The Atomists: Leucippus and Democritus.* Toronto: University of Toronto Press, 1999.

Vermes, Geza. *The Complete Dead Sea Scrolls in English.* New York: Penguin Press, 1997. *See for the Dead Sea Scrolls.*

Wente, Edward F. "Funerary Beliefs of the Ancient Egyptians." *Expedition* Winter, 1982.

West, M.L. *Early Greek Philosophy and the Orient.* Oxford: Clarendon Press, 1971.

_______. *Hesiod: Theogony and Works and Days.* Oxford: Oxford University Press, 1988.

Wilken, Robert L. *The Christians as the Romans Saw Them.* Yale University Press, New Haven and London, 1984.

Wilson, A. N. *Paul: The Mind of the Apostle.* W.W. Norton & Company, 1997. *See for importance of St. Paul.*

Wilson, John A. In *Ancient Near Eastern Texts.* Ed. James B. Pritchard. Princeton: Princeton University Press, 1955.

Zabkar, Louis V. *A Study of the Ba Concept in Ancient Egyptian Text*. Chicago: University of Chicago Press, 1960.

Zhmud', Leonid. "Orphism and grafitti from Olbia," *Hermes* 120, 1992.

INDEX

B

C

D

E

I

J

K

L

M

N

O

P

Q

R

S

T

U

V

W

X

Y

Z

0-595-33376-1

Printed in the United States
42940LVS00003B/91-108

9 780595 333769